Strategic Stability in South Asia: Challenges and Implications for India

Strategic Stability in South Asia: Challenges and Implications for India

by

Zubin Bhatnagar

(Established 1870)

United Service Institution of India
New Delhi

Vij Books India Pvt Ltd
New Delhi (India)

Published by

Vij Books India Pvt Ltd
(Publishers, Distributors & Importers)
2/19, Ansari Road
Delhi – 110 002
Phones: 91-11-43596460, 91-11-47340674
Fax: 91-11-47340674
e-mail: vijbooks@rediffmail.com

Copyright © 2017, United Service Institution of India, New Delhi

ISBN   : 978-93-86457-35-6 (Hardback)
ISBN   : 978-93-86457-37-0 (ebook)

Contents

Foreword   vii

Acknowledgments   xi

Introduction   xiii

Chapters

1   South Asia and the Concept of Strategic Stability   1

2   Situation in Af- Pak Region: An Appraisal   9

3   India and Pakistan Relations: Seven Decades of Unrest   52

4   Littoral States of Indian Ocean in South Asia   73

5   Himalayan Kingdoms of South Asia   88

6   Security Environment in Bangladesh & Myanmar   102

7   China Factor in South Asia   120

8   Role of Major Powers in South Asia   155

9   Strategic Stability in South Asia: Options For India   175

Conclusion   202

Bibliography   205

Index   223

Foreword

The conceptualization of the project '**Strategic Stability in South Asia: Challenges and Implications for India**' is a result of the felt need to analyse the implications of the global power shift and unprecedented geopolitical developments in the region. Coming specifically to the dynamics of peace and security in South Asia, it can be said that contemporary strategic environment in the region is in ferment and can be described as that of elusive peace and fragile security. Much of this security dilemma stems from South Asia's chequered history. A cradle of rich civilization that South Asia is -multiple faiths and ethnicities, impart an interconnected cultural matrix to the region and paradoxically this very attribute is also causative of a regional divide.

Since the time of de-colonization the fledgling nation states have been embroiled in internal conflicts, partition and re-partition of the Indian subcontinent, and even conventional wars. The region today faces far more virulent form of hybrid threats that combine asymmetric conflicts with conventional wars, under a nuclear overhang. Although peace in this versatile region is not an option but a necessity, deep religious and ideological underpinnings, ethno-regional divide, heightened cartographic consciousness, and "ZeroSum" mind-sets are hampering conflict resolution and peace building. We need visionary and transformational leadership to steer the nations out of this 'insecurity logjam'. In this endeavour academia and strategic community play an important role to deconstruct or demystify vexed problems and help in articulating a broad range of options for governments to pursue the path of conflict resolution, attaining comprehensive humanitarian security and usher peace and prosperity for its people.

In geopolitics, geography plays a significant role in shaping peace and security environment of a region. From a geostrategic perspective, South

Asia and the Indian Ocean Region (IOR) form part of the same strategic space. In this strategic space, India enjoys a strategic centrality. It shares borders with all other states and dominates the Indian Ocean. However, on the flipside, India besets unresolved boundaries with China and Pakistan. Boundary disputes have been and continue to be a key driver of regional conflicts. Looking from a broader strategic perspective, it can be seen that the South Asian landmass abuts continental China's non – Han periphery with the Indian Ocean through Xinjiang-Gwadar Economic Corridor and Kunming-Kyaukphyu-Dhaka Corridor. On the Eastern flank of India; Nepal and Bhutan are the two strategic buffers that border strategically sensitive Siliguri Corridor, whereas, Bangladesh and Myanmar form strategic bridges between Indian Peninsula and Southeast Asia.

On the Western frontier, Pakistan's strategic location lends itself a pivotal advantage for access to Afghanistan, Gulf Region, and Central Asia. Pakistan has rented this strategic advantage to extra regional powers like China to access the Arabian Sea and the US to play a Great Game in Afghanistan and Central Asia. On the Western flank, India is geographically disadvantaged due to lack of physical connectivity with Afghanistan and Central Asia. Therefore, Iran assumes an overwhelming importance for India in its "Connect Central Asia Policy" and sustained engagement in Afghanistan.

From a maritime perspective, Indian Ocean is the hub of global maritime trade and energy flow. The US has always maintained a strong naval presence in the IOR to serve its strategic objectives in South Asia and Middle East. China too is emerging a key player in the Indian Ocean purportedly to meet its energy security demands, mitigate its Malacca Dilemma and accomplish its "Two Ocean Strategy". China's enhanced naval deployment in the Gulf of Aden for counter piracy missions and its much-touted 'Maritime Silk Route' project should be seen in that context. China is constructing a number of ports and strategic infrastructure assets in the IOR, what Booz Allen called as the "String of Pearls". China's no strings attached dollar diplomacy is aimed to flood the smaller South Asian countries with economic aid, which they will not be able to pay back in cash but in terms of giving China, political, diplomatic, economic and military concessions.

When and how will this String of Pearls or Maritime Silk Route assume a military dimension merits a close watch? At this juncture, it will not be naive to say that major powers will continue to be stakeholders in peace and security of South Asia, be it IOR or Af-Pak region. While the geostrategic advantage confers South Asia with a multitude of opportunities for building peace and regional cooperation, the environmental realities point to the contrary.

On the security front, Af-Pak region has infamously come to be known as an epicentre of international terrorism. The security situation in Afghanistan remains worrisome with a resurgence of Taliban and a fragile government and security setup. Pakistan is in the mid of a serious internal crisis. Sunni and Shia sectarian conflict, secessionist movements in Baluchistan and Khyber–Pakhtunkhwa and rising spectre of Jihadi violence are threatening the very existence of Pakistan as a viable nation state. Pakistan will continue to be a major source of instability in the region with Jihadi terrorism as the biggest threat to South Asian security.

Bangladesh, India's eastern neighbour remains prone to political violence and Islamist activism, which has a potential to acquire an anti-India rhetoric. Maldives, another Muslim majority state also runs the risk of radicalization with spill over effect into India.

Sri Lanka, a majority Sinhala state remains paranoid about a perceived threat from Tamil majority in South India, across Mannar strait. This pushes Sri Lanka's foreign policy orientation towards China to hedge against perceived hostility from India. The security scenario in Sri Lanka has internal and external dynamics with implications on the strategic balance in the IOR.

The nascent democracy in Nepal is getting traction and is in the process of addressing the legitimate demands of various stakeholders in its new constitution. However, the economically deprived country remains susceptible to instability. China's growing influence in the country remains a cause of concern for India.

The security environment in Myanmar has implication on South Asia especially India. The majority Burmans and other ethnicities (Kachin and Karen) remain at loggerheads. Buddhist militant nationalism has led to clashes with Rohingya Muslims. Indian insurgent groups find safe havens in Myanmar. Contraband and drug trafficking from Myanmar adds to

India's security concerns in the northeast region. Myanmar nevertheless holds the key to India's Act East Policy.

In South Asia, India is the only state that has witnessed democratic rise, economic growth and relative internal stability. The country, however, continues to face myriad of socio-political, religious, and ethno-regional fault lines. Good governance, inclusive growth, dealing with the Left Wing Extremism, containing proxy war in Kashmir, and pan India terrorism are the major internal security challenges faced by India.

Apart from the above stated security issues, issues like human development, unemployment, climate change, pandemics etc too play an essential role in determining the stability of the region. South Asia is home to one-fifth of the world's population and as per the World Bank, the region is home to half of the world's poor. With intra-regional trade at less than 5 percent of total trade, South Asia is the least integrated region in the world. One fifth of the population is between the ages of 15 and 24, with unemployment rate as high as 9.6 per cent. Regional countries rank low on Human Development Index while most find a high ranking on Failing State Index. Lack of good governance, political instability, and ethnic strife are perennial sources of internal conflicts which have serious ramifications on the strategic stability of the region.

The book is an important and valuable contribution as it attempts to bring under one volume a holistic understanding of the concept of strategic stability; various issues that challenge the peace and security in South Asia; a 'sine qua non' for India to retain its pre–eminence in South Asia.

I appreciate Col Zubin Bhatnagar's efforts for his timely work of immense value to the geo-strategic community and the Centre for Strategic Studies and Simulation (CS3), USI of India, New Delhi for their support and encouragement to the author.

New Delhi
15 June 2017

Lt Gen PK Singh,
PVSM, AVSM (Retd)
Director, USI of India
New Delhi

Acknowledgments

I am indeed grateful to the USI of India for having given me an opportunity to express my small research effort through their portal. It is difficult to express in words the feeling of immense satisfaction on the culmination of the project, which is but a stepping stone for further endeavours.

The topic for the research was crafted by Maj Gen BK Sharma, AVSM, SM** (Retd), Deputy Director CS3 who very painstakingly explained to me the nuances of the subject. Lt Gen PC Katoch, PVSM, UYSM, AVSM, SC (Retd), my guide for the project, channelized my reading, patiently perused and corrected my drafts and goaded to write my ideas. I immensely benefitted from the valuable papers on the subject, authored by these General Officers, a result of years of their hands on experience which they readily shared with me.

I will like to acknowledge the efforts of Lt Gen Chander Prakash, SM, VSM (Retd), Maj Gen RPS Bhadauria, VSM (Retd) and Maj Gen SB Asthana, SM, VSM (Retd) and other colleagues at the USI of India who were always available to discuss and share their views on the subject. I will also like to thank Dr. Smruti S Pattanaik from IDSA for reviewing the entire work in detail. Her comments have done the much needed value addition to the book.

My special acknowledgements for the role played by Dr Roshan Khaneijo, our research coordinator, who not only created an ideal environment for research but was always available to share her wealth of knowledge to provide the much needed guidance on a day to day basis.

Lastly, I owe the successful completion of the book to the blessings of my parents and the encouragement by my better half and the children; their role has been immeasurable.

Introduction

South Asia represents the southern region of the Asian continent comprising of sub-Himalayan SAARC countries to include Afghanistan, Bangladesh, Bhutan, Maldives, Nepal, India, Pakistan and Sri Lanka. Topographically, it is dominated by the Indian Plate, which rises above sea level as Nepal and northern parts of India situated south of the Himalayas and the Hindu Kush. South Asia is bounded on the south by the Indian Ocean and on land (clockwise, from west) by West Asia, Central Asia, East Asia, and Southeast Asia. It covers about 5.1 million km², which is 11.51 percent of the Asian continent or 3.4 percent of the world's land surface area. South Asia has the largest population of both Hindus and Muslims in the world at about 1 billion and 507 million respectively as per 2010 records.

The South Asian region is generally perceived to be a volatile area of the world. This perception derives from the numerous geopolitical developments which the region has experienced. The chronic instability between India and Pakistan, the two nuclear armed states is a cause of major concern. This instability has episodically surfaced in acute form, with two states having fought four major wars since their independence in 1947. Pakistan continues its nuclear brinkmanship and wage a proxy war against India over Kashmir issue. In Afghanistan, Pakistan's role in politics of dispute resolution and continued instability is adversely impacting regional security dynamics of South Asia and other regional states as well.

While the Af-Pak region remains the arc of vulnerability, growing Islamic fundamentalism in Bangladesh, political instability in Nepal and Chinese increasing footprints in India's immediate neighbourhood have strategic ramifications both regional and global. Moreover, the geopolitical developments in regions adjoining South Asia; namely the rise of ISIS in West Asia, ongoing Ukraine imbroglio and increasing Chinese assertiveness in South China Sea, impact the region's strategic stability. Not surprisingly, therefore, South Asia is invariably viewed by many observers and strategists as an explosive 'flashpoint' in global politics. These have implications not only on the overall strategic stability of the region but also India's twin goals of development and stability in South Asia. India's intention to play a proactive role in providing leadership and governance structure to the region characterised by fragmentation and tension is a challenge but an imperative to realise its stature of global pre-eminence.

Chapter 1

South Asia and the Concept of Strategic Stability

"In South Asian context, talks on conventional military confidence building cannot be divorced from terrorism... The route of the escalatory process is militancy"

- Bharat Karnad

Strategic Balance – Definition and Concept

In the game of Chess, strategic balance is defined as a situation where advantages held by one's opponent are compensated for by developing one's advantages, the position is then considered to be balanced. It is only after the balance of the positions has been disturbed, that one player holds an uncompensated advantage, and may this player attack with intent to win[1]. According to M Sheehan[2], the balance of power theory sees international society as unequal; power versus weakness. But this basic inequality among states can be balanced, that is, all states can be kept in check regarding each other's position, and this can therefore prevent hegemony, allowing states to preserve their identity, integrity and independence, and perhaps deterring aggression or war. Some classic definitions of Strategic Balance are discussed in the following paragraphs.

A state in which long-term and short-term (or high risk and low risk) elements, factors, or objectives are judiciously combined to achieve a desired level of equilibrium[3].

The term "strategic balance" refers to the relative capabilities of the two sides to achieve their respective strategic objectives in relation to the other[4].

The purpose of balancing is to prevent a rising power from assuming hegemony, and if and when that prevention effort succeeds, a balance of power is expected to be present.[5]

Conceptually strategic balance can be achieved through hard balancing or soft balancing. Hard balancing is a behaviour in which states form and maintain military alliances to balance a stronger state or check the rise of a potential threat. According to T V Paul,[6] traditional hard balancing, albeit in a weakened form, seems to be present only in conflict-ridden regions of the world; the Middle East, South Asia, and East Asia; where enduring rivalries persist. In South Asian context, Pakistan has been hard balancing India while India is making efforts now to close down their defence gap vis-à-vis China.

Soft balancing is used to describe non-military forms of balancing evident since the end of the Cold War, particularly during and after the 2003 Iraq War. Soft balancing occurs when weaker states decide that the dominance and influence of a stronger state is unacceptable, but that the military advantage of the stronger state is overwhelming that traditional balancing is not feasible or even impossible. Soft balancing is undertaken not to physically shift the balance of power but to undermine, frustrate, and increase the cost of unilateral action for the stronger state. Soft balancing is not undertaken via military effort, but by a combination of economic, diplomatic, and institutional methods. States can adopt different means to engage in soft balancing: tacit understandings or alliances etc. The Indian neighbours like Nepal, Sri Lanka and Bangladesh have been trying to soft balance India by playing the China card and extracting economic and military benefits from both, India and China.

Another way to look at types of balancing is by internal and external efforts and means. Internal balancing involves efforts to enhance state's power by increasing ones economic resources and military strength in order to be able to rely on independent capabilities in response to a potential hegemon and be able to compete more effectively in the international system. India has been trying to modernise its defence forces but the process has been marred by decline in economic growth and due to lack of consensus among political leadership. With Bharatiya Janata Party, a majority government at the centre, it is expected that pro-reform policies will gain required momentum and India's economic growth will revive that will strengthen Indian efforts for internal balancing of China. External balancing is done by forming alliances with other states to deter the rival state. India, Japan, South Korea, USA and Vietnam are the countries that could potentially strengthen their alliances with each other in future on the pretext of a Chinese threat.

Accordingly Strategic Balance of a country is the achievement of a desired state in critical strategic space over a time horizon which enables it to pursue its national interests and strategic objectives vis-a-vis its competitors from a position of relative advantage. This is essential to prevent hegemony. Further the process entails internal balancing which is as a result of Comprehensive National Development (CND), external balancing formed out of alliance as also strategic partnership, soft balancing as a result of economics combined with cultural relations and finally asymmetric balancing including disruptive instruments. Asymmetric balancing includes efforts by sub national actors and their state sponsors to challenge and weaken established states using asymmetric means such as terrorism.

Strategic Balance in South Asia

The current dynamics of Strategic Balance in South Asia is governed by certain important aspects. Turbulent and unstable Af-Pak region, Sino-India mistrust, Pakistan sponsored cross border terrorism in India, Sino-Pak bonhomie unstable political situation in Nepal, growing Islamic radicalisation in Bangladesh and role of major powers especially the increasing Chinese footprints in South Asia have ramifications on the region's strategic stability. Further, the geopolitical developments in regions adjoining South Asia; namely the rise of ISIS in West Asia, ongoing Ukraine imbroglio and increasing Chinese assertiveness in South China Sea too impact the region. Not surprisingly, therefore, South Asia is invariably viewed by many observers and strategists as an explosive 'flashpoint' in global politics.

Geographically, China is not a part of South Asia but its engagement with South Asian States and strategic nexus with Pakistan make it an important player in the region. China has the potential to alter the strategic balance in South Asia in its favour. Former Indian Prime Minister, Dr Manmohan Singh had said in 2010 that China would like to gain a foothold in South Asia and India needed to be aware of this reality. He said China could be tempted to use India's soft underbelly (neighbourhood), Kashmir issue and Pakistan to keep India in low-level equilibrium[7].

From India's perspective, its strategic security can be visualised in terms of concentric circles in which the country's defence perimeter lies not at India's border but at the outer boundaries of its regional neighbours[8]. China's gravitational pull is weaning the Governments of Bangladesh, Nepal and Sri Lanka. However, the smaller countries of South Asia too on their part use China as a balancer against India in the region. A number of South Asian countries namely Pakistan, Nepal, Bangladesh and Sri Lanka, primarily driven by their desire to have a credible balance against India's comparatively huge capabilities, have even advocated treating China as a South Asian country[9]. This proposal was supported by Pakistan and Bangladesh[10]. This has given these countries a better bargaining power in dealing with political, economic and security issues with India. China's geographical proximity to the region and its growing military, economic and diplomatic presence in South Asia undermine India's strategic interests in the region.

India-China relations have improved after the 1962 war but they are marked by 'mistrust' and 'suspicion'. China's military posturing in Tibet, strategic forays in the Northern areas and Indian Ocean and nuanced policy on No First Use (NFU)[11] are issues of strategic concern for India. China also has a strategic partnership with India's traditional foe, and the China-Pakistan nexus has been at work to limit Indian influence not only in South Asia but in Central Asia as well. The China-Pakistan Economic Corridor, through disputed areas will give China access to Arabian Sea through Pakistan's port of Gwadar. Chinese forays in Northern areas of POK have the potency of assuming a security dimension. While a smaller and resource less Pakistan has always tried to seek a status on par with India, China has been trying to keep India engaged in South Asia so that it can emerge as the predominant power in Asia. It will not be incorrect to say that China-Pakistan strategic nexus poses a hybrid threat to India.

It is safe to conclude that China's foreign and defence policy initiatives will continue to be designed to reduce India to the status of a sub-regional power by increasing Chinese influence and leverage in the South Asian region[12]. Instability in India's periphery tends South Asia to socio-political turmoil which can be exploited by inimical state and non-state actors using inter-alia asymmetric capabilities to harm India. U.S. sees India as a strategic partner in Asia[13] and as a potential balancer to rising China. However, there are issues of divergence like climate change, trade barriers; US lenient stand on cross-border terrorism from Pakistan and transfer of high end military technology to India. These issues can be ironed out through astute diplomacy, as was the case in Indo-US nuclear deal. Keeping the nature of U.S. relations with Pakistan and China in view, it would be unrealistic to expect U.S. to get directly embroiled in the South Asia strategic quagmire. India has to hold on its own.

The next major issue for regional stability is chronic instability between India and Pakistan, the two nuclear armed states; a cause of major concern. This instability has episodically surfaced in acute form, with two states having fought four major wars since their independence in 1947. Pakistan continues its nuclear brinkmanship and wage a proxy war against India over Kashmir issue. Jihadi terrorism and nuclear weapons have increased the risks of hybrid wars in the region. India follows a 'no first use' policy in its nuclear doctrine while Pakistan advocates the doctrine of 'first strike' against India[14]. India's Military superiority and nuclear deterrence is challenged by cross-border terrorism sponsored by Pakistan.

While the 'strategic mistrust' in India-Pakistan and India-China relationship can be explained by realist theory of international relations[15], the economic interdependence between these countries has not given expected results, especially in context of India-China.

India's own engagement in the region has been found wanting, even though it has evolved over the years. India's intention to play a proactive role in providing leadership and governance structure to a region characterised by fragmentation and tension is a challenge but an imperative to realise its stature of global pre-eminence. However India, the biggest player in the region is punching below its weight and seems to be lacking the desired pedestal in regional leadership. As brought out earlier, India's ambitions have been confronted by external and internal challenges which pose threats to emergence of India as a regional leader.

However, what primarily goes in India's favour is its ability to govern the diverse and multi-ethnic states which benefit better through democracy rather than through repressive and authoritarian regimes. Apart from governance, India is better at creating the "software" of development namely technology, law and services. Since all South Asian countries are multi-ethnic states, India can become a role model of development for them by better managing its society and economy. Further, it must be noted that India being a democracy naturally finds acceptance with other democracies like the US, Japan, Australia, South Korea and other European countries. Moreover, India by virtue of its size, geographical location and economic growth is a pre-eminent power in South Asia. India is considered as the third largest economy in purchasing power parity terms[16].

According to C Raja Mohan[17], Asia is seeing the consolidation and rise of powerful nationalisms that are somewhat less amenable to integrative impulses arising from the economic imperative. This has made it difficult to overcome the deep historical animosities in Asia. Further, unlike in Europe there is no broad consensus in Asia that liberal democracy is the only acceptable form of governance. Barring India, the South Asian countries are struggling to institutionalise strong and effective democracy. These two factors explain the failure of regional co-operation in South Asia.

South Asian strategic stability is also influenced by incremental erosion of strategic buffers, such as Nepal and Bhutan, political instability in Nepal and growing Islamic instability in Bangladesh. The execution of the String of Pearls Strategy in the Indian Ocean Region by China with aspirations to improve its geo-strategic position in the world has added a new dimension to regional competitions[18]. The underlying purpose/intention of China is to project its power overseas and protect its oil shipments[19]. Recently, China has also mooted the idea of Maritime Silk Route. Creation of transportation corridors along Eastern and Western strategic flanks of India has political dimensions.

Though there are a number of factors influencing the strategic stability of South Asia; in the present geo-political environment it is the Af-Pak region that remains the arc of vulnerability.[20] While the security dynamics of an unstable Af-Pak region remains a cause of global concern; policy directives reflecting international resolve seem to be missing. In Afghanistan, Pakistan's role in politics of dispute resolution and continued instability is adversely impacting regional security dynamics of South Asia and other regional states as well.

Therefore to sum up, South Asia one of the most volatile regions of the world shall remain in the present state of 'Unpleasant Stability', in the foreseeable future. This peculiar form of stability derives substantially from the inability of both India and Pakistan, the two big players in the region, to attain what may be desired political objectives. Strategic stability in South Asia is vital for emerging India's own growth, peace and stability. However, despite India's endeavours to assume regional leadership; its proactive policies in the region shall remain marginalised due to interests of extra regional players like China, growing religious fundamentalism and dynamics of partisan bilateral relations.

Endnotes

1   Hayes, Harold (1991) "Strategic Balance in Chess and Fencing"[Online: web] Accessed 30 Nov 2016 URL :http://saf.pair.com/chess.htm

2   Sheehan, Michael (1995), "The Balance of Power: History and Theory" [Online: web] Accessed 30 Nov 2016 URL :https://www.scribd.com/ document/331162074/SHEEHAN-The-Balance-of-Power-History-and-Theory-pdf

3   (2015) "Strategic Balance"[Online: web] Accessed 30 Nov 2016 URL:http:// www.businessdictionary.com/definition/strategic-balance.html

4   (2014) "Strategic Balance"[Online: web] Accessed 30 Nov 2016 URL :http:// csis.org/programs/international-security-program/asia-division/cross-strait-security-initiative-/strategic-ba

5   Paul, TV (2004), "Balance of Power – Theory and Practice in 21st Century," Stanford University Press, California

6   ibid

7   (2011)"China wants India in a low level equilibrium" [Online: web] Accessed 30 Nov 2016 URL: http://timesofindia.indiatimes.com/india/China-wants-India-in-state-of-low-level-equilibrium-PM/articleshow/6508868.cms.

8   Ghosh, Partha S (2013), "An Enigma that is South Asia: India versus the Region", Asia Pacific review, 20:1, 100-120

9   Nayak, Nihar (2013), "Cooperative Security Framework for South Asia," Pentagon Press, New Delhi.pp- 9.

10 (2010) "India foils attempt to bring China into South Asian group"[Online: web] Accessed 30 Nov 2016 URL : http://www.scmp.com/article/712578/india-foils-attempt-bring-china-south-asian-group

11 Anthony H. Cordesman, Steven Colley *(2015) "Chinese Strategy and Military Modernization in 2015: A Comparative Analysis"* [Online : web] Accessed 30 Nov 2016 URL :*https://books.google.co.in/books?id=i5RDCwAAQBAJ&pg=PA328&lpg=PA328&dq=China percent27s+nuanced+policy+on+No+First+Use+(NFU)*

12 Malik, Mohan (2001) "South Asia in China's Foreign Relations," Pacifica Review, 13(1): 73–90.

13 Sharip, Mohd Mansor HjMohd (2015) "United States - India Strategic Partnership: Implications For Asian Security" [Online: web] Accessed25 Oct 2016 URL:http://search.proquest.com/openview/ff7ff5cdd69ab7d316046f61c51d5f38/1?pq-origsite=gscholar&cbl=1456373

14 Alam, Mohammed Badrul(2012) ''India and Pakistan's Nuclear Doctrines: A Comparative Analysis" [Online : web]Accessed 25 Oct 2016 URL: http://sspconline.org/opinion/India_Pakistans_NuclearDoctrines_11042012

15 "Realism (international relations)" [Online : web]Accessed 25 Oct 2016 URL: http://en.wikipedia.org/wiki/Realism_(international_relations)

16 "List of countries by GDP (PPP)" [Online : web]Accessed 25 Oct 2016 URL: http://en.wikipedia.org/wiki/List_of_countries_by_GDP_(PPP)

17 Mohan, C. Raja(2000) "The Asian balance of power"[Online : web]Accessed 25 Oct 2016 URL: http://www.india-seminar.com/2000/487/487 percent20raja percent20mohan.htm

18 Chaturvedi, Rajeev Ranjan(2014) "Reviving the Maritime Silk Route"[Online : web]Accessed 30 Nov 2016 URL:http://www.thehindu.com/opinion/op-ed/reviving-the-maritime-silk-route/article5896989.ece

19 Bo Zhou (2014) "The String of Pearls and the Maritime Silk Road"[Online : web]Accessed 30 Nov 2016 URL: http://www.chinausfocus.com/foreign-policy/the-string-of-pearls-and-the-maritime-silk-road/

20 (2016) "News- Afghanistan" [Online: web] Accessed 25 Oct 2016 URL :http://www.tolonews.com/en/afghanistan/25826-us-general-nicholson-submits-his-assessment-of-the-situation-in-afghanistan

Chapter 2

Situation in Af- Pak Region: An Appraisal

"Afghanistan has moved forward and Afghanistan will defend itself. And the progress that we have achieved, the Afghan people will not allow it to be put back or reversed"

- Hamid Karzai

Introduction

The term Af-Pak was coined within US foreign policy circles to designate Afghanistan and Pakistan as a single theatre of operations. The term had reflected the policy approach introduced by the Obama administration, which regarded the region of Afghanistan and Pakistan as having a single, dominant political and military situation that required a joint policy in the War on Terror.[1] US Government stopped using the term in 2010 respecting Pakistan's sensitivities. However, in any case the efforts of US have primarily remained directed towards Afghanistan

Figure 2.1

and no substantial steps have been initiated towards Pakistan and its policy of state sponsored terrorism.

Since the end of the ISAF mission, Afghanistan continues to face significant complex challenges of governance, economy, security and regional dynamics. The Taliban has not been defeated militarily or politically and these challenges exist in the midst of an ongoing, resilient and entrenched Taliban-led insurgency.[2] The security situation in the region remains precarious despite more than 15 years of international community's efforts in Afghanistan. Further, the country's economy and society have been left fragile after decades of warfare that has left about two million dead, 700,000 widows and orphans, and about one million Afghan children raised in refugee camps outside Afghanistan. More than 3.5 million Afghan refugees have since returned, although a comparable number remain outside Afghanistan.[3]

Not only has Afghanistan seen ever increasing levels of violence and loss of life, the virus of instability and culture of violence has also spread across the Durand line into Pakistan which has a history of complex relations with Afghanistan having seen many ups and downs over the period of time. The fates of these two nations are inextricably tied. The two countries have many things in common: religion, ethnicity, and thousands of kilometres of border. The border and security issues have always overshadowed the relations between these two neighbours. The current situation has offered no cure to the ailment of mistrust rather it has widened the cracks and created more security fault lines between Pakistan and Afghanistan.

To sum up, a deadly insurgency, unstable government, poor economy, higher opium production, increasing civilian casualties, rampant corruption, an unstable neighbourhood remain the defining features of the complex and combustible situation in the Af-Pak region.[4]

The paper proposes to bring forth the prevailing environment in the region to include the political, economic and security situation with special emphasis on operations being conducted by the security forces of Afghanistan, Pakistan and NATO, major security fault lines between these two countries, the external political dynamics, implications, prognosis and a suggested way ahead.

Political Situation in Afghanistan

The presidential elections held on 05 April 2014 saw a repeat on 14 June 2014 as no candidate had won more than fifty percent votes. The second round saw Mr Ashraf Ghani wining the disputed elections decisively. However, both Mr Ghani and Mr Abdullah claimed victory which plunged the country into political crises which United Nations feared could descend the country into ethnic unrest of the 1990s civil war. However, a 'unity government' was formed with Mr Ghani serving as the next president and Mr Abdullah taking up the new role of chief executive, similar to that of prime minister. The elections were marred by widespread fraud, repeating serious problems seen in previous elections since the Taliban regime was ousted from power in 2001.[5]

The governance in the country is plagued by corruption, nepotism, and cronyism which remains rampant at all levels of government.[6] However, President Ashraf Ghani and CEO Abdullah Abdullah are institutionalising processes to establish rule of law and good governance. Amongst first of such efforts has been the creation of National Procurements Commission to review big government contracts, reopening of the messy Kabul Bank case, firing of a number of central as well as provincial high officials suspected of corruption or incompetence and improved communications with provincial officials.[7] Recently, the Afghan president elevated the role of governors in decision-making and monitoring of provincial affairs and started a process of budgetary devolution. In turn, he has placed more responsibility on his governors to curb local corruption. However, tangible progress demands earnest action against major instigators of corruption which remains to be taken. To establish rule of law requires tackling the political elite and their well-entrenched patronage networks. This task, in turn, requires a full, honest and sustained partnership between the Afghan government and its international supporters.[8]

Apart from tackling issues of corruption, the government has to remain focused on balancing complex ethnic dynamics in the country as ethnic fragmentation can exacerbate the fragile security situation. However, attempts to balance ethnic divisions are likely to adversely impact the governance. While power struggles between ethnic blocs can affect business operations at the provincial level and adversely impact the already fragile economy; ethnic fragmentation at the government level could lead to corresponding splits within the Afghan Security Forces.[9]

The stability of the government itself is questionable. Its writ does not extend to the entire country with many areas either governed by militia or non-state actor.[10] Desired governance in war-torn Afghanistan demands synergy between various organs of the government especially the President and the Chief Executive. Reportedly all is not well amongst the two with Mr Abdullah openly criticising President Ghani for being out of touch with the deteriorating situation in the country, failing to work collaboratively and deemed him undeserving to serve the government; raising fresh questions about the stability of the coalition formed in 2014.[11]

One key challenge facing the NUG is the timely convening of a Constitutional Loya Jirga to establish constitutional legality for the power-sharing arrangement. The political deal that created this government was originally for a two-year period that is set to expire in September 2016. Under the terms of that deal, the government was supposed to implement electoral reforms and hold district council and parliamentary elections to allow a Constitutional Loya Jirga to be convened. However, the reform process has stalled; the current term of parliament has expired without new elections being held, and district boundaries have not been drawn. The situation may lead to a constitutional crisis with uncertain consequences.[12]

Economic Situation in Afghanistan

Afghanistan remains one of the least developed countries in the world, ranking 175th on the United Nations' Human Development Index.[13] However, country's economy has recovered since 2001, largely because of the infusion of international assistance, the recovery of the agricultural sector and service sector growth. Nevertheless, 36 percent Afghans live below the national poverty line with 35 percent unemployed and suffer from shortages of housing, clean water, electricity, medical care and jobs. Criminality, insecurity, weak governance, lack of infrastructure, and Afghan Government's difficulty in extending rule of law to all parts of the country pose challenges to future economic growth.[14]

Despite the international community's commitment to Afghanistan's development, the country's growth rate showed sluggishness in 2014-15.[15] The deteriorating security environment and persisting political uncertainty continue to undermine private sector confidence. Economic growth increased only marginally from 1.3 percent in 2014 to an estimated 1.5 percent in 2015. Domestic demand remains weak, with no signs of a pick-up in private consumption and investment. Though, the number of new firms registration indicates small increase in new investment activities in 2015, it remains significantly below the levels of 2012-2013. Consumer prices dropped to -1.5 percent, down from 4.5 percent in 2014, due to lower private consumption and global commodity prices.[16] The drawdown of international security forces that started in 2014 has negatively affected economic growth, as a substantial portion of commerce, especially in the services sector, has catered to the ongoing international troop presence in the country.[17]

Agriculture, the second largest contributor to GDP growth after services, also declined by about 2 percent in 2015. With 45 percent of the poor relying on agriculture for their livelihood, sluggish GDP growth and a decline in agriculture production has put continuous upward pressure on poverty. However, all is not that bleak. The fiscal position has improved significantly. Domestic revenues rebounded to 10.6 percent in 2015, after a significant decline to 8.7 percent in 2014. The government also continued to exercise prudent expenditure controls in 2015. Improvement in revenue collection, more realistic budgeting and restraints on expenditures helped to balance the budget.[18]

As per the World Bank, a medium-term outlook of Afghanistan points towards a slow recovery over the next three years. Growth is projected at 1.9 percent in 2016, assuming adjustment in domestic consumption and investment. Growth is projected to gradually increase from 1.9 percent in 2016 to 3.6 percent in 2018, predicated on political stabilization and stronger reform efforts. However, further deterioration in the security environment pose significant downside risks and could weaken growth prospects.[19]

Security Situation in Afghanistan

The insurgent challenge to stability in Afghanistan has been sustained by a number of factors. These include public resentment against corruption in the Afghan government and unrealized economic expectations (discussed above), small numbers of security forces in many rural areas, logistical and other shortfalls on the part of the ANDSF, a backlash against civilian casualties caused by military operations and lastly safe haven enjoyed by militants in Pakistan.[20]

Security in Afghanistan is challenged by several armed groups that are allied with each other. Insurgency continues to take a heavy toll on the population and Afghan security forces. The Taliban's increased activity and military gains in the country as well as activity by Al-Qaeda and the ISIS have been resisted by Afghan security forces with the assistance of NATO.[21] However, loses sustained by ANDSF have been significant. As per the US Commander of the NATO Resolute Support Mission, "the ANDSF still cannot handle the fight alone without American close air support and a special operations counter terrorism force to hit the Taliban leadership". It will take time for them to build their human capital in logistics and managing their forces in the field, meaning Afghan forces will need international assistance well beyond this year [2015]."[22]

The various stakeholders and players in the security situation in Afghanistan are discussed in the subsequent paras.

Taliban

Taliban continues to be the main threat to ANDSF and the Afghan Government, exploiting its weaknesses particularly in rural areas. The new leadership under Mullah Haibatullah Akhunzada has announced that it would remain committed to battlefield operations and would not return to peace talks. As per US Department of Defense the strength of Taliban forces could be assessed at some 22,000 hard-core element members. The real strength of the Taliban, however, is not its numbers but its ability to 'influence and intimidate the population and to co-opt local support'.[23] The Taliban operates throughout Afghanistan, with the majority of its forces located in the Pashtun homeland in the country's south and east. However, as a result of the Taliban's successful capture of Kunduz in September 2015, it is evident that the Taliban has established itself outside its traditional Pashtun heartland and has been recruiting non-Pashtuns from Afghanistan's Northern provinces.[24] These non-Pashtun Taliban factions are reportedly said to be less ideological than the core of the Taliban movement in implementing Islamic law and other restrictions in areas under their control.[25]

Afghanistan's frontier provinces along the Pakistan border are of particular importance to the Taliban. It has established sanctuaries in these areas, adjacent to its safe havens in Pakistan (which have the patronage of Pakistan ISI patronage and Pakistani Taliban (Tehrik-e-Taliban Pakistan,

TTP), where it continues to plan, train, re-equip and seek refuge from ANDSF and US offensive operations.[26]

Haqqani Network

The 'Haqqani Network' was founded by Jalaludin Haqqani, a mujahedin commander and US ally during the US backed war against the Soviet occupation. Jalaluddin Haqqani served in the Taliban regime as Minister of Tribal Affairs and his network has fought against the current Afghan government. Over the past few years, Jalaludin's son Sirajuddin, now has largely taken over the group's operations and has become increasingly influential in setting overall insurgency strategy. Sirajuddin is also the deputy leader of the Taliban under its new leader, Mullah Akhunzada which has further strengthened Haqqani influence within the Taliban allowing it to increase its area of operations within Afghanistan. The network shares similar goals as the Taliban: namely, to expel coalition forces, destabilise the Afghan Government and re-establish an Islamic Emirate of Afghanistan.[27]

Haqqani Network, an arm of Pakistan's ISI, provides the Taliban with additional operational and planning capabilities. It enjoys safe havens in Pakistan and often acts as a tool of Pakistani interests in Afghanistan. Targeting of several Indian interests in Afghanistan is a proof of the same. The network claimed responsibility for July 2008 and October 2009 attacks on India's Embassy in Kabul. It is also considered the likely perpetrator of the August 4, 2013 attack on India's consulate in Jalalabad.[28]

The Haqqani Network had about 3,000 fighters and supporters between 2004-2010, but it is believed to have far fewer than that currently. Haqqani commanders had earlier indicated that the network may be prepared to participate in peace talks with the US and the Afghan Government, contingent on the Taliban leader Mullah Omar deciding to do so. However, Omar reportedly died in 2013, so its current willingness to negotiate is uncertain. Regardless, US officials assess that the Haqqani Network; the key facilitator of foreign fighters into Afghanistan will remain a major threat to Afghan security and coalition forces via its demonstrated capability for high-profile, complex attacks, particularly if it cannot be denied its safe haven in Pakistan.[29]

Al Qaeda

The post 2014 US counterterrorism mission in Afghanistan had been directed primarily against Al Qaeda and its associates and it was considered that as a result groups' presence within Afghanistan was minimal and focused on facilitating other insurgent forces, rather than acting as a fighting force itself. However, in late 2015, US Special Operations forces and their ANDSF partners discovered and destroyed a large Al Qaeda training camp in Kandahar Province, an indicator that Al Qaeda had expanded its presence in Afghanistan. In April 2016, US commanders publicly raised their estimates of Al Qaeda fighters in Afghanistan to 100-300, and said they are seeing an increasingly close relationship between Al Qaeda and the Taliban.[30]

The Islamic State-Khorasan Province (ISKP)

The Islamic State acting under the name of-Khorasan Province has increased its influence in Afghanistan since mid-2014. As per mid 2016, ISKP fighters in Afghanistan can be estimated at approximately 1000.[31] The group mostly comprises of foreign fighters and a small number of disaffected Taliban commanders and their supporters, operating in eastern Afghanistan in Nangarhar province. The group's goal in Afghanistan is likely to expand its presence further in north-eastern Afghanistan as well as in areas east of Kandahar.[32] As per press reports of late 2015, Afghan affiliates of the ISKP have started receiving financial assistance from the core organization located in the self-declared "caliphate" in parts of Iraq and Syria.[33] To address the apparent growing threat from ISKP, US conducted approximately 70 counter-terrorism strikes from January-March 2016 reducing ISKP presence to two to three provinces, from six to eight provinces three months ago.[34] Press reports indicate that Afghans consider the Taliban's practices as moderate compared to the brutality practiced by ISKP. On July 24, 2016, ISIS attacked a peaceful demonstration by Hazara protestors in Kabul which left over 80 killed; reviving fears about the continued strength of the group and the extent of its reach in Afghanistan. Worryingly, the attack also shows intentions of ISIS to inflame sectarian tensions and its capacity to carry out large-scale attacks in Kabul. But this is not necessarily indicative of its strength in Afghanistan, nor a prelude to any greater foothold of the group in the country.[35]

Hezb-i-Islami

Hizb-e-Islami-Gulbuddin (HIG) is another group under significant insurgent leader, a former mujahedin party leader Gulbuddin Hikmatyar. The faction received extensive US support against the Soviet Union, but turned against its mujahedin colleagues after the Communist government fell in 1992. The Taliban displaced HIG as the main opposition to the 1992-1996 Rabbani government. In the post-Taliban period, HIG has been ideologically and politically allied with the Taliban insurgents, but HIG fighters sometimes clash with the Taliban over control of territory. Not considered a major factor on the Afghanistan battlefield, the group has focused primarily on high-profile attacks. HIG is widely considered amenable to reconciliation with Kabul. In May 2016, it was reported that the government and Hikmatyar were close to finalizing a 25-point reconciliation agreement that could potentially serve as a model for reconciliations between the government and other groups.[36] In September 2016, Afghan government and the Gulbadin Hekmatyar-led Hezb-i-Islami Afghanistan (HIA) group inked the historic deal, when Ghani signed the deal and Hekmatyar affixed his signature to the document via a video link into the presidential palace. A nine-article decree has been issued by President Ghani on implementation of his government's peace agreement.[37]

Other Insurgent / Terrorist Groups

Islamic Movement of Uzbekistan (IMU)

The Islamic Movement of Uzbekistan (IMU) is a militant group active primarily against the authoritarian government in Uzbekistan. In Afghanistan, the IMU has been affiliated with Al Qaeda, although in recent months some of its fighters have aligned with the Islamic State branch there. The IMU might have as many as 300 fighters in Konduz Province alone. It is virtually active in all the northernmost provinces of Afghanistan. The IMU contingent in Afghanistan reportedly is led by Qari Balal, who escaped from a Pakistani jail in 2010. A splinter IMU group, the Jamaat Ansarullah, is active in Central Asia and northern Afghanistan.[38]

Lashkar-e-Tayyiba

Laskhar-e-Tayyiba (LET) is a Pakistani Islamist militant group which is becoming increasingly active inside Afghanistan. The group was initially focused on operations against Indian control of Kashmir. The group was responsible for the May 23, 2014, attack on India's consulate in Herat.[39]

Lashkar-i-Janghvi

Lashkar-i-Janghvi is another Pakistan-based group that is somewhat active in Afghanistan. It has conducted some suicide attacks in Afghanistan and was accused of several attacks on Afghanistan's Hazara Shiite community during 2011-2012.[40]

Harakat ul-Jihad Islami

Harakat ul-Jihad Islami is a Pakistan-based militant group that trained in Al Qaeda camps. Its former leader, Ilyas Kashmiri, was killed in U.S. drone strike in June 2011. He had earlier been indicted in the United States for supporting LET operative David Coleman Headley, who planned a terrorist attack on a Danish newspaper (Jyllands-Posten).[41]

ANDSF – An Update

On January 1, 2015, the Afghan National Defence and Security Forces (ANDSF) took over full security responsibility in Afghanistan, after the US officially concluded Operation Enduring Freedom and the North Atlantic Treaty Organization (NATO) ended the International Security Assistance Force (ISAF) mission.[42] The follow-on, NATO-led Resolute Support (RS) mission provides further training, guidance, and assistance to Afghan security forces and institutions. The U.S. Forces in Afghanistan transitioned to Operation Freedom's Sentinel, contributing to both the NATO's RS mission and continuing U.S. counterterrorism efforts against the remnants of al-Qaeda and the ISIS.[43]

The security situation in Afghanistan is synonymous with the effectiveness of ANDSF which primarily comprises of the Afghan National Army (ANA) and Afghan National Police (ANP). The current authorized strength of the ANDSF is 195,000 for the ANA (including 7,800 Afghan Air Force personnel) and 157,000 for ANP. Additionally, the ALP are authorized an additional 30,000 personnel.[44] The size of the forces less the ALP is about 10 percent below the authorised strength. About 1,700 women serve in the ANDSF, of which about 1,370 are police.[45]

From inception, the ANDSF have experienced shifting political and security conditions that have impacted their size, structure, mission and capacity. The force has long been dependent on U.S. financial and operational assistance, as well as support from the North Atlantic Treaty Organization. They are expected to remain dependent on foreign aid for many years. Although well-designed on paper, the ANDSF's command and control structure does not function as intended. The structure is bureaucratically heavy at the top and weak at the bottom. Political interference and the circumventing of formal command levels often prevent the carrying out of established procedures, plans and unit functions. Further, coordination across the ANA, ANP and National Directorate of Security forces in the field is dangerously lacking. The nature of shared decision making within the National Unity Government has led to delays in appointments, thus inhibiting the ability of Afghan security ministries and their forces to effectively exercise command and control.[46]

The force faces major human resource management issues as almost one third of the force does not reenlist each year and therefore the sheer need for rapid recruitment impinges adversely on the selection of desirable personnel. The ANDSF continue to experience major logistics, air power and intelligence shortfalls, undermining their operational posture and the combat effectiveness of their troops.[47] Further, as per the US DOD report ANDSF suffered about 5,500 combat deaths in 2015, which is unsustainable.[48]Afghan Army Gen Shir Mohammad Karimi, the former general staff chief of operations, said that to stem casualties, improve capacity and boost morale, Afghanistan needs close air support, heavy weaponry and, most of all, training which needs to be done on the front line. Military experts say that the lack of modem technology and weapons have created major challenges to Afghan forces in their struggle against the militants.[49]

However, it was encouraging to see that despite the heavy losses no units or groups of units collapsed or conducted any disorganized retreats in the face of Taliban offensives. The statement by Afghan Army Chief of Staff Gen Qadam Shah Shaheem, while speaking during a ceremony to mark the 97th Independence Day of Afghanistan in Kabul that ANDSF were turning Afghanistan into a graveyard of terrorism; reflects the resolve of the force.[50]Nevertheless, ANDSF needs to urgently avoid overextension and improve the space-to-force ratio. It should change its operational posture from being defensive to offensive. This would mean prioritizing some areas and leaving other areas for local forces to cover. Remote, hard to reach locations should only be watched and hit where the enemy shows concentration.

Role of Regional and Extra Regional Players in Afghanistan

Pakistan

Pakistan is considered as the most important neighbour of Afghanistan, crucial for its security. However, experts and officials of many countries debate whether Pakistan is committed to Afghan stability or to exerting control of Afghanistan through ties to insurgent groups. Afghan militant safe haven in Pakistan is identified by experts as a threat to Afghan stability. Afghan President Ashraf Ghani has blamed Pakistan for providing safe havens to terrorists and has said that state-to-state ties with the neighbouring country a "bigger challenge" for his government than combating terror groups such as al-Qaeda and Taliban.[51]

Many Afghans had viewed positively Pakistan's role as the hub for US backing of the mujahedin that forced the Soviet withdrawal in 1988-1989, but later came to resent Pakistan as one of only three countries to formally recognize the Taliban as the legitimate government. Its support to the Taliban continues unabated. The failure of Quadrilateral Coordination Group (QCG) which involves China, Pakistan and the U.S. in addition to Afghanistan – is not only due to the pursuit of individual objectives by certain QCG member states but primarily the apparent obstinacy of the Taliban.

The failure is an indication that Afghanistan will not be able to come to an agreement with the Taliban on peace initiates, as long as there is a Western footprint in the country. Pakistan's role in facilitating peace talks is critical, given its clout within the Taliban. However, Pakistan is not inclined to make efforts commensurate with that clout and push the Taliban towards peace talks. This suggests two hypotheses about Pakistan's role. First, an important issue to consider is the extent to which Pakistan has the will to help facilitate peace talks. It appears that Islamabad is questioning its interest in reconciliation between the Taliban and the government of Afghanistan under the current constitution. Pakistan calculates that a post reconciliation role for the Taliban in the Afghan government would not give Islamabad the influence it wants in Afghanistan. Given this policy paradigm, even if elements within the Taliban show interest in peace talks without the behest of Pakistan, events in the past have shown that Pakistan will target and neutralize these elements if peace talks are truly Afghan-led and Afghan owned.[52]

The second hypothesis is whether Pakistan really does not have the influence, as it claims it does not, with the Taliban to push the group towards negotiation. This hypothesis seems unlikely. However, as per a report in the Guardian dated 18 October 2016, the Afghan government and the Taliban have restarted the secret talks in Qatar. Interestingly it did not have any representative from Pakistan and only one senior diplomat from the US side to facilitate the talks was present. Therefore the possibility of both Afghan government and the Taliban releasing the futility of Pakistan's role in the peace process seems high.[53] As far as Pakistan is concerned it continues to see the Taliban as a strategic asset and proxy to promote the country's interests and help it counterweigh India's perceived influence in Afghanistan. On the other hand, it talks of having only marginal influence with the group and using it as an excuse not to fulfil the promises it made as a member of QCG.[54]

The India factor in Afghanistan is a cause of major concern for Pakistan. President Ghani has publically stated that Kabul was proud of its friendship with India, as India shares Afghanistan's democratic aspirations.[55] Analysts suggest that Pakistan uses proxy forces in Afghanistan to counter Indian influence there. Some argue that Pakistan sees Afghanistan as potentially providing it with strategic depth against India.[56] Pakistan wants to limit India's influence in Afghanistan. It has long asserted that India is using its Embassy and four consulates in Afghanistan (Pakistan says India has nine consulates) to recruit anti-Pakistan insurgents, and that India is using its aid programs only to build influence there. At a February 2013 meeting in Britain, Pakistan had demanded that Afghanistan scale back relations with India and sign a strategic agreement with Pakistan that includes Pakistani training for the ANDSF. Pakistan's Defence Secretary stated in January 2014 that Pakistan would not accept a robust role for India in Afghanistan as international forces wind down involvement in Afghanistan.[57]

Settling of the International Border between Afghanistan and Pakistan is another issue of discord. There are no indications the two countries are close to settling the long-standing issue. Pakistan has long sought that

Afghanistan formally recognize as the border the 'Durand Line'. However, though the Durand Line is recognized by the United Nations, Afghanistan continues to indicate that the border was drawn unfairly to separate Pashtun tribes and should be renegotiated.[58] The issue of 'Pashtunistan' is linked to this unresolved border issue. Pakistan has always considered Afghanistan's support for Pashtunistan as a threat to its national security. While there is little support for an independent Pashtunistan in Pakistan now, elements in Afghanistan still think it to be a useful future.[59]

However, there have been some positive developments as well between the two states. Afghanistan-Pakistan Transit Trade Agreement (APTTA) signed on 18 Jul 2010 is one such example. The agreement allows for easier exportation via Pakistan of Afghan products, which are mostly agricultural products that depend on rapid transit and are key to Afghanistan's economy. It is expected to greatly expand the $2 billion in trade per year the two countries were doing prior to the agreement. The agreement represented a success for the Canada-sponsored 'Dubai Process' of talks between Afghanistan and Pakistan on modernizing border crossings, new roads and a comprehensive border management strategy to meet IMF benchmarks. However, a drawback to the agreement is that Afghan trucks, under the agreement, are not permitted to take back cargo from India after dropping off goods there. The Afghanistan-Pakistan trade agreement followed agreements to send more Afghan graduate students to study in Pakistan, and a June 2010 agreement to send small numbers of ANA officers to train in Pakistan.[60]

Pakistan is faced with dilemmas in its Afghanistan policy. Its leaders sometimes appear to believe that instability in Afghanistan will rebound to Pakistan's detriment and therefore it was essential to promote a political settlement within Afghanistan. Pakistan has begun training small numbers of ANA officers in Pakistan. In May 2015, a demonstration of improving cooperation came in the form of a Memorandum of Understanding for Afghanistan's NDS Intelligence Service to be trained by Pakistan's Inter-Services Intelligence Directorate (ISI), its key intelligence arm. The agreement came despite Pakistan's complaints that militants expelled by the Pakistani military are being given safe haven in Afghanistan.[61]

Pakistan's emerging economic ambitions in Afghanistan is driving its security strategy in the country and in some ways adds to its dilemmas. Pakistan needs energy for its own economic revitalisation and the

Turkmenistan-Afghanistan-Pakistan-India pipeline [TAPI], with all its hurdles, provides an energy source that will be in Pakistan's capital stock for fifty more years. The pipeline is expected to complete by 2019. In recent years, the abundant energy resources in Central Asia, largely untapped, have triggered a race amongst the big powers for gas and oil pipelines in and around the region. Moreover, Pakistan and Afghanistan's geostrategic setting between the energy-loaded Middle East and Central Asia, and the energy-keen and growing economies of India and China naturally triggers some strong potential drivers for economic development in both Afghanistan and Pakistan.[62]

The Afghan government's relationship with Pakistan remains a critical aspect of enhancing security and stability in Afghanistan. Though, in December 2015, Heart of Asia Conference in Islamabad, Pakistan, President Ghani and Pakistani Prime Minister Nawaz Sharif reaffirmed their commitment to Taliban peace talks; results have been mixed.[63] Pakistan's ongoing counterterrorism and counterinsurgency operations in the Federally Administered Tribal Areas (FATA) and other areas technically reduce some militant groups' ability to use Pakistani territory as a safe haven for terrorism and a base of support for the insurgency in Afghanistan. However, desired results are not forthcoming.

To summarise the three point agenda suggested by President Ghani to build trust with Pakistan is the essence. Firstly, to take action against declared terrorist groups to build trust. Secondly, all countries should act on the quadrilateral process, regarding reconcilable and irreconcilable (groups). Thirdly those who reject peace talks should be evacuated from Pakistan.[64]

China

China's involvement in Afghanistan is aimed at securing access to Afghan minerals and other resources help Pakistan avoid encirclement by India and reduce the Islamist militant threat.[65] It remains concerned about Islamic militants operating in Afghanistan assisting restive Uighur community. The East Turkestan Islamic Movement (ETIM) is an opposition group in China, some of whose operatives are based in Afghanistan.[66]

Since 2012, China has deepened its involvement in Afghan security issues with signing of security and economic agreements. Chinese forces have never been deployed in Afghanistan. Nevertheless, China has been training small numbers of ANP at a People's Armed Police facility since 2006, with a focus on counter narcotics. However, China is now willing to play more prominent role as a potential mediator in Afghan reconciliation. As part of Beijing's commitment to provide millions of dollars of assistance to help Kabul fight terrorism; on 03 Jul 2016, Afghanistan received its first batch of Chinese military equipment; comprising of logistical equipment, parts of military vehicles, ammunition and weapons for the Afghan National Defence and Security Forces (ANDSF).[67]

Perhaps because of China's growing role in Afghanistan's affairs, CEO Abdullah said in May 2016 that Afghanistan supports China's position on the SCS and China's efforts to resolve issues through peaceful means.

Chinese activities in Afghanistan are primarily economically driven. From 2002 to 2014, China provided about $255 million in economic aid to Afghanistan. A fresh aid package of $2.2 million has been pledged by China to Afghanistan in Aug 2016 as the country attempts to expand its role in civilian and military domains in the country.[68] China has built border access routes and supply depots to facilitate China's access to Afghanistan through "Wakhan Corridor".

Cornerstone of China's investment to date has been the development of the Aynak copper mine south of Kabul. At present, the Afghan government is locked in a contractual struggle with the company, Metallurgical Corporation of China Limited (MCC), over royalties from the $3 billion effort, which is said to undergird potential copper resources in excess of $100 billion. Delays have plagued the ambitious project since a deal was inked in 2007, though the government claims 7,000 jobs are being created, with a $1.2 billion impact on the national economy. MCC may not be in a hurry, as it holds a 30-year lease for the site.[69] China has made inroads in oil sector as well. In 2012, China National Petroleum Company was awarded the rights to develop oil deposits in the Amu Darya basin.[70]This project is estimated to yield about $7 billion in profits.

Transportation and trade routes through Afghanistan complement China's vision of a "One Belt, One Road" regional network linking East, Central, and South Asia.

Iran

Iran's national interests in Afghanistan are primarily two. Firstly, to deny US use of Afghanistan as a base from which to pressure or attack Iran (Iran strenuously but unsuccessfully sought to scuttle the May 1, 2012 US-Afghanistan SPA and the US-Afghanistan BSA) and secondly to export its political ideology into Afghanistan and contain Salafism and Sunni extremism.[71]However, Iran has failed to develop a coherent long term strategy which is a cause of distrust on the Afghan side. Tehran's power projection in Afghanistan through Shiite symbolism has turned Shiite communities into vulnerable religious islands, making them outsiders within their own country. In May 2015, a political organization, Afghan Milli Ghorzang launched protest in front of Iranian embassy in Kabul to end cultural invasion of Afghanistan by Iran.[72]

Iran's interests in Afghanistan also need to be analysed from its regional rival, Saudi Arabia's point of view as well. Iran's sponsorship of religious madrasas and clerics in Afghanistan has not gone ignored by Saudi Arabia. Iran-Saudi rivalry is an extension of the Shia-Sunni divide which has portends of intensifying radicalization of religious communities in Afghanistan that have traditionally coexisted in relative harmony.[73] While Karzai maintained a friendly relationship with Iran, President Ghani has supported Saudi-led coalition attacks on Yemen's Houthi insurgency which undermines the Iran-Afghan neighbourly relationship to some extent.

Iran's support to Taliban too is a cause of concern. Reportedly it has been arming and providing training to the Taliban cadres. It has also allowed a Taliban office to open in Iran, and high-level Taliban figures have visited Iran.[74] While some see the contacts as Iranian support to the insurgency, others see it as an effort to exert some influence over reconciliation efforts. Iran cannot afford to get side-lined from political, security and economic developments in Afghanistan. A Stable Afghanistan is in Iran's interest. However, there is an apparent duality of symbolism and development in Iranian's foreign policy vis-à-vis Afghanistan. [75]

Nevertheless, Iran has had success in building ties to the Afghan government, despite its heavy reliance on US support. Ghani has generally endorsed the approach of his predecessor on Iran, which was to call Iran a "friend" of Afghanistan and to assert that Afghanistan must not become an arena for the broader competition and disputes between the US and

Iran.[76] The two states have a consistent pattern of high level visits which has facilitated better understanding of mutual interests. Ghani visited Tehran during April 19-20, 2015, and held meetings with President Rouhani and Supreme Leader Ali Khamene'i, yielding agreement to work jointly against the organization, which Iran is helping combat in Iraq and, to a lesser extent, in Syria.[77]

Iran remains committed towards Afghanistan's reconstruction. It has pledged about $1 billion in aid to Afghanistan, of which about $500 million has been provided to date. The funds have been used mostly to build roads and bridges in western Afghanistan. In cooperation with India, Iran has been building roads that would connect western Afghanistan to Iran's port of Chahbahar and provide goods from Afghanistan an easier outlet to the Persian Gulf.[78] Trade and Transit Treaties, cooperation in energy and education is bringing balance to the overall relations.[79]

Russia

Russia firmly believes that a stable and secure Afghanistan is in its national interest. The two states have become friends again, putting behind their past enmity and bitter memories from the decade-long Soviet occupation. The two countries today share good relations, and they even signed a security agreement last year.[80] It is sensitive to Talibanisation, increase in Wahhabism and role of Islamic Jihadists in Afghanistan. During the 1990s, after its 1989 withdrawal and the breakup of Soviet Union, Russia supported the Northern Alliance against the Taliban with some military equipment and technical assistance in order to blunt Islamic militancy emanating from Afghanistan.

However, increasing presence of ISIS in Afghanistan has led to convergence of Russia's interests with those of the Taliban as per Zamir Kabulov, a department chief at Russia's Foreign Ministry and President Vladimir Putin's special representative to Afghanistan. Reportedly, Russian government apart from urging the Taliban to participate in peace talks is also seeking information on (IS) terrorist group.[81] Russians view IS as a bigger threat to their interests. And therefore they seek to use the Taliban, as a hedge against the growing influence of IS in the neighbourhood. As per September 2015 UN report IS fighters were operating in 25 of Afghanistan's 34 provinces. Many of these militants are former Taliban members. It is estimated that there are currently some 2500 IS fighters in the country.[82]

Though Russia seeks to contain US power in Central Asia; it tacitly accepts its presence for furthering the battle against radical Islamists based in Afghanistan. There are no indications of Russia's military intervention in Afghanistan; however it has publicly offered to play a role in combatting affiliates in Afghanistan which appears as an effort to justify its military intervention in Syria.[83]

Russia's cooperation in developing the Northern Distribution Network supply line to Afghanistan has been significant. About half of all ground cargo for US forces in Afghanistan flowed through the Northern Distribution Network from 2011-2014, despite the extra costs as compared to the Pakistan route. US equipment during the 2014 US/NATO troop drawdown was also removed through this route. [84]

Russia is investing $1 billion in Afghanistan to develop its electricity capacity and build out other infrastructure. It is also investing in housing construction sector in Afghanistan which is seen as a critical step forward considering the previous engagements in which 11,000 housing units in the form of blocks in Macroryan were constructed.[85]

Central Asian States

The Central Asian States of Tajikistan, Uzbekistan, Turkmenistan and Kyrgyzstan worried are worried about the spill over effects of NATO forces withdrawal from Afghanistan, especially with the growing influence of the terrorists.[86] These fears are further accentuated with the growing number of Tajik, Uzbek, Chechen and Kyrgyz fighters on battlefields of Afghanistan fighting for either ISIS or the Taliban. It will not be naïve to assume that the security situation in the region can get extremely precarious if extremists find safe havens and training grounds in Afghanistan's Northern provinces. Poor cross border security coordination and intelligence sharing mechanisms, regional trust deficit, coupled with organized crime and drug trafficking further exacerbate this problem.[87]

Ties between Afghanistan and Central Asia are driven more by security imperatives than by trade and energy. In 1996, several of the CARs banded together with Russia and China into the SCO because of the perceived Taliban threat. Many in Central Asia quietly welcomed the arrival of NATO forces in Afghanistan as an alternative to Russia and China. Also earned sizeable revenues in security, economic and trade deals to supply equipment and facilitate trade and supply routes to ISAF/NATO forces in the country.

Today ANDSF is fighting Chechen, Uzbek, Tajik and Kyrgyz extremists in Northern provinces at huge costs. However, there is little acknowledgement from Central Asian neighbours. In the present geostrategic environment cooperation amongst CARs and with Afghanistan is crucial. Success of New Silk Road (NSR) strategy that seeks to help Afghanistan become a trade crossroads between South and Central Asia, successful realisation of TAPI which will help Afghanistan earn vital transit fees and custom duties depends upon this cooperation.

United States

US is undoubtedly the most important player in Afghanistan. Successful transition as also stability in Af-Pak region will depend upon its policies in the region. In last 10-12 years, US diplomacy has followed military objectives leading to engagement with Taliban and Pakistan, relegating or neglecting engagement with India, China, Russia, Iran and Central Asian Republics; hindering regional cooperation. US has decided to keep 8400 troops in Afghanistan through 2016.

Preserving a military stalemate in Afghanistan is a major challenge to US drawdown with increase in Taliban offensive and consequent loss of territory. US today seeks greater role of regional stakeholders in Afghan reconciliation, albeit without losing strategic space in Afghanistan.[88]

India

India's national interests in Afghanistan are a part of its strong geopolitical and strategic interests in South Asian and Central Asian Regions. Moreover, it shares deep cultural and historical relations with Afghanistan and therefore; India's engagement in Afghanistan is neither transitory nor transient. It aims at fostering a sphere of influence across South Asia to promote regional stability.

India cannot afford to let Afghanistan get into chaos, for it will not be safe from the spill over. Therefore, it is imperative for India to assist Afghanistan in building sound political structures, a strong military and economy, along with human resources. It cannot afford to let Afghanistan slide back to the days of Taliban rule after 15 years of Western intervention.[89]

India's apprehensions about Afghanistan's instability are primarily driven by its own pragmatic security concerns. On March 2, 2016, the Indian consulate in the city of Jalalabad in Afghanistan was attacked, leaving nine dead and many more injured in the fourth attack on the Indian consulate in the city.[90]

An unstable backyard is not only pernicious to India's larger strategic interests abroad and future goals but can also impact its internal security. Afghanistan has served as springboard not only for al-Qaeda and the Taliban but also for Kashmir-focused terrorist groups. After the withdrawal of Soviet forces from Afghanistan in 1989, jihadists moved to new conflict zones, including Kashmir. Following 9/11, Pakistani militant groups moved to Afghanistan to fight against the Western coalition. After the withdrawal of ISAF forces from Afghanistan, it is highly likely that they could focus their attention back on Kashmir. Groups like Jaish-e-Mohammad (JeM), Harkat ul-Mujahideen (HUM), and Lashkar-e-Taiba (LeT) might increase their activities in Indian Kashmir.[91]

The emergence of the Islamic State terrorist group's local franchise, IS-Khurasan, and al-Qaeda's South Asian affiliate, AQIS, has further complicated the regional threat environment. However, the presence of traditional groups like the Taliban and geopolitical conflicts in the Af-Pak region and Kashmir lessen Islamic States' traction.

Another aspect of India's interest in Afghanistan relates to its need to reduce Pakistani influence in the region. Afghanistan has been the battleground for an India-Pakistan proxy war since 2001. New Delhi needs Kabul to get a better view of Islamabad and hence it is pertinent that it fosters positive relations.

From the economic point India looks at Afghanistan as a hub for its economic integration with Eurasia. Economic / transportation corridor with Iran-Afghanistan- Central Asian States, South-South corridor linking Eurasia-Afghanistan-Pakistan-India- Southeast Asia and oil pipelines with Central Asian States, Russia, Iran for energy security are few such examples. These projects can see the light of the day only if stability is established in Afghanistan.

Afghanistan not only serves security and economic interests of Indian but is also closely tied to its vision of being a regional leader and a great power. India is whole heartedly assisting Afghanistan in reconstruction and stability. It is the fifth-largest bilateral donor to Afghanistan with over $2 billion in pledged support. It has recently during President Ghani's visit to India on 14 September 2016 pledged fresh $1 billion in economic assistance to strengthen already close ties between the two countries.[92]

Security Situation across the Durand Line – 'Pakistan in Turmoil'

Since its birth in 1947, having been carved out of mostly Hindu India, as a homeland for Muslims when India gained independence from Britain, Pakistan has lived in constant turmoil. Conceived as a democracy, it has been ruled by the military for half its life having experienced three successful military coups till date. Even when elected governments have ruled, the military, especially the Inter-Services Intelligence agency, has played a forceful role.

Figure 2.2

The government has made major investments in nuclear arsenal although many citizens still lack access to clean drinking water or a toilet. Engaged in off-and-on talks with its traditional foe India, its leaders have deep suspicions of the fellow nuclear power next door that continue to drive national priorities. [93]

India routinely accuses Pakistan of backing anti-India militants in the fight over the border state Kashmir. Pakistan supported the Taliban in the early 1990s to subvert Afghanistan's Soviet-backed government.

After the 2001 U.S.-led invasion of Afghanistan brought to power a government friendlier to India, Taliban remnants found refuge in Pakistan.

So did al-Qaeda leader Osama bin Laden — until U.S. forces killed him in a 2011 raid. The policy of using extremists to pursue strategic goals has blown back on Pakistan. Militant groups have metastasized and struck within the country, largely against security forces and Muslims of the minority Shiite sect. By one estimate, more than 59,000 people have died in terrorist violence in Pakistan since 2003. [94]

The ongoing insurgency in Balochistan, Pak forceful occupation of Gilgit-Baltistan and the critical terrorist threat in northwest Pakistan, dominates the overall security environment in the country.

Northwest Pakistan

Northwest Pakistan consists of Khyber Pakhtunkhwa Province (KP), the provincial capital Peshawar and the Federally Administered Tribal Areas (FATA). KP shares borders with the FATA to the west; Gilgit–Baltistan the northeast; Azad Kashmir, Islamabad and Punjab to the east and southeast. KP also shares an international border with Afghanistan, connected through the Khyber Pass.[95]

FATA shares border with the restive province of Balochistan to the east and south, Afghanistan's provinces of Kunar, Nangarhar, Paktia, Khost and Paktika to the west and north. The territory is almost exclusively inhabited by the Pashtuns, who also live in the neighbouring provinces of KP and Northern Balochistan.[96]

The security situation in Peshawar is tenuous at best. Northwest Pakistan is a dangerous region with Pakistani authorities having only minimal control in many areas of KP province and FATA, including the Swat Valley and North and South Waziristan. The presence of Al-Qaeda, ISIS, Afghan and Pakistani Taliban elements and other indigenous militant sectarian groups and geographic proximity to the Afghanistan border, continue to pose a danger. These areas act as a safe haven for these terrorist groups to prepare, train and carry out attacks. Targeted attacks against government officials, property, military, law enforcement and soft targets (educational facilities) are common. [97]

A historical review shows that terrorist incidents rose dramatically from 2007-2010, with late 2009-mid-2010 marking a high point of large-scale attacks on the outskirts of Peshawar. Subsequently, from mid-2012-

early 2014, brazen attacks against high-level Pakistani targets in Peshawar rose, despite perceived better security near the city. The summer of 2014 saw a decline in militant activity and a relatively stable period, which was shattered on 16 December 2014 when seven Taliban gunmen killed 150 children and teachers at the Army Public School inside a military-controlled area of Peshawar.

Following this attack, the government implemented the National Action Plan and focused efforts by the security apparatus on targeting militants and their sanctuaries across the province. As reported by the Office of the Inspector General of Police, this concerted effort captured or killed thousands of militants and seized some 20,000 weapons and thousands of kilograms of explosives.[98]

Balochistan

Balochistan is Pakistan's largest region, rich in mineral resources but one of its most impoverished provinces. The region remains plagued by constant acts of violence. But insurgency and armed conflicts in Balochistan are not a new phenomenon. The violence dates back to late 19th century when the region came under the administration of the British Empire. During the early 20th century, Balochistan strove to become a "British free" region; later on, it was forcibly annexed by newly founded Pakistan in 1948 and ever since the inhabitants of this region are striving for provincial autonomy as promised by the father of the nation and the constitution of Pakistan. However, continuous suppression by the federal government through military might has turned this quest into a separatist movement.[99]

Andrew Small, in his book 'The China-Pakistan Axis', has maintained that the biggest concern for the China, Pakistan's closest ally is growing terrorism in the region, where Beijing has agreed to invest $46 billion for CPEC.[100] Pakistan has repeatedly accused India of fomenting insurgency and terrorism in Balochistan (through Afghanistan). The Pakistani government claims that Baloch separatists receive training in camps in Afghanistan established by India. Interestingly, in 1970s, Afghan President Daoud Khan had established militant camps in his country to train Baloch separatists. This continued to be the case until President Hamid Karzai's government, when he assured Islamabad that Afghan soil would not be used against their neighbour.[101]

Indian PM's words of support to Baloch freedom movement from the ramparts of the Red Fort on the 15 Aug 2016; which immediately saw protests in Dera Bugti, Khuzdar, Quetta, Chaman and other parts of the province by the tribesmen further exacerbate Pakistan's concern.[102]

In response the authorities registered cases against separatist Baloch leaders Brahamdagh Bugti, Harbiyar Marri and Banuk Karima Baloch in Pakistan for supporting Indian PM's statements.[103] Incidentally exiled Baloch leader Brahamdagh Bugti, (the grandson of Baloch nationalist leader Nawab Akbar Khan Bugti who was killed by Pakistani forces 10 years ago), who is leader of Baloch Republican Party (BRP), heading the movement in Balochistan is seeking an asylum in India not only for himself but other Baloch leaders currently staying in Balochistan, Afghanistan and in some other countries.[104]

On August 8, 2016 a blast in Balochistan's capital, Quetta, killed at least 95 people. The same day Pakistan's PM and Army Chief visited the injured and labelled the attack an attempt to sabotage CPEC in an official statement. Balochistan's Chief Minister accused India's intelligence agency RAW of being behind the attack whereas national media linked the bombing to "India backed Afghanistan".[105]

Interestingly, Pakistan has now linked such activities to Iran also, whose Sistan province borders Balochistan; the only land route that connects both countries travels through this region. However, the same is surprising keeping into view Iran's interests in joining the CPEC which it feels will facilitate regional growth.[106]

The issue of Balochistan is not restricted between the regional players. The U.S. has also expressed concerns regarding human rights violations in Balochistan, making Pakistan wary of an intrusion into the Islamic Republic's internal matters. On Feb 08, 2012, the U.S. House of Representative Committee on Foreign Affairs convened a congressional hearing on Balochistan where it was argued that Balochistan is under siege by the Pak federal government and rights of the Balochs were restricted. Pakistan's military was also accused of using "American arms" against their own people in Balochistan. The event's chair, Dana Rohrabacher, has advocated for self-determination in Balochistan, even up to independence. Given the U.S. track record of meddling in the internal affairs of many countries under the guise of human rights, Islamabad assumes that the US agenda in Balochistan is far greater that just human rights violations.[107]

India's stance on Balochistan is significant keeping into view the CPEC and the ongoing Kashmir imbroglio in an overall environment of endemically strained relations between India and Pakistan and mutual distrust between India and China. Emerging India's growing interests in Afghanistan (Pakistan's backyard) and the strategic partnership with the US further accentuate concerns of both Pakistan and China.[108]

Among all the speculations, apprehensions, assumptions, and accusations, peace in Balochistan means a peaceful South Asian region. Its importance has grown beyond all estimates for a successful CPEC. However, the big question is whether India will like to exploit this trump card and build up a diplomatic challenge (under a veiled sub conventional threat) for Pakistan in the prevailing geostrategic environment? At the UN human rights council on 20 September 2016, India sent out a strong message to Pakistan asking it to stop promoting terrorism and human rights violations in Balochistan and PoK.[109]

Statements by Indian leadership on Balochistan in wake of the terror attack in Uri represent some bold and out-of-the-box thinking by the Indian government. India can be expected to regularly highlight the plight of Balochs on the international stage to create momentum around their cause.

Gilgit-Baltistan

As per Senge H. Sering, a cultural activist from Baltistan, who currently is President, Institute for Gilgit-Baltistan Studies, Washington, while giving details of the massacre of local Shia population by the Taliban and other Punjabi and Pashtun Sunnis, highlights that, "Baltistan is experiencing an artificial social osmosis". While poverty and Taliban threats are causing Shia exodus from their ancestral homes, an increasing number of Pakistanis are acquiring land in Baltistan and claiming their stake as its citizens as a result of the abrogation of State Subject Rule (SSR) which barred outsiders from acquiring land in Baltistan to preserve its unique identity.

Such a government sponsored strategy has damaged the social fabric of Baltistan and provoked religious feuds which continue to simmer.

Many of these wealthy newcomers exert power and influence in the socio-political arena by imposing their language and customs upon the locals, which further exacerbate the identity crisis. To counter such trends, leading religious leaders of Gilgit-Baltistan have been demanding the reinstatement of SSR. They are concerned about the increasing number of Pashtuns and Punjabis control over local commerce. Similar views are being expressed by religious students of Imamia Students Organization (ISO) and Nurbakhshi Youth Federation (NYF).[110]

It is interesting to note that in 1998 Shia resentment in Gilgit-Baltistan against the creeping demographic shock and the injection of Sunni-fundamentalist tendencies by Pakistan took the form of demands for an autonomous Shia province to be called 'Karakoram State'. Zia-ul Haq responded to Shia mobilisation with military force. Pakistan's former President, General Pervez Musharraf in 1988 (as Brigadier) led a ruthless campaign against Shia dissent with the assistance of Islamist militia groups led by a then-obscure Saudi jihadi named Osama bin Laden destroying crops, houses, lynching and burning people to death in the villages around Gilgit town. The number of dead and injured was put in hundreds.[111]

Recently, Balawaristan National Front (BNF), a dissident group from the Gilgit region based in Belgium has written to the United Nations Secretary General Ban Ki-moon, urging UN intervention in saving two million people of the Pakistan-occupied territory where China has been developing infrastructure under the CPEC project. The BNF claims that Pakistan has hatched a conspiracy to sell the whole region to China on the pretext of the CPEC without taking the UN or people of Gilgit-Baltistan into confidence.[112] Pakistan had earlier violated the territorial integrity and sovereignty of Jammu and Kashmir by giving 2,500 square miles of Shimshaal, Hunza and Gilgit-Baltistan to China in 1963 to construct the Karakoram highway for its own military benefits.[113]

Highlighting the grave human right violations, BNF chairman Abdul Hamid Khan has urged the world body and European Union to put pressure on Pakistan to end the occupation of Gilgit-Baltistan and withdraw its civilians and military forces by fulfilling its obligations under United Nations Commission for India and Pakistan (UNCIP) resolutions. The letter says political leaders are being treated as terrorists and real terrorists are free to torture and kill political and religious opponents who do not obey the 'enslaving orders of the occupying forces and their intelligence agencies'.[114]

Echoing the same sentiments, Shaukat Kashmiri, Chairman, United Kashmir People's National Party, says emphatically that "In our view, the Republic of India has a constitutional responsibility to unify the whole state of Jammu and Kashmir, to push back all infiltrators, to ask the government of Pakistan to vacate the occupied areas, so that until the final settlement, these areas are administered in accordance with the international law on disputed territories and entities; and to ensure that the democratic, progressive and secular forces of 'Azad' Kashmir and Gilgit-Baltistan are supported by the civil society and democratic forces of India and Jammu and Kashmir".[115]

India's moral support to the people of Balochistan in their struggle against the tyrannical Pakistani regime has been welcomed as a long overdue and sound tactical position. However, it is the territory of Pak occupied Kashmir and Gilgit-Baltistan, where India's legal, legitimate and strategic interests lie.[116] Due to preoccupation in countering cross border terrorism sponsored by Pakistan over the years in the State of Jammu and Kashmir, India has not been able to focus much on the miseries on the other side of the Line of Control[117]. However, the present situation in Gilgit-Baltistan and India's legal right over the territory makes a strong case for India's intervention in the region and exposes nefarious designs of Pakistan – China.

Assessment and Prognosis

To summarise the situation in Afghanistan, it may not be incorrect to say that the road to peace and stability is rather long. The security situation continues to be dominated by a resilient insurgency (terrorism?); but the Afghan government remains in control of all major population centres and key lines of communication and the ANDSF continues to deny the Taliban strategic ground throughout the country.[118]

The country continues to face major challenges of transition on the political, economic and security front. The fault-lines have become particularly visible since the drawdown of US and NATO forces and the end of their combat mission in Afghanistan. The political environment has become increasingly fractious and polarized. The economy too remains to be characterized by low growth, poverty and high unemployment. Afghanistan is overwhelmingly dependent on external aid. It relies on external funding sources for 69 percent of its government expenditures.[119] The Brussels Conference was held on 04 and 05 October 2016 where the international community pledged to sustain international support and funding at or near current levels through 2020 {US$15.2 billion}.[120]

The security situation in Afghanistan is becoming increasingly volatile. Though ANDSF is improving its capabilities, the conflict has grown in intensity and scope with a resurgence of Taliban causing high casualties and internally displaced people. The situation is becoming even more precarious with ISIS having announced the formation of its Khorasan branch in South Asia; a loose coalition of defections from Taliban. Its presence is mainly restricted to eastern provinces of Nangarhar and Nuristan at the moment. The degrading security situation can also be assessed by the fact that as per Pajhwok news ageny, between January and October 2016, 13 journalists have been murdered and 292 forced to suspend jobs; an unprecedented development in the past eight years.[121]

The Afghan-led, Afghan-owned peace process with the Taliban has not made much headway as it continues to remain firm on its demands and refuses to negotiate unless its preconditions are met which include withdrawal of foreign troops, release of prisoners and removal from international sanctions list.[122] However, there are reports of secret talks between Taliban and the government and interestingly without representation from Pakistan.[123] Reportedly Pakistan is quite upset over the issue and has warned the Taliban that unless they consult with Islamabad during the negotiations all top Taliban leaders will be forced to leave Pakistan along with their families.[124]

The Quadrilateral Coordination Group too has not yielded any worthwhile dividends. But this is not surprising as Pakistan will subvert all effort towards reconciliation and peace in its desire to exercise full control and authority over the Afghan negotiations and its outcome. It will obstruct negotiations that do not further its interests. The statement by Dr Umar Zakhilwal, Afghan ambassador to Pakistan sums up the current role of Pakistan in Afghanistan peace process. As per the ambassador despite repeated promises, Pakistan has not taken practical steps to help Afghanistan restore its peace and stability. The ambassador has also alleged that Pakistan has not taken any action against the Haqqani network as requested by them.[125]

The situation in a nuclear armed Pakistan is actually becoming more worrisome as a result of its policy of state sponsored terrorism and fear of nuclear weapons falling into the hands of radical elements within and outside the organisation. It is today the epicentre of terror in the world, posing a grave threat to the region and humanity.

The presence of Islamic State in Pakistan which has been admitted by its military[126] for the first time, has added a new dimension to the strategic stability of South Asia which has scope of forming deeper linkages with the ongoing turmoil in West Asia. Fazal Ahmad Shirzad, the Police Chief of Eastern Nangarhar province in Afghanistan is on record stating that Pakistan's ISI is leading the Islamic State militant group in his province.[127]If the threat of Islamic State in Af-Pak region is not checked now, Russia and China will be the worst affected resulting in containment of these two powers in Central Asia.[128]

Escalation of violence and radicalisation are fraught with risks of state collapse in Pakistan and Afghanistan. Destabilisation of the region will have unintended consequences for China's One Belt and Road initiative, flow of energy resources from the Caspian region and operationalisation of China-Pakistan Economic Corridor (CPEC). Likewise emboldened terrorists have the potential to escalate violence in Kashmir, push India- Pakistan towards a military confrontation, heighten the risk of nuclear terrorism, scuttle the prospects of Turkmenistan-Afghanistan-Pakistan-India(TAPI), Iran-Pakistan-India(IPI) pipelines and Central Asia South Asia Electricity Transmission and Trade project (CASA 1000MW) electricity project.

The emerging security situation in Af-Pak region has major implications for Indian sub-continent, Iran, Fergana Valley in Central Asia, Caucasus and Xinjiang province. Therefore, it is pertinent that regional countries are cognizant of this larger 'Trans-national threat' that can destabilise the region. Defeat of Taliban in Af-Pak region is a 'sine quo non' for regional security.

However, the Taliban, once a pariah, now finds itself courted by several powerful regional players. Even Russia, the group's historical enemy, has recently turned to the group for intelligence sharing against a common foe:

the Islamic State.[129] Earlier Putin is said to have met Mansour over dinner at a late night meeting on a military base in Tajikistan in September 2015, with Russia promising arms and financial support to the Taliban.[130] Is Russia planning to employ the Taliban to counter Islamic State and, in the process, counter the U.S.'s undisclosed containment policy against Russia and China in Central Asia?

Even China is not far behind. Though some strategists argue that China's role in Afghanistan is more economic than security, it has taken up a proactive role in promoting peace talks between the Afghan government and the Taliban. According to recent reports, an Afghan Taliban delegation led by the leader of the group's Qatar-based political office, Sher Mohammad Abbas Stanikzai, visited China in mid-July 2016.[131] With Afghanistan's National Unity Government (NUG), its security relations are closer than ever before.[132]

The geo-political and off late the geo-economic environment in Afghanistan has led to the regional stakeholders especially Russia and China jostle for strategic space. There is a possibility of partnerships (even issue based in certain cases) emerging between the states which will marginalise the role of US and its allies in Afghanistan and question the efficacy of their overall approach towards the Global War on Terrorism.

In all likelihood, it may not be incorrect to state that probably the present situation in Afghanistan may have reached a stalemate which cannot be broken or handled by any single country. The present form of terrorism is not an isolated event or confined to a limited area. It has affected a large number of countries in the world, cutting across continents in one form or the other. This menace cannot be tackled piecemeal or with countries of the world pulling in different directions.[133]

Therefore the big question is what is the way ahead? Whether the present strategy needs a relook? As it cannot and should not be an endless war since the selective approach by the US led West operations have achieved limited results that seem unsustainable.

A viable strategy for Afghanistan cannot be crafted without the international community unequivocally agreeing to the fact that terrorism in Afghanistan is shaped, aided, and armed from across the border by Pakistan's military, with its intelligence arm, the ISI controlling the war.[134]

With Pakistan providing shelter to militants across the Durand Line and the terror commanders tucked into safe houses inside Pakistan, how could any military operation in Afghanistan succeed without the terror bases in Pakistan being tackled in tandem?[135]

Synergised operations, categorising the entire area of operations as one single entity, as Af-Pak region in the real sense is an imperative; if the threat from Taliban, al Qaeda and now ISIS has to be stemmed. [136]Though, Pakistan is carrying out operations in FATA and adjoining areas; these need to be more transparent. Pakistan needs to come out clean on its understanding of good and bad terrorists. The international community has to pressurise Pakistan to decisively act on de radicalisation of its society and mitigate the impact of a militant culture on young minds. Further, Pakistan while targeting the roots and hatcheries of terrorism has to focus on its economic development.

U.S. needs to maintain the current force levels if not increase them. As per the October 2016 three-month assessment of the situation by Gen John W. Nicholson, US commander in Afghanistan, surge in Taliban insurgency demands that US maintain current American force levels in Afghanistan to remain where they are. He is also seeking more authority for US forces in their campaign against the militants. As per Brig Gen Charles Cleveland, deputy chief of staff for communications for Operation Resolute Support, the NATO mission in Afghanistan, it was important to help the Afghans create the sustainable capability not just to win a fight tonight, not just to win a battle next month, but to have an enduring security capability that will allow the Afghans to defend themselves and deal with these transitional threats.[137] Therefore, it was important that support to the ANDSF in terms of a 10 year block budget, sharing of intelligence, technology, joint exercises between the militaries of the regional stakeholders, establishment of counter terrorism centres with linkages and enhancement of its air arm and logistic capabilities be put into urgent focus.

Improvement in present security situation in Afghanistan is a priority as it overshadows the political and economic developments in the country. However, Afghanistan's long-term security strategy needs to focus on reducing threat levels through political settlement and building indigenous security capacity to respond to emerging threats.[138]

This in turn demands crafting of a multipronged, multinational, inclusive and collaborative approach as an imperative. Interestingly, it may be noted that the US has been struggling to 'degrade and defeat' Islamic State for nearly two years in Iraq with very little success until the Russian intervention which showed that the war against Islamic State could indeed be fought better.

Organisations like the Shanghai Cooperation Organisation (SCO), Collective Security Organisation (CSTO) between Russia and three Central Asian States (Kazakhstan, Tajikistan and Kyrgyzstan) along with NATO need to shed their traditional mind-sets and create collaborative security framework and mechanisms. These organisations should therefore work on sharing intelligence, combating terrorism, nuclear terrorism, curbing terror financing networks, cyber security, capacity building, interoperability and conducting counter-terrorism exercises.

To sum up, the road to peace in Afghanistan is rather long. However, an Afghan led and Afghan owned peace process with honest indulgence away from petty domestic politics by the global and regional stakeholders can make a change to the ongoing imbroglio and bring lasting peace and stability to the war torn country.

Endnotes

1 Prados John(2009) "The AfPak Paradox",[Online: web] Accessed 01 Sept. 2016 URL: http://fpif.org/the_afpak_paradox/

2 Goodson and Johnson(2014) "US Policy and Strategy Towards Afghanistan after 2014" [Online: web]Accessed 07 Sept. 2016URL:http://www.strategicstudiesinstitute.army.mil/pubs/display.cfm?pubID=1233

3 (2016) "General Security Situation in Afghanistan and Events in Kabul",[Online: web] Accessed 01Sept.2016 URL:http://www.ecoi.net/news/188769::afghanistan/101.general-security-situation-in-afghanistan-and-events-in-kabul.htm

4 Shamin Imran (2011) "Af-Pak Regional Security Fault lines",[Online: web] Accessed 01 Sept.2016 URL: http://www.academia.edu/824937/Af-Pak_Regional_Security_Fault_lines

5   (2016)"General Security Situation in Afghanistan and Events in Kabul",[Online: web] Accessed 01Sept.2016 URL:http://www.ecoi.net/news/188769::afghanistan/101.general-security-situation-in-afghanistan-and-events-in-kabul.htm

6   (2015) "Afghanistan Country Report 2015",[Online: web]Accessed 01 Sept. 2016 URL: https://freedomhouse.org/report/freedom-world/2015/afghanistan

7   (2016) "Afghanistan Country Report 2016",[Online: web]Accessed 01 Sept. 2016 URL: https://freedomhouse.org/report/freedom-world/2016/afghanistan

8   (2016)"What corruption indexes don't tell us about Afghanistan", [Online: web]Accessed 01 Sept.2016 URL:http://www.aljazeera.com/indepth/opinion/2016/02/corruption-indexes-don-afghanistan-ashraf-ghani-160204132917875.html

9   Yusuf Huma(2015) "Ethnic Fault Lines: Overlapping Risks in Afghanistan and Pakistan",[Online: web] Accessed 01 Sept.2015 URL:https://www.controlrisks.com/en/our-thinking/analysis/ethnic-fault-lines.pdf

10 Naseri Huma (2016) "The story of Democracy in Afghanistan and Pakistan", [Online: web] Accessed 02 Sept.2016 URL: http://www.khaama.com/the-story-of-democracy-in-afghanistan-and-pakistan-6692

11 (2016) "Afghanistan's Abdullah Abdullah chides Ashraf Ghani",[Online: web] Accessed 01 Sept.2016 URL: http://www.aljazeera.com/news/2016/08/afghanistan-abdullah-abdullah-chides-ashraf-ghani-160812064503457.html

12 Jalali Ali A (2016) "Afghanistan National Defence And Security Forces Mission, Challenges and Sustainability", [Online: web] URL : http://www.usip.org/sites/default/files/PW115-Afghanistan-National-Defense-and-Security-Forces-Mission-Challenges-and-Sustainability.pdf

13 (2016)"Economy of Afghanistan"[Online: web] Accessed 02 Sept. 2016 URL:https://en.wikipedia.org/wiki/Economy_of_Afghanistan

14 (2016) "The World Fact Book: South Asia-Afghanistan"[Online: web] Accessed 02 Sept. 2016 URL: https://www.cia.gov/library/publications/the-world-factbook/geos/af.html

15 ibid

16 (2016) "The World Bank Report on Afghanistan"[Online: web] Accessed 02 Sept.2016URL: http://www.worldbank.org/en/country/afghanistan/overview

17 (2016) "The World Fact Book: South Asia-Afghanistan"[Online: web] Accessed 02 Sept. 2016 URL: https://www.cia.gov/library/publications/the-world-factbook/geos/af.html

18 (2016) "The World Bank Report on Afghanistan"[Online: web] Accessed 02 Sept.2016URL: http://www.worldbank.org/en/country/afghanistan/overview

19 ibid

20 (2015) "Progress Towards Security and Stability in Afghanistan" [Online: web] Accessed 07 Sept. 2016 URL: http://www.defense.gov/Portals/1/Documents/pubs/1225_Report_Dec_2015_-_Final_20151210.pdf.

21 (2016) "Security Situation in Afghanistan"[Online: web] Accessed 07 Sept. 2016 URL:http://www.securitycouncilreport.org/monthly-forecast/2016-09/afghanistan_18.php

22 (2015) "Top US Commander: American troops need to stay in Afghanistan", Foreign Policy [Online: web] Accessed 07 Sept.2016URL:http://foreignpolicy.com/2015/10/06top-u-s-commander-american-troops-stay-afghanistan

23 (2016) Kenny Stuart Instability in Afghanistan: Why Afghanistan matters and what Australia can do to address the causes of Instability [Online: web] Accessed 07Sept.2016 URL:www.defence.gov.au/ADC/Publications/IndoPac/Kenny percent20Afghanistan percent20IPSP.pdf

24 (2015) Pillalamarri Akhilesh "Here's the Most Disturbing Thing About the Taliban Takeover of Kunduz"[Online: web] Accessed 05 Sept.2016 URL:http://thediplomat.com/2015/10/heres-the-most-disturbing-thing-about-the-taliban-takeover-of-kunduz

25 Katzman Kenneth (2016) "Afghanistan: Post-Taliban Governance, Security, and U.S. Policy" [Online: web] Accessed 06 Sept.2016 URL:https://www.fas.org/sgp/crs/row/RL30588.pdf

26 ibid

27 ibid

28 ibid

29 (2016) Kenny Stuart Instability in Afghanistan: Why Afghanistan matters and what Australia can do to address the causes of Instability [Online: web] Accessed 07Sept.2016 URL:www.defence.gov.au/ADC/Publications/IndoPac/Kenny percent20Afghanistan percent20IPSP.pdf

30 Katzman Kenneth (2016) "Afghanistan: Post-Taliban Governance, Security, and U.S. Policy" [Online: web] Accessed 06 Sept. 2016 URL:https://www.fas.org/sgp/crs/row/RL30588.pdf

31 (2016) "Transcript of the Briefing by General Cleveland via teleconference from Afghanistan" [Online: web] Accessed 09 Sept. 2016 URL:http://www.defense.gov/News/Transcripts/Transcript-View/Article/721738/department-of-defense-press-briefing-by-general-cleveland-via-teleconference-fr

32 ibid

33 (2015) Gordon Michael "ISIS Building 'Little Nests' in Afghanistan" [Online: web] Accessed 09 Sept.2016 URL:http://www.nytimes.com/2015/12/19/world/asia/afghanistan-ash-carter.html?_r=0

34 (2016) "Transcript of the Briefing by General Cleveland via teleconference from Afghanistan" [Online: web] Accessed 09 Sept. 2016 URL:http://www.defense.gov/News/Transcripts/Transcript-View/Article/721738/department-of-defense-press-briefing-by-general-cleveland-via-teleconference-fr

35 (2016) "A Shift in Tactics for ISIS in Afghanistan?" [Online: web] Accessed 07 Sept.2016 URL:http://www.newsweek.com/shift-tactics-isis-afghanistan-483594

36 Katzman Kenneth (2016) "Afghanistan: Post-Taliban Governance, Security, and U.S. Policy" [Online: web] Accessed 06 Sept.2016 URL:https://www.fas.org/sgp/crs/row/RL30588.pdf

37 Kakar, Javed Hamim (2016) "Ghani Issues Decree on Peace Deal's Enforcement" [Online: web] Accessed 21 Oct 2016 URL: http://www.pajhwok.com/en/2016/10/21/ghani-issues-decree-peace-deal   percentE2   percent80 percent99s-enforcement

38 Katzman Kenneth (2016) "Afghanistan: Post-Taliban Governance, Security, and U.S. Policy" [Online: web] Accessed 06 Sept.2016 URL:https://www.fas.org/sgp/crs/row/RL30588.pdf

39 ibid

40 ibid

41 ibid

42 ibid

43 Jalali Ali A (2016) "Afghanistan National Defence And Security Forces Mission, Challenges and Sustainability", [Online: web] URL : http://www.usip.org/sites/default/files/PW115-Afghanistan-National-Defense-and-Security-Forces-Mission-Challenges-and-Sustainability.pdf

44 ibid

45 Katzman Kenneth (2016) "Afghanistan: Post-Taliban Governance, Security, and U.S. Policy" [Online: web] Accessed 06 Sept.2016 URL:https://www.fas.org/sgp/crs/row/RL30588.pdf

46 Jalali Ali A (2016) " Afghanistan National Defence And Security Forces Mission, Challenges and Sustainability", [Online: web] URL : http://www.usip.

org/sites/default/files/PW115-Afghanistan-National-Defense-and-Security-Forces-Mission-Challenges-and-Sustainability.pdf

47 ibid

48 Katzman Kenneth (2016) "Afghanistan: Post-Taliban Governance, Security, and U.S. Policy" [Online: web] Accessed 06 Sept.2016 URL:https://www.fas.org/sgp/crs/row/RL30588.pdf

49 (2016) "News- Afghanistan" [Online: web] Accessed 25 Oct 2016 URL :http://www.tolonews.com/en/afghanistan/25826-us-general-nicholson-submits-his-assessment-of-the-situation-in-afghanistan

50 (2016) "Afghan Forces Turning Afghanistan into Graveyard of Terrorism says Afghan Army Chief of Staff" [Online: web] Accessed 19 Sept 2016 URL : http://usiblog.in/2016/08/afghan-forces-turning-afghanistan-into-graveyard-of-terrorism-says-afghan-army-chief-of-staff/

51 (2016) "Ashraf Ghani slams Pakistan for harbouring terrorists; praises India"[Online: web] Accessed 03 Oct 2016 URL: http://www.firstpost.com/world/ashraf-ghani-slams-pakistan-for-harbouring-terrorists-praises-india-2913030.html

52 Kousary Halimullah (2016) "The Afghan Peace Talks, QCG and China-Pakistan Role" [Online: web] Accessed 03 Oct 2016 URL: http://thediplomat.com/2016/07/the-afghan-peace-talks-qcg-and-china-pakistan-role/

53 (2016) "Taliban and Afghanistan restart secret talks in Qatar[Online: web] Accessed 20 Oct 2016 URL https://www.theguardian.com/world/2016/oct/18/taliban-afghanistan-secret-talks-qatar

54 Kousary Halimullah (2016) "The Afghan Peace Talks, QCG and China-Pakistan Role" [Online: web] Accessed 03 Oct 2016 URL: http://thediplomat.com/2016/07/the-afghan-peace-talks-qcg-and-china-pakistan-role/

55 ibid

56 Katzman Kenneth (2016) "Afghanistan: Post-Taliban Governance, Security, and U.S. Policy" [Online: web] Accessed 06 Sept.2016 URL:https://www.fas.org/sgp/crs/row/RL30588.pdf

57 ibid

58 ibid

59 Jamal Umair (2016) "Understanding Pakistan's strategic interests in Afghanistan" [Online: web] Accessed 03 Oct 2016 URL: http://tns.thenews.com.pk/understanding-pakistans-strategic-interests-afghanistan/#.V_IZdvl97cc

60 Partlow, Joshua (2010) "Afghans Build Up Ties With Pakistan." [Online: web] Accessed 03 Oct2016 URL: http://www.washingtonpost.com/wp-dyn/content/article/2010/07/20/AR2010072003548.html

61 (2016) Katzman Kenneth "Afghanistan: Post-Taliban Governance, Security, and U.S. Policy" [Online: web] Accessed 06 Sept.2016 URL:https://www.fas.org/sgp/crs/row/RL30588.pdf

62 Jamal Umair (2016) "Understanding Pakistan's strategic interests in Afghanistan" [Online: web] Accessed 03 Oct 2016 URL: http://tns.thenews.com.pk/understanding-pakistans-strategic-interests-afghanistan/#.V_IZdvl97cc

63 (2016) "Enhancing Security and Stability in Afghanistan" [Online: web] Accessed 03 Oct2016 URL: http://www.defense.gov/Portals/1/Documents/Enhancing_Security_and_Stability_in_Afghanistan-June_2016.pdf

64 (2016) "Ashraf Ghani slams Pakistan for harbouring terrorists; praises India"[Online: web] Accessed 03 Oct 2016 URL: http://www.firstpost.com/world/ashraf-ghani-slams-pakistan-for-harbouring-terrorists-praises-india-2913030.html

65 Katzman Kenneth (2016) "Afghanistan: Post-Taliban Governance, Security, and U.S. Policy" [Online: web] Accessed 10 Oct 2016 URL:https://www.fas.org/sgp/crs/row/RL30588.pdf

66 Beina Xu, Holly Fletcher, and Jayshree Bajoria (2014) "The East Turkestan Islamic Movement (ETIM)" [Online: web]Accessed 10 Oct2016 URL:http://www.cfr.org/china/east-turkestan-islamic-movement-etim/p9179

67 (2016) "China Delivers First Batch of Military Aid to Afghanistan" [Online: web] Accessed 10 Oct 2016 URL:http://www.voanews.com/a/china-military-aid-afghanistan/3402178.html

68 (2016) "China pledges $2.2 million in fresh aid to Afghanistan" [Online: web] Accessed 10 Oct2016 URL: http://www.khaama.com/china-pledges-2-2-million-in-fresh-aid-to-afghanistan-01645

69 Piven Ben(2015) "Chinese company and Taliban battle over Afghanistan's underground riches"[Online: web] Accessed 10 Oct 2016 URL:http://america.aljazeera.com/articles/2015/7/11/chinese-company-taliban-battle-afghanistan.html

70 Shalizi, Hamid (2012) "China's CNPC begins oil production in Afghanistan" [Online: web]Accessed 10 Oct2016 URL: http://www.reuters.com/article/us-afghanistan-oil-idUSBRE89K08G20121021

71 Seerat, Rustam Ali (2016)' "Iran and Saudi Arabia in Afghanistan" [Online: web]Accessed 03Oct2016 URL :http://thediplomat.com/2016/01/iran-and-saudi-arabia-in-afghanistan/

72 ibid

73 ibid

74 Katzman Kenneth (2016) "Afghanistan: Post-Taliban Governance, Security, and U.S. Policy" [Online: web] Accessed 10 Oct 2016 URL:https://www.fas.org/sgp/crs/row/RL30588.pdf

75 Seerat, Rustam Ali(2016)" Iran and Saudi Arabia in Afghanistan" [Online: web]Accessed 03Oct2016 URL: http://thediplomat.com/2016/01/iran-and-saudi-arabia-in-afghanistan/

76 (2009) "Afghan President Karzai at Brookings Institution"[Online: web] Accessed 10 Oct2016 URL: http://www.enduringamerica.com/may-2009/2009/5/6/video-afghan-president-karzai-at-brookings-institution-5-may.html

77 Katzman Kenneth (2016) "Afghanistan: Post-Taliban Governance, Security, and U.S. Policy" [Online: web] Accessed 10 Oct 2016 URL:https://www.fas.org/sgp/crs/row/RL30588.pdf

78 (2015) "Ready to take forward Chahbahar Port Project" [Online: web]Accessed 10 Oct2016 URL:http://economictimes.indiatimes.com/news/politics-and-nation/afghanistan-president-ashraf-ghanis-visit-ready-to-take-forward-chabahar-port-project-says-pm-narendra-modi/articlesho

79 Seerat, Rustam Ali (2016) "Iran and Saudi Arabia in Afghanistan" [Online: web]Accessed 10 Oct2016 URL: http://thediplomat.com/2016/01/iran-and-saudi-arabia-in-afghanistan/

80 Hasrat-Nazim Waslat(2016) "Russia's new role in Afghanistan"[Online: web] Accessed 13 Oct 2016 URL: http://www.dw.com/en/russias-new-role-in-afghanistan/a-19087432

81 ibid

82 (2016) "Rise of ISIS in Afghanistan is threat to Russia – Moscow" [Online: web] Accessed 13 Oct 2016 URL: https://www.rt.com/news/359220-russia-afghanistan-us-isis/

83 Katzman Kenneth (2016) "Afghanistan: Post-Taliban Governance, Security, and U.S. Policy" [Online: web] Accessed 13 Oct 2016 URL:https://www.fas.org/sgp/crs/row/RL30588.pdf

84 (2015) "Northern Distribution Network" [Online: web]Accessed13 Oct 2016 URL:https://www.csis.org/programs/transnational-threats-project/past-projects/northern-distribution-network-ndn

85 (2015) "Russia pledges major investment in Afghanistan housing"[Online: web] Accessed 13 Oct 2016 URL: http://www.khaama.com/russia-pledges-major-investment-in-housing-construction-sector-of-afghanistan-1476

86 Asey, Tamim (2015) "Central Asia's Stake in Afghanistan's War" [Online: web] Accessed 13 Oct 2016 URL: http://thediplomat.com/2015/07/central-asias-stake-in-afghanistans-war/

87 ibid

88 (2016) "Enhancing Security and Stability in Afghanistan" [Online: web] Accessed 03 Oct2016 URL: http://www.defense.gov/Portals/1/Documents/Enhancing_Security_and_Stability_in_Afghanistan-June_2016.pdf

89 Narain, Akanksha (2016) "Afghanistan's Growing Unrest: Implications for India's Security"[Online: web] Accessed 25 Oct 2016 URL: http://thediplomat.com/2016/05/afghanistans-growing-unrest-implications-for-indias-security/

90 ibid

91 Narain, Akanksha (2016) "Afghanistan's Growing Unrest: Implications for India's Security"[Online: web] Accessed 25 Oct 2016 URL: http://thediplomat.com/2016/05/afghanistans-growing-unrest-implications-for-indias-security/

92 (2016) "India Promises $1 Billion in Aid During Afghan President's Visit"[Online: web] Accessed 25 November 2016 URL: http://www.voanews.com/a/india-promises-1-billion-dollars-in-aid-during-afghan-president-s-visit/3508969.html

93 Kay Chris (2016) "Pakistan's Turmoil"[Online: web] Accessed 19 Oct 2016 URL: https://www.bloomberg.com/quicktake/pakistans-turmoil

94 ibid

95 (2016) "Khyber Pakhtunkhwa"[Online: web] Accessed 19 Oct 2016 URL: https://en.wikipedia.org/wiki/Khyber_Pakhtunkhwa

96 (2016) "Federally Administered Tribal Areas" [Online: web] Accessed 19 Oct 2016 URL: https://en.wikipedia.org/wiki/Federally_Administered_Tribal_Areas

97 (2016) "Pakistan 2016 Crime and Safety Report: Peshawar" [Online: web] Accessed 19 Oct 2016 URL: https://www.osac.gov/pages/ContentReportDetails.aspx?cid=19396

98 ibid

99   Shahid Usman (2016) "Balochistan: The Troubled Heart of the CPEC", [Online: web] Accessed 20 Sept. 2016 URL: http://thediplomat.com/2016/08/balochistan-the-troubled-heart-of-the-cpec/

100 ibid

101 ibid

102 Hariharan R (2016) "Balochistan – Pak's untold story", [Online: web] Accessed 21 Sept. 2016 URL: http://www.asianage.com/editorial/balochistan-pak-s-untold-story-544

103 (2016) "Baloch leaders who supported PM Modi's comments booked in Pakistan" [Online: web] Accessed 22 Sept. 2016 URL : http://timesofindia. indiatimes.com/world/pakistan/Baloch-leaders-who-supported-PM-Modis-comments-booked-in-Pakistan/articleshow/53810280.cms

104 (2016) "Baloch leader Brahamdagh Bugti approaches India for asylum" [Online: web] Accessed 22 Sept. 2016 URL: http://timesofindia.indiatimes.com/india/Baloch-leader-Brahamdagh-Bugti-approaches-India-for-asylum/articleshow/54432342.cms

105 Shahid Usman (2016)"Balochistan: The Troubled Heart of the CPEC", [Online: web] Accessed 20 Sept. 2016 URL: http://thediplomat.com/2016/08/balochistan-the-troubled-heart-of-the-cpec/

106 AbbaSyed Sammer(2016) "Iran wants to be part of CPEC, says Rouhani" [Online: web] Accessed 23 Sept. 2016 URL : shttp://www.dawn.com/news/1285404

107 Shahid Usman (2016) "Balochistan: The Troubled Heart of the CPEC", [Online: web] Accessed 20 Sept. 2016 URL: http://thediplomat.com/2016/08/balochistan-the-troubled-heart-of-the-cpec/

108 ibid

109 Sehrawat Yashaswani (2016) "India slams Pakistan at UN rights council after Uri attack, rakes up human rights violations in Balochistan" [Online: web] Accessed 21 Sept. 2016 URL : http://indiatoday.intoday.in/story/un-rights-council-india-pakistan-uri-balochistan-human-rights-violation/1/768466.html

110 Kaul Ravinder (2016) "A Path Breaking Study of Politics, Society and Culture in PoK" [Online: web] Accessed 22 Sept. 2016 URL : http://www.dailyexcelsior.com/412465-2/

111 ibid

112 Hakhoo Sumit (2016) "Opposition to China corridor in Gilgit-Baltistan"[Online: web] Accessed 22 Sept. 2016 URL : http://www.

tribuneindia.com/news/jammu-kashmir/community/opposition-to-china-corridor-in-gilgit-baltistan/288340.html

113 ibid

114 ibid

115 Kaul Ravinder (2016) "Path Breaking Study of Politics, Society and Culture in PoK" [Online: web] Accessed 22 Sept. 2016 URL : http://www.dailyexcelsior.com/412465-2/

116 ibid

117 ibid

118 (2016) "Enhancing Security and Stability in Afghanistan" [Online: web] Accessed 01 Nov 2016 URL : http://www.defense.gov/Portals/1/Documents/Enhancing_Security_and_Stability_in_Afghanistan-June_2016.pdf

119 Chadha, Pavneet (2016) "Long Road to Peace in Afghanistan"[Online: web] Accessed 25 Oct 2016 URL: http://www.claws.in/1595/long-road-to-peace-in-afghanistan-pavneet-chadha.html

120 (2016) "Brussels Conference on Afghanistan, 04-05/10/2016" [Online: web] Accessed 25 Oct 2016 URL: http://www.consilium.europa.eu/en/meetings/international-summit/2016/10/05/

121 Bashardost, Naheed (2016) "13 journalists murdered, 292 forced to suspend jobs" [Online: web] Accessed 31 Oct 2016 URL: http://www.pajhwok.com/en/2016/10/30/13-journalists-murdered-292-forced-suspend-jobs

122 Chadha, Pavneet(2016) "Long Road to Peace in Afghanistan"[Online: web] Accessed 25 Oct 2016 URL: http://www.claws.in/1595/long-road-to-peace-in-afghanistan-pavneet-chadha.html

123 Sharma, Raj Kumar (2016) "Pakistan Sidelined: Afghanistan-Taliban Secret Talks at Qatar?" [Online: web] Accessed 31 Oct 2016 URL: http://usiblog.in/2016/10/pakistan-sidelined-afghanistan-taliban-secret-talks-at-qatar/

124 (2016) "All top leaders will be forced to leave: Upset at being sidelined in talks, Pakistan warns Taliban"[Online: web] Accessed 01 Nov 2016 URL:http://timesofindia.indiatimes.com/world/pakistan/All-top-leaders-will-be-forced-to-leave-Upset-at-being-sidelined-in-talks-Pakistan-warns-Taliban/articleshow/55162518.cms

125 Shah, S. Mudassir Ali (2016)"Pakistan has taken no action against Haqqanis" [Online: web] Accessed 31 Oct 2016 URL: http://www.pajhwok.com/en/2016/10/31/pakistan-has-taken-no-action-against-haqqanis-zakhilwal

126 (2016) "Pakistan admits for the first time that ISIS is active in the country after foiling planned attack on foreign embassies" [Online: web] Accessed 31 Oct 2016 URL: http://www.dailymail.co.uk/news/article-3769308/Pakistan-military-admits-IS-presence-country.html Follow us: @MailOnline on Twitter | DailyMail on Facebookhttp://www.dailymail.co.uk/news/article-3769308/Pakistan-military-admits-IS-presence-country.html

127 Mahalingam, V(2016) "Afghanistan: A Tale of Pakistan's Lies and Deceit"[Online: web] Accessed 25 Oct 2016 URL: http://www.claws.in/images/publication_pdf/1192209486_MP59-VMahalingam-14-03-16.pdf

128 ibid

129 Ahmad, Javid(2016) "Moscow's New Ally in Afghanistan" [Online: web] Accessed 31 Oct 2016 URL:https://www.foreignaffairs.com/articles/afghanistan/2016-01-31/russia-and-taliban-make-amends

130 (2015) "Taliban leader gains Vladimir Putin's help at secret meeting" [Online: web] Accessed 31 Oct 2016 URL: http://www.theaustralian.com.au/news/world/the-times/taliban-leader-gains-vladimir-putins-help-at-secret-meeting/news-story/c212a1f20b685fae034c63ea7b0cdb89

131 (2016) "What to Make of China's Latest Meeting With the Taliban" [Online: web] Accessed 31 Oct 2016 URL :http://thediplomat.com/2016/08/what-to-make-of-chinas-latest-meeting-with-the-taliban/

132 Khalil, Ahmad Bilal (2016) "The Rise of China-Afghanistan Security Relations" [Online: web] Accessed 31 Oct 2016 URL: http://thediplomat.com/2016/06/the-rise-of-china-afghanistan-security-relations/

133 Mahalingam, V(2016) "Afghanistan: A Tale of Pakistan's Lies and Deceit"[Online: web] Accessed 25 Oct 2016 URL: http://www.claws.in/images/publication_pdf/1192209486_MP59-VMahalingam-14-03-16.pdf

134 ibid

135 ibid

136 ibid

137 (2016) "News- Afghanistan" [Online: web] Accessed 25 Oct 2016 URL :http://www.tolonews.com/en/afghanistan/25826-us-general-nicholson-submits-his-assessment-of-the-situation-in-afghanistan

138 ibid

Chapter 3

India and Pakistan Relations: Seven Decades of Unrest

"Whatever language Pakistan understands India should teach in that language"

- Narendra Modi

Introduction

Pakistan came into being in 1947 along with India after gaining independence from the British. Pakistan which has 1,046 km of coastline along the Arabian Sea, the Gulf of Oman as also land boundaries with Afghanistan (2410 km), Iran (999 km), China (523 km) apart from India (3323 km); today is the epicenter of international Jihadi terrorism.

Since its inception in 1947, India and Pakistan have had troubled relationship. At the core of these animosities lies the question of Kashmir. Geopolitics of Pakistan devolves around its strategic location as a frontline state, chronic animosity towards India, Jihadi ideology and ethno-regional and sectarian conflicts. The state of Pakistan has been dominated by its military establishment which has locked the country in an enduring rivalry with India. Pakistan has fought four wars with India in the past - 1947, 1965, 1971 and 1999 and failed to win any of these. Today the army continues to prosecute the dangerous policy of employing non state actors under the security of its ever expanding nuclear umbrella to wrest control over Kashmir. However, the animosity is not just limited to territorial revisionist goals only; as Pakistani army has committed itself to resisting India's slow but inevitable rise on the global stage.

Despite Pakistan's efforts to coerce India, it has achieved only modest successes at best. Even though India vivisected Pakistan in 1972, Pakistan continues to see itself as India's equal and demands the world do the same[1]. An analysis of the military balance between India and Pakistan suggests that for strict military reasons alone, premeditated conventional wars between India and Pakistan are unlikely in the foreseeable future.[2] However, the relations between India and Pakistan are not just limited to the Kashmir issue and the border dispute; to comprehend these relations in its full earnest issues related to Pakistan's geostrategic importance, its economy, society, culture, its relations with China etc too are relevant and are discussed in the chapter.

Geo-Strategic Importance of Pakistan

Pakistan's pivotal location at the cross roads of South Asia, Arabian Sea, the Middle East and Central Asia endows it with critical significance. Pakistan connects South Asia to Central Asia and China to West Asia. It also has potential to influence shipping lanes in the Arabian Sea. Bolan Pass and Khyber Pass connect Afghanistan and Pakistan. The supply routes passing through these passes are vital for sustenance of US and NATO forces in Afghanistan. It is one of the major leverages used by Pakistan against US-NATO forces in Afghanistan. Around 80 percent of food supplies and military armaments to US-NATO forces go through this pass. Pakistan from time to time has closed these passes and denied flow of US logistics supplies into Afghanistan. These passes are also crucial for smooth de-induction of US/NATO troops from Afghanistan.[3]

Pakistan's importance to China, Central Asian Republics and Afghanistan from the point of view of connectivity to the Arabian Sea is immense. The upcoming China- Pakistan Economic Corridor (CPEC) assumes strategic importance. Energy supplies from Iran or Africa across Strait of Malacca take 16-25 days to reach China through Indian Ocean and Western Pacific. The domination of SLOCs by the US Navy poses maximum concern, what is commonly known as Malacca Dilemma for China. Once Gwadar and Karakoram rail and pipeline route is operationalised, it will take only 48 hours for energy resources to reach Kashgar in Xinjiang province across Kunjerab pass[4].

However, the ethno-regional fault lines have the potential to undermine Pakistan's strategic advantage in many ways. The dispute over

Durand line can spark off a strong movement for independent Pashtunistan with Pashtun's in Afghanistan and Khyber Pakhtunkhwa joining ranks. Sectarian violence in Karachi, secessionist movement in Baluchistan and ethnic strife in northern areas can destabilise Pakistan and thwart much-touted CPEC project. These developments can potentially pose multiple criticalities and multi front dilemmas for Pakistan and undermine China-Pakistan strategic nexus.

Pakistan as a Society

Pakistan has a population of 194 million. Ethnic groups in Pakistan constitute Punjabi 45 percent, Pashtun 15 percent, Sindhi-15 percent, Saraike-10 percent, Muhajir 7 percent, and Baloochs 4 percent and other 4 percent. 80 percent of Pakistani population is Sunni and 20 percent are Shias which is one of the fault lines in Pakistan. Another ethnic fault line is between Sindhis and Muhajirs in Sindh province. Integration has not taken place in these communities. Further Baluchistan which has two naval bases would like to be an independent country. Pashtuns on either side of Afghanistan and Pakistan would like to merge, thus forming another fault line. Literacy in the country is 55 percent and there is need to focus on education. Population greater than 25 is 56 percent which would be a youth bulge to be gainfully employed.

Economy of Pakistan

Pakistan's economic outlook is not encouraging and its economic growth is sluggish. Agriculture employs 40 percent of the people with an output of 20 percent of GDP which as per 2013 figures is $ 232.3 billion and growth rate is 4.34 percent as of 2016. China has emerged as Pakistan's largest trading partner replacing the US in 2012. The China–Pakistan Free Trade Agreement is a major trade agreement that exists between the two countries. Trade volume due to this agreement was $13 billion in 2013, while is expected to reach $15 billion by 2015.[5] However, the trade deficit is continuously increasing in China's favour. Pakistan's economy is facing a balance of payment crisis. There is no FDI. Bangladesh could overtake Pakistan by 2025, as the second largest economy of South Asia behind India. High unemployment ratio of 5.7 percent has social ramifications apart from the obvious economic fallouts. Pakistan remains dependent on US grants for clearance of loans.

Pakistan's Political Outlook

The Islamic Republic of Pakistan has four provinces. Democracy in the country has not flourished due to interference from the Army. Pakistan has witnessed three military coups and the Army has an important say in defence and foreign policy. Pakistan counters India's conventional edge by Jihadi terrorism and nuclear weapons which makes it an important player in this region. Pakistan with its proximity to China has developed a collusive two front strategy to fight a war with India. China uses Pakistan as a 'proxy' to keep India bogged down in South Asia and thwart Indian attempts to rise as a global player. China has provided extensive economic, military and technical support to Pakistan. China is largest defence supplier to Pakistan. As per SIPRI 2014 report 47 percent of total Chinese arms exports go to Pakistan[6]. China facilitated Pakistan's nuclear program which is essentially an extension of Chinese one.[7]

China-Pakistan interests coalesce in Pakistan Occupied Kashmir where there is presence of Chinese troops. CPEC has further deepened this interest. After Indo-US nuclear deal, China promised to build two nuclear power reactors in Karachi despite knowing the history of Pakistan's proliferation record.[8] After Bin Laden's assassination, China was perhaps the only powerful country that openly expressed its support for Pakistan for having its territorial integrity violated. As per 2014 Pew Global Attitudes Survey, 78 percent of Pakistanis view China favourably with only 14 percent sharing the same view for the US.[9] Not surprisingly calls are being heard in Pakistan to make China, not the US, the strongest ally in its foreign policy[10]. The Chinese Dream of becoming a global power and India's increasing closeness with the US have further increased such demands in Pakistan. There is a growing feeling in Pakistan that US uses it in times of need and can desert it for a policy that favors better relations with India.

Talibanisation of Pakistan- A Myth or Reality

"Talibanisation" indicates the influence of Islamic radicals aiming at radicalisation and weaponisation of the society. There are various definitions of Talibanisation. Some of these which are widely accepted especially in the west are "A firestorm of ideologically driven violence and intimidation", "The Taliban philosophy is representative of Muslim political thought except that it is heavily influenced by the tribal traditions — not only of the Pashtuns but also the Arabs" and "It is about the 'imposition' of tribal and rural values on the public at large".[11] The debates over the Talibanisation of Pakistan have been prompted by the increasing incidents of religious extremism, fundamentalism and sectarianism, which generate the feeling that the country is gradually moving towards Talibanisation, as has happened in Afghanistan.

Gen Musharraf while he was the President of Pakistan had termed Talibanisation as a potential threat to national security of Pakistan in view of the Taliban having regrouped and reorganised. He had further stressed that Talibanisation was also casting its dark shadows over FATA and areas adjoining the tribal belt.[12]

There are many reasons behind the threat of Talibanisation of Pakistani society such as political and social perpetration by some governments and social groups, within a socio-political environment of unjust cultural norms, injustice in the society, ideological contradictions and rigid religious beliefs. While, socioeconomic factors like poverty, unemployment, ignorance and unequal social opportunities have added in the deterioration of situation. Though unlikely; the emergence of similar movement as witnessed in the tribal areas of Pakistan, cannot be ruled out in other parts of the country, where poverty, unemployment and illiteracy are common, and where the feudal hold remains strong. Such areas could be the southern parts of the Punjab, interior Sindh and in the remote areas of Baluchistan.[13]

The Talibanisation of Pakistan is the blowback of their powerful military and intelligence establishment's flawed policy of using Jihadi indoctrination to advance its geo strategic agenda in the region.[14]Pakistan's own security is at risk due to the threat from Taliban and Al Qaeda. As the menace of Islamic militancy spreads across their country like a jungle fire, the Taliban militia and the Al Qaeda network continues to thrive.

As far as India is concerned, though the Talibanisation of Pakistan is unlikely; however if it happens, will considerably increase the probability of a full scale war between India and Pakistan which might escalate the risk of use of nuclear weapons. Or, there will be rise in militancy in Kashmir and pan-Indian terrorism fully sponsored by Taliban controlled Pakistan.

Another possibility is Balkanisation of Pakistan.[15] Western experts have been talking about it for quite some time now. The nexus between military dominance and Islamic extremism has weakened the country to the extent that it may break-up. In such an event, the attitude of the Pakistan Army will be crucial for the future course of action. It may engineer a conflict with India in a bid to reunite the 'nationalistic' sentiment among different ethnicities. Break-up of Pakistan will be strategically favourable for India as Pakistan's ability to launch conventional military threat against India will diminish. In such a scenario, the entity controlling the nuclear weapons will be important and its attitude towards India will define the strategic balance in South Asia. An anti-India group holding nuclear weapons after Pakistan disintegrates can blackmail India.

India-Pakistan Border Dispute

The India and Pakistan Border, known locally as the International Border (IB), is an international border running between India and Pakistan that demarcates the Indian states and the four provinces of Pakistan. The border runs from the Line of Control (LoC), which separates the Indian controlled Kashmir from Pakistan occupied Kashmir (PoK), in the north, to Wagah, which partitioned the Indian Punjab state and Punjab Province of Pakistan, in the east. The Zero Point separates the Indian states of Gujarat and Rajasthan from Sindh province of Pakistan, in the south.[16]

The border based on artificial Radcliffe line of 1947, runs 1225 km in Jammu and Kashmir, 553 km in Punjab, 1037 km in Rajasthan and 508 km in Gujarat, making a total 3323 km. It is one of the most complex borders in the world. The border traverses a variety of terrains ranging from major urban areas to inhospitable deserts and has been site of numerous conflicts and wars between each country. From the Arabian Sea, the naval border follows the course of Manora Island of Pakistan to the course of the Mumbai Harbour, in the south east.[17]

India claims the entire state of Jammu and Kashmir including PoK and at present, administers approximately 43 percent of the region, including most of Jammu, the Kashmir Valley, Ladakh, and the Siachen Glacier. Pakistan controls approximately 37 percent of Kashmir, namely PoK and the northern areas of Gilgit-Baltistan.

From Indian perspective, the dividing line between India and Pakistan occupied Kashmir is called Line of Control (LC). It runs from Akhnoor sector till NJ9842, the northernmost demarcated point of the India-Pakistan cease fire line. Beyond this point, the current position that divides Indian and Pakistani troops in the Siachen Glacier region is called Actual Ground Position Line (AGPL). The line extends from the northernmost point of the LC to Indira Col. In other states (Punjab, Rajasthan and Gujarat), the border dispute has been settled and it is called international border.

On the other hand, from NJ9842 to Akhnoor sector, Pakistan refers to the dividing line as Line of Control (LoC). From Akhnoor to Punjab border in India, Pakistan calls it working boundary. India argues that the southern frontier in Jammu and Kashmir is a border, because it has remained unchanged ever since the accession of the state into the Indian Union. Pakistan accepted this position until the rise of insurgency in the late 1980s. It now describes the border as a "working boundary"[18]. Pakistan accepts the rest of the line as international border.

Shaksgam Valley, an area of Baltistan, was illegally ceded by Pakistan to the People's Republic of China on 03 March 1963. The Siachen glacier in the proximity of Shaksgam valley is an issue which is of immense strategic importance to India. The conflict in Siachen arose from the incompletely demarcated territory on the map beyond the map coordinate known as NJ9842. The 1972 Simla Agreement did not clearly mention who controlled the glacier, merely stating that from NJ9842 the boundary would proceed "thence north to the glaciers". Pakistan interprets this line running northeast to Karakoram pass, the trijunction where boundaries of India- Pakistan and China converge. India, based on watershed principal believes this line running northwards along the Saltoro ridge[19].

These two interpretations have great strategic bearing for all the three countries. Indian interpretation of line has a great bearing on its claims over the international border that existed at the time of undivided state of J&K. Pakistan's interpretation on the other hand lends it to share borders with China and make India's presence northwest of Khardungla pass untenable and poses a collusive bidirectional threat to Leh. India was alerted by Pakistan Army's attempts to capture Siachen and Indian Army successfully launched 'Operation Meghdoot' and pre-empted the capture of this strategically important glacier in 1984. Not only Siachen but all its tributary glaciers, as well as the three main passes of the Saltoro

Ridge immediately west of the glacier—Sia La, Bilafond La, and Gyong La are controlled by Indian Army. India's presence in Siachen is essential for access to Karakoram pass, pose a threat to Karakoram highway and maintain the legitimacy of our claims over Shaksgam valley that borders China's western highway and Xinjiang province[20].

Sir Creek is another dispute between India and Pakistan. It is a 96 km strip of water that is disputed between the two countries in the Rann of Kutch marshlands in Gujarat. The creek, which opens up into the Arabian Sea divides the Kutch region of India and Sindh province of Pakistan. The dispute lies in the interpretation of the maritime boundary line between Kutch and Sindh. There is the possibility of the presence of an enormous quantity and volume of oil and gas along the sea-bed in this zone. The area, therefore, has a bearing on the energy potential of the two countries[21]. Also once the boundaries are defined; it would help in the determination of the maritime boundaries which are drawn as an extension of onshore reference points.

Pakistan has made several unsuccessful attempts to change the alignment of LoC in Jammu and Kashmir by force but it has not been successful. Since Pakistan could not match India's conventional military might, it embarked upon a course of well strategized form of asymmetric warfare; and from 1989, started state-sponsored terrorism in Jammu and Kashmir, infiltrating terrorists in the state. Following increasing terrorist violence and Pakistan's attempts to highlight the Kashmir dispute, both houses of the Indian Parliament unanimously adopted a resolution on February 22, 1994, emphasizing that Jammu and Kashmir was an integral part of India, and that Pakistan must vacate parts of the State under its occupation[22].

India has taken effective steps to guard its border with Pakistan. In order to prevent illegal immigration and anti-India activities from Pakistan, India has constructed a fence with flood lighting along the borders to include the international border and the LoC. The fence is backed by several other protective measures including the presence of troops and sophisticated surveillance equipment. Though the fence did bring down the level of infiltration especially in the state of Jammu and Kashmir, gaps still exist due to the nature of the terrain as well as requirement of maintenance. The government has now declared that the entire India-Pakistan border is to be completely sealed by December 2018. The announcement may be viewed in the context of India-Pakistan relations reaching a particular low and uncertain threshold post the Uri incident and cross-LC operations by India on 28-29 September 2016. The decision of the Union Government is reported to have been taken after a review of gaps in border management by a high-level Committee on Security and Border Protection of the Union Ministry of Home Affairs popularly known as the Madhukar Gupta Committee set up in March 2016 to overcome the lacunae observed consequent on the Gurdaspur and Pathankot infiltration occurrences[23].

Indo-Pak border is replete with flash points to trigger a broad spectrum of conflicts. It lends itself to a collusive hybrid threat from Pakistan and China. Heightened proxy war through this border has major implications on the stability of South Asia.

Pakistan's highly indoctrinated army believes in finding its relevance in keeping the Kashmir issue alive. It regularly resorts to cross-border firing; despite the 2003 ceasefire between the two countries, as a cover to infiltrate militants in Jammu and Kashmir. Pakistan wants to link the issue of peace and stability in Afghanistan with the Kashmir issue and vehemently tries to sell it to the West. Continuation of ceasefire violations as well as attempts by Pakistan based terrorists' strikes to worsen the already deteriorating India-Pakistan relations cannot be ruled out.

Sir Creek and Siachen are the leverages held by India against Pakistan in their border disputes. India must insist that Pakistan dismantles its terrorist infrastructure before any concessions are accorded on these issues. Therefore, solving these issues before the Kashmir issue is not in India's interest.

Pak: Epicentre of Terrorism

Terrorism can be defined as the systematic use or threatened use of violence to intimidate a population or government and thereby effect political, religious, or ideological change.[24] South Asia has been a victim of terrorism and terrorist organisations continue to pose a big challenge to the South Asian states in their efforts to provide security to their citizens. The most serious terror threat, however, presently exists is in Pakistan and Afghanistan. The Taliban are active in both these countries. There are other Islamist radicals as well in Pakistan—some of whom are sectarian whereas others have an anti-India agenda.

Pak as an epicentre of terrorism has direct bearing on India. External terrorism in India emerges from Pakistan which is sponsored by the state. Internal terrorism which emulates from religious or communal violence, left-wing extremism and insurgency in the north-eastern states too is abetted by Pakistan. The government has identified 65 terror groups active in the country, out of which a maximum of 34 are in Manipur[25]. Pakistan and China are covertly involved in providing help to internal terrorists in India. Reportedly, through the LeT, Pakistan has been providing material support to the Maoists in India and has also arranged for mine / IED training of the core group. Pakistan has also been supporting Khalistan movement which seeks to create a Sikh country in the Punjab region of South Asia.

Pakistan, under the tutelage of its Army continues to wage a proxy war in India's state of Jammu and Kashmir. Unable to seek a conventional parity with India is has sought to exploit this low cost option to bleed India by a thousand cuts. Terrorists trained in Pakistan continue to fight their Jihad in Kashmir. For India, the Lashkar-e-Taiba (LeT) is the central hub of militant groups like Harkat-ul-Mujahideen (HuM), Jaish-e-Mohammed (JeM), Harkat-ul-Jihad-al-Islami (HuJI) in Pakistan and Bangladesh, Tehrik-e-Taliban Pakistan, anti-Shia Lashkar-e-Jhangvi and multinational organized crime syndicates like D-Company, ISI, Pakistani Army and   Al Qaeda itself[26]. LeT being the covert arm of Pakistan's ISI is well established as evident from the testimony of David Headley and radio intercepts during 26/11 Mumbai terrorist attacks. The Indian Mujahideen (IM) is the creation of Pakistan[27] while the HuM is openly headquartered in Muzaffarabad with units in 43 districts in Pakistan. LeT and Markaz Dawat Wal Irshad (JD) have joined hands, with the latter having support of Saudis.

These trans-border terrorist groups serve to escalate tensions between India and Pakistan; which have portents of manifesting themselves into an all-out conventional war under a nuclear umbrella; with disastrous outcome, threatening South Asian region.

Moreover, there is also danger of nuclear terrorism looming large over the South Asian countries and India in particular. Pakistan is on the frontline of this proliferation-terrorism adequacy since its P-3 and P-4 facilities produce nuclear material which don't need further enrichment and can be handled by non-state actors without major technical requirements.

If it is believed that reliable security measures have been implemented, there is little information on the level of material control and accountability mechanisms. With a lack of nuclear material accountability and a possible "intersection of nuclear weapons and terrorism", as mentioned by the US Senate Commission on the Prevention of Weapons of Mass Destruction, Proliferation and Terrorism in a 2008 report, it is also believed that a small scale terrorist group will be able to undertake the manufacturing of a "dirty bomb". The scientific and technical means of some State entities can be used by non-state actors towards the aim of constructing and using a dirty bomb.[28]

Pakistan undoubtedly is the epicentre of terrorism in the world today.[29] Pakistan-based militant groups with a proven ability to strike at home, in India, and beyond, and with demonstrable links to international terrorist networks pose the most significant threat to stability in South Asia. Pakistan itself has been a victim of terrorism in recent past. The terror outfits it once created are targeting Pakistan itself. Terrorist acts stemming from Sunni-Shia sectarian strife and ethnic tensions have become a major concern in Pakistan.

Despite being a victim of terrorism itself, Pakistan has not initiated any credible cooperation mechanism with India to tackle this menace. It continues to use cross-border terrorism as a state policy, not learning from its mistakes. It is not clear to what extent Pakistan can control terrorist organizations now, since it is being targeted itself now.

To sum up, Pakistan is a nuclear weapon state beset by underdevelopment, poor socio-economic conditions, rising population and growing unemployment. This has been exacerbated by lack of robust governance. Foreign terrorist organisations including Al-Qaeda and its affiliates continue to operate and carry out attacks in Pakistan. Pakistan is going through a churning process where an elected government, the Army and the terrorist outfits are trying to establish their dominance.

From the Indian point of view, it needs to be clearly understood that a clear Pakistani approach against terrorists is unlikely to appear until a strong democratic government comes to power and realises that terrorists are nobody's friends. While there is no chance that military will give up its hold over Pakistan's power reigns, the civil society in the country can make a difference. If it strongly stands against the terrorists, the civil society can build up the pressure on the government which in turn will force the Army to act against terrorists.

Indo-Pak-China: Collusive Hybrid Threats and Challenges

Hybrid warfare is a military strategy that blends conventional warfare, irregular warfare and cyber warfare. The collusive hybrid threat to India as a result of the Sino-Pakistan nexus would be a combination of politico-diplomacy, conventional, asymmetric, disruptive technologies and nuclear, biological as also chemical warfare. It is pertinent to note that both these countries are playing some aspects of hybrid warfare currently. Pakistan is currently playing the Jihadi card through which she can heighten the proxy war in J&K, fuel the militancy in Punjab, abet pan-India terrorism as also launch social cyber-attacks as occurred in Bengaluru in 2013 where employees from the North East fled to their native states due to threatening communal text messages[30].

These non-contact means can be fused with escalation of violence at the LoC and forward aggressive military posturing to perpetuate India's two front dilemma. China on the other hand is possibly assisting Left Wing Extremism which is spread in over 200 districts of India. There are indications of possible Chinese help to groups in the North East to compound our problems as part of its non-contact unrestricted warfare strategy. These asymmetric threats can be blended with upping the ante on the LoC and adopting aggressive military posture on the LAC as also the Indian Ocean. Further cyber espionage and sabotage as also other asymmetric capabilities can be employed with an attempt to subdue India.

Weapons of Mass Destruction (WMD) have never been ever used in South Asia. India verifiably destroyed its declared chemical weapons arsenal in 2009 under the supervision of the Organization for the Prohibition of Chemical Weapons (OPCW)[31].India and Pakistan are signatories to the treaties of Biological and Toxic Weapons Convention Treaty of 1975 and the Chemical Weapons Convention Treaty of 1997. However, though debatable intelligence inputs indicate that Pakistan has manufactured weapons for blister, blood choking and nerve agents. Baloch nationalists have often accused Pakistani security forces of using chemical weapons, namely phosphorus gas against Baloch rebels and civilians.[32]

China –Pakistan Collusion

China and Pakistan describe their relationship as higher than the mountains and deeper than the oceans. Politically, the two have always been a staunch supporter for each other. The Sino-Pak overlapping geostrategic and geo-economic interests are at cross roads with India's national interests. While the bilateral relations between India and Pakistan are fraught with animosity, India's relations with China too are characterised by mutual distrust. An emerging India is a challenge to Chinese interests in South Asia and therefore it has all along followed a policy of marginalising and containing India's growth. It is therefore no surprise that it finds Pakistan as a natural partner in this process.

China has been responsible for Pakistan's nuclear programme which has changed the complexion of security dynamics in South Asia. China has also been abetting the proxy war by Pakistan in Jammu and Kashmir. Both the countries have a border dispute with India. China has been issuing stapled visas to residents of J&K thus questioning the legitimacy of India's legal claims over PoK, northern area and Ladakh.[33]

The congruence of mutual interest in PoK has further deepened by the ongoing China-Pakistan Economic Corridor (CPEC) which will pass through disputed territory in PoK. On 13th November 2016, CPEC was partially operationalised as Chinese cargo was transported to Gwadar Port for onward maritime shipment to Africa and West Asia.[34] Improvement of roads and other infrastructure projects along the CPEC are underway; some have been completed as well. Upgradation of Karakoram highway project costing $ 350 bn by China[35] while completion of the construction of 800 Km long railway link from Havellian in Pakistan to Khunjerab Pass are a few such examples.

The developments have security implications for India. There are uncorroborated reports of presence of Chinese troops at Khunjerab Pass (15,397 ft) on Karakoram highway.[36] Tunnels which are being constructed as infrastructure development projects can be used for hiding missiles and silos. Construction of rail road network from China to Gwadar Port reducing travel time to 48 hours instead of 16-25 days as at present has obvious security implications.

In the present geopolitical environment emergence of collusion against India in case of hostilities emerging against either China or Pakistan cannot be ruled out. Simultaneous border tensions and violations by Pakistan and China can lead to a two-front war dilemma for India. The probability of this scenario has increased further keeping in mind the increasing cooperation between Pakistan-China in the disputed areas of Jammu and Kashmir.

Indian Ocean Region: Emerging Competitions

Indian Interests in the Indian Ocean

India in the Indian Ocean Region (IOR) has a strategic geographical advantage. Located in the centre its peninsula juts into the Indian Ocean flanking the Arabian Sea on one side and the Bay of Bengal on the other side. India has a coastline of 7516.6 km. India has the potential to dominate the Sea Lanes of Communication (SLOC) from Strait of Hormuz to Strait of Malacca and even beyond. An emerging India is seeking to establish itself on the global stage as the main resident power of the Indian Ocean, willing to cooperate with all external powers while aligning with none to prevent strategies that might polarize the Indian Ocean region.

Other important players are China, USA and now Pakistan as well due to the emerging Chinese interests coupled with Sino-Pak collusion of interests. While the US supports rise of Indian power in the IOR, China is a competitor seeking to establish its presence in IOR much to India's discomfort.[37]China's 'String of Pearls strategy' seeks to limit Indian influence in the IOR. It is developing ports in Sittwe (Myanmar), Chittagong (Bangladesh), Hambantota (Sri Lanka) and deep water port in Gwadar in Pakistan. Its nuclear powered submarines are on constant patrol in the IOR. Construction of CPEC from Xinjiang to Gwadar port to Arabian Sea and the second from Kunming to Sittwe to Bay of Bengal are part of China's endeavour to dominate the IOR.

IOR has strategic importance for India. The Indian Ocean cannot be considered as a single entity from strategic point of view. Security considerations weigh on three separate parts of Indian Ocean to India.[38]SLOCs from the Middle East and African continent carrying India's energy needs pass through the Arabian Sea. These face security challenges from traditional adversary Pakistan and non-state actors. The Central

Indian Ocean Region is vital as India's sphere of influence and suitable for projection of power. However, it is the Bay of Bengal and Malacca Strait where India's strategic strength lies in this region, which has the potential to create vulnerability for China. This is also an area of cooperation with ASEAN and Asia Pacific countries.

Andaman and Nicobar islands situated in the Bay of Bengal have a very strategic role to play in Indian security calculus. The Islands are closer to a number of countries than the Indian mainland namely Myanmar, Indonesia and Thailand. The Malacca Strait is also very near to these islands and Indian presence at Andamans further aggravates China's Malacca dilemma. Apart from their location, these Islands also have an Exclusive Economic Zone (EEZ) of 300,000 sq. km. Thus, any country controlling these Islands would be able to control the Bay of Bengal. Due to their proximity to South East Asian countries, these Islands can serve as a bridgehead for any country wishing to either attack mainland India or carry out subversive activities.[39] Indian Navy based at Port Blair can carry out joint operations for security of Straits of Malacca, Lombok and Sunda during times of crisis in conjunction with navies of Indonesia, Vietnam and other ASEAN nations.

An emerging India with great power aspirations has to look at IOR with a view to upgrading its relations with mineral and energy rich Africa, the Middle East, the Persian Gulf and Southeast Asia. These reserves are critical to India's economic development and great power aspirations. India-Africa trade volume is around $ 75 billion[40]. India-ASEAN trade volume which stood at $ 58.7 billion is expected to further grow in future[41]. The security of SLOCs is therefore critical for India and it seeks to position itself as the dominant Indian Ocean power in the decades ahead. Modernisation of Indian Navy is an imperative. This is all the more essential as India and China have same sources of oil import with similar trade destinations.

Pakistan's Interests in Indian Ocean

Pakistan's interests emanate from its coastline that is over 1000 km long, an Exclusive Economic Zone (EEZ) of around 300,000 square km, the Karachi port and the newly built deep sea port of Gawadar. Pakistan's only coastal access point is Indian Ocean for its trade and energy supplies. 95 percent of its trade and 100 percent of its energy supplies are dependent on Indian Ocean.[42] Therefore it is but natural that Pakistan intends to prevent India from dominating areas close to its own coastline so that its trade and energy routes are safe. As per Pakistan India's evolving "expansionist" maritime security strategy and un-demarked border of Sir Creek pose "threat" to the security of the Indian Ocean.[43]

Since Pakistan does not have naval capability to stop India in the IOR, it has depended on external balancers. In the current scenario, the US is not a reliable partner for Pakistan due to increasing US-India bonhomie, ongoing security dialogue and shared mutual interest to contain China. Pakistan is therefore using China as a balancer against India in the IOR.

The construction of CPEC which shall give China access to the Arabian Sea has changed the complexion of the ongoing competition between India and Pakistan in the IOR. Pakistan stands to benefit from China's string of pearls strategy and has therefore, handed over operational rights of the Gwadar port to China[44]. Pakistan is developing its naval power to exploit India's 'Hormuz dilemma'. Indian trade and energy imports pass through the narrow Strait of Hormuz. It is close to Pakistan's Makran coast where the Chinese are helping them to develop deep-water ports.

India-Pakistan Water Issues

Water issues between India and Pakistan are historically constructed, emotionally charged, and politically divisive. The Indo-Pakistan water relations are governed by Indus Water Treaty which came into existence in 1960.[45] The eastern rivers (Ravi, Satluj, and Beas) have been assigned to India under the treaty while the control over the western rivers (Chenab and Jhelum) has been given to Pakistan. The treaty has survived three wars and is often cited as an example of 'cooperation' among the states who are sworn enemies. Indian projects on the western rivers have evoked objections from Pakistan, the latest being Baglihar dam on Chenab river.[46] All fears raised by Pakistan including the height of the dam were allayed by a World Bank appointed neutral expert, giving a go-ahead to Indian project. Water availability has dropped from about 5,000 cubic metres per capita to in early 1950s to 1,500 today. Pakistan is expected to become water scarce by 2035. However, the situation is not any better in India.

Most of the dams in Pakistan like Tarbela are silted; consequently flow in Indus in lower reaches has reduced to the extent that sea ingress has affected the fertile Sukkur belt in Sind. Mismanagement is the root cause of such a state. Indus River System Authority (IRSA) and Water and Power Development Authority (WAPDA) the two organisations responsible for the management of water resources in Pakistan are highly corrupt organizations.[47] Food security challenge will become more daunting for Pakistan in future if water resources are not better managed.

Water insecurity also spawns different manifestations of militancy and nationalism in Pakistan. Extremists in Pakistan's Punjab province have issued violent threats, angrily blaming India for 'stealing' Pakistan's water and vowing aggression against India. Not only the militants, but also the country's government, have blamed India for their water woes, (even though the IWT allots it 80 percent of the total Indus basin river flow).

Prognosis

Indo – Pak relations are unlikely to see a qualitative change in the short to midterm. The Pakistan military in the foreseeable future shall continue to remain the most important factor in Pakistan and will continue to adversely impact the desired democratic transition in the country. The internal security situation will continue to be plagued by ethno-sectarianism and jihadi violence. The country's economic situation will remain dim and fuel social unrest and disillusionment amongst the people. Pakistan will maintain its current policy towards India and Afghanistan and relations with the two neighbours will remain tense, with the incidence of violence following a sine curve. Relations with US will also remain uneasy with ambiguity increasing further under the Trump administration. Relations with China and Saudi Arabia shall remain strong. The strategists feel that Pakistan runs the risk of an Arab Spring like situation. The same is debatable; however, Pakistan shall remain in turmoil, posing a major challenge for India.

Endnotes

1 Fair Christine, C "Fighting To The End-The Pakistan Army's Way of War" Oxford University Press

2 Tellis Ashley J(2005) "Stability in South Asia" [Online : web] Accessed 23 Jan 2017 URL : https://www.rand.org/content/dam/rand/pubs/documented_briefings/2005/DB185.pdf

3 (2013) "Pakistani protests threaten NATO supply lines to Afghanistan" [Online : web] Accessed 23 Jan 2017 URL : http://www.csmonitor.com/World/Asia-South-Central/2013/1203/Pakistani-protests-threaten-NATO-supply-lines-to-Afghanistan

4 http://tacstrat.com/content/index.php/2012/10/10/indian-predictions-for-the-next-major-conflict/

5 http://en.wikipedia.org/wiki/China percentE2 percent80 percent93Pakistan_Free_Trade_Agreement

6 books.sipri.org/files/FS/SIPRIFS1403.pdf

7 Pant, Harsh (2012), "The Rise of China: Implications for India," Cambridge University Press India Pvt. Ltd, pp

8 http://sinosphere.blogs.nytimes.com/2013/11/27/behind-the-chinese-pakistani- nuclear-deal/?_php=true&_type=blogs&_r=0

9 (2014) "How Asians View Each other"[Online: web] Accessed 23 Jan 2017 URL: http://www.pewglobal.org/2014/07/14/chapter-4-how-asians-view-each-other

10 http://www.diplomaticourier.com/news/regions/asia/2193-how-china-and-pakistan-shift-the-balance-of-power-in-south-asia

11 Khawaja, Asma Shakir (2009) "Talibanisation of Pakistan: Myth or Reality"[Online : web] Accessed 31 Jan 2017 URL : http://wcms.itz.uni-halle.de/download.php?down=9047&elem=1986859

12 ibid

13 ibid

14 (2015) "Talibanisation Of Pakistan: A Threat To India's Security"[Online : web] Accessed 31 Jan 2017 URL : https://www.ukessays.com/essays/history/talibanisation-of-pakistan-a-threat-to-indias-security-history-essay.php?utm_expid=309629-

15 (2015) "Factors For Balkanisation And Future Of Pakistan"[Online : web] Accessed 31 Jan 2017 URL : https://www.ukessays.com/essays/politics/

factors-for-balkanisation-and-future-of-pakistan-politics-essay.php?utm_expid=309629-

16 Khan MH (2006) "Back on Track" [Online : web] Accessed 06 Feb 2017 URL : http://www.dawn.com/weekly/dmag/archive/060305/dmag6.htm

17 (2015) "Indo-Pakistani border"[Online : web] Accessed 06 Feb 2017 URL :https://en.wikipedia.org/wiki/Indo-Pakistani_border#cite_note-Dawn_News_archives-1

18 Swamy, Praveen(2001) "Border Barriers"[Online : web] Accessed 31 Jan 2017 URL : http://www.frontline.in/navigation/?type=static&page=flonnet&rdurl=fl1819/18191290.htm

19 (2005) "All about the Siachen Glacier: the conflict, perspectives of India and Pakistan, geography, history and the possible resolutions"[Online : web] Accessed 06 Feb 2017 URL : http://www.siachenglacier.com/

20 ibid

21 Mishra, Raghavendra (2015) "The 'Sir Creek' Dispute: Contours, Implications and the Way Ahead" [Online : web] Accessed 06 Feb 2017 URL : http://www.idsa.in/strategicanalysis/39_2/TheSirCreekDispute

22 (1994) "Parliament Resolution on Jammu and Kashmir" [Online: web] Accessed 06 Feb 2017 URL : http://www.satp.org/satporgtp/countries/india/document/papers/parliament_resolution_on_Jammu_and_ Kashmir.htm

23 Sen, Gautam(2016) "Implications of a Complete Sealing of the India-Pakistan" [Online : web] Accessed 06 Feb 2017 URL : Borderhttp://www.idsa.in/idsacomments/complete-sealing-of-the-india-pakistan-border_gsen_181016

24 http://www.britannica.com/EBchecked/topic/588371/terrorism

25 (2013) "65 terror groups active in India"[Online : web] Accessed 13Feb 2017 URL : http://www.thehindu.com/news/65-terror-groups-active-in-india-govt/article5064769.ece

26 Padukone Neil (2011) "The Next al-Qaeda? Lashkar-e-Taiba and the Future of Terrorism in South Asia" [Online : web] Accessed 13Feb 2017 URL : http://www.worldaffairsjournal.org/article/next-al-qaeda-lashkar-e-taiba-and-future-terrorism-south-asia

27 (2012) "ISI created Indian Mujahideen to spread terror in India: Anti-terrorism squad" [Online : web] Accessed 13 Feb 2017 URL :http://timesofindia.indiatimes.com/india/ISI-created-Indian-Mujahideen-to-spread-terror-in-India-Anti-terrorism-squad/articleshow/13714739.cms

28 Lavern, Martin de(2012) "The Non-Traditional Nuclear Threat in South Asia: Managing the Focus" [Online : web] Accessed 13Feb 2017 URL : http://www.

ipcs.org/article/terrorism/the-non-traditional-nuclear-threat-in-south-asia-managing-the-3633.html

29 (2016) "Pakistan has distinction of being 'epicentre' of terrorism" [Online : web] Accessed 13 Feb 2017 URL : http://www.newindianexpress.com/nation/2016/oct/25/pakistan-has-distinction-of-being-epicentre-of-terrorism-india-at-ipu-1531611.html

30 Singha Rajib (2014) "Indian Businesses Lost $4 Billion Due to Cyberattacks in 2013; 2014 to be Worse"[Online : web] Accessed 13 Feb 2017 URL :http://blogs.quickheal.com/indian-businesses-lost-4-billion-due-cyberattacks-2013-2014-worse/

31 (2015) "South Asia 1540 Reporting"[Online : web] Accessed 13 Feb 2017 URL : http://www.nti.org/analysis/reports/south-asia-1540-reporting/

32 (2016) "WMD Terrorism: Could South Asia be the Next Target?" [Online : web] Accessed 13 Feb 2017 URL : http://www.bharatdefencekavach.com/news/beyond-headlines/story/58561.html

33 Raman, B (2010) "China supports Pakistan's claim on Kashmir!" [Online : web] Accessed 07 Feb 2017 URL : http://idr.qburst.com/news/china-supports-pakistans-claim-on-kashmir/

34 Ramachandran Subha (2016) "CPEC takes a step forward as violence surges in Balochistan" [Online: web] Accessed 07 Feb 2017 URL: http://www.atimes.com/cpec-takes-step-forward-violence-surges-balochistan/?platform=hootsuite

35 (2015) "Chinese firms to get contracts for two CPEC projects" [Online : web] Accessed 07 Feb 2017 URL : http://www.dawn.com/news/1200203

36 (2016) "Game changers: Pak tactical nukes, Chinese troops in PoK" [Online : web] Accessed 07 Feb 2017 URL : http://www.tribuneindia.com/news/sunday-special/kaleidoscope/game-changers-pak-tactical-nukes-chinese-troops-in-pok/243608.html

37 (2017) "Indian Navy's Largest-Ever Exercise vs Enemy Submarines" http://www.ndtv.com/india-news/off-goa-the-largest-ever-naval-exercises-with-a-focus-on-the-chinese-navy-1657264

38 http://www.claws.in/index.php?action=master&task=580&u_id=36

39 Kukreja, Dhiraj (2013) "Andaman and Nicobar Islands: A security challenge for India" [Online : web] Accessed 08 Feb 2017 URL :http://www.indiandefencereview.com/news/andaman-and-nicobar-islands-a-security-challenge-for-india/

40 (2016) "India, Africa rekindle trade ties"[Online : web] Accessed 13 Feb 2017 URL : http://www.un.org/africarenewal/magazine/august-2016/india-africa-rekindle-trade-ties

41 (2016) "Why India needs to expand its engagement with ASEAN"[Online : web] Accessed 13Feb 2017 URL : http://www.dnaindia.com/india/comment-why-india-needs-to-expand-its-engagement-with-asean-2252804

42 (2017) "Pak Concerned Over Peace In Indian Ocean"[Online : web] Accessed 13Feb 2017 URL :http://www.indiandefensenews.in/2017/02/pak-concerned-over-peace-in-indian.html

43 ibid

44 (2016) "Gwadar Port to be Operational by 2017" [Online : web] Accessed 13Feb 2017 URL :http://www.dawn.com/news/1251723

45 (2016) "10 things to know about Indus Water Treaty"[Online : web] Accessed 13Feb 2017 URL : http://www.thehindu.com/specials/10-things-to-know-about-Indus-Water-Treaty/article15000672.ece

46 Shaukat, Sajjad (2017) "Pak-India Water Dispute Accelerates"[Online : web] Accessed 13Feb 2017 URL : http://www.kashmirawareness.org/pak-india-water-dispute-accelerates/

47 Sharma,Raj Kumar (2016) "South Asia's Water Problem" [Online : web] Accessed 13Feb 2017 URL : http://usiblog.in/2016/02/south-asias-water-problem/

Chapter 4

Littoral States of Indian Ocean in South Asia

"There is a new awakening in South Asia, a new recognition of inter-linked destinies and a new belief in shared opportunities"

- Narendra Modi

MALDIVES

Introduction

Maldives, located to the South West of India, is vital for our strategic and security interests. It is a Muslim country strategically located in the Indian Ocean and the smallest member of SAARC. It is an Island country with 1192 low lying coral Islands grouped into 26 atolls, out of which only 199 are inhabited.

The importance of Maldives is derived from its strategic location in the Indian Ocean astride the SLOC from Persian Gulf, Red Sea and East Africa.[1] For India, the strategic importance of Maldives also stems from its close geographic location to India. The Islands lie only 114 Km from Minicoy Islands and 640 Kms from the mainland, as compared to 770 Km from Sri Lanka. The dispersed nature of the Islands, the fact that only 199 Islands are inhabited, and the difficulty in effectively patrolling/monitoring them implies these could be used by forces inimical to India, in case bases are leased to them.

The population of Maldives is approximately 369,812[2] which is almost 100 percent Salafist Sunni Muslims. Though Maldives has generally had a pro-India leaning in spite of a Muslim population, lately Islamisation of society is taking hold, with influence from Pakistan and the Middle-East. Yet, India has a clear advantage as the people do identify themselves more with India than with any other country. This is due to the close geographical proximity combined with ethno-religious similarities (akin to Malabar Muslims of Kerala).

Indians are the largest expatriate community in the Maldives; with a total strength of approximately 29,000, followed by Sri Lanka 8350 and Bangladesh 7000[3]. The Indian expatriate community consists of doctors, nurses and technicians, teachers, etc spread over the islands. This results in substantial influence of India in the country as well as the aspect of their security in case of an emergency.

Political Stability

In February 2012, the country's first democratically elected president, Mohamed Nasheed, was forced to resign amid an alleged police coup and was swiftly replaced by his former deputy, Mohamed Waheed. The elections in Maldives, after two earlier aborted attempts, were finally held on 10 and 17 November 2013 wherein Abdullah Yameen emerged as the surprise winner and was sworn in as the President.[4] Mohd Nasheed, the ousted President, was leading in the first round of polls, and was expected to win; however, the elections have been widely acknowledged as free and fair and the newly elected government has been accepted by all including India and also by Mohd Nasheed and his party. The new President visited India from 01-04 January 2014, wherein he met PM Manmohan Singh. This was H.E. Mr Abdulla Yameen Abdul Gayoom's first visit abroad after assuming Office.

It was widely believed that the ousted President, Mohd Nasheed, who had also sought refuge in the Indian Embassy in Maldives, was pro-India and a moderate, and therefore his re-election as President was in India's interests. However, India's neutral stand during the election and only an insistence on conduct of a free and fair election, and thereafter a quick acceptance of the new government under Abdullah Yameen, has had a positive influence in Maldives. Yameen, is the half-brother of Gayoom who ruled Maldives for 30 years, and is seen as a hardliner with Islamic leanings.[5] India needs to continually engage with the new government, provide necessary assistance, leverage its influence and ensure that

Indian economic and security interests are met. Continued political and democratic stability in Maldives is an imperative for India.

Security Dynamics

Strategic Vulnerability

Maldives strategic vulnerability is primarily a derivative of its geographic vulnerability due to dispersed location of islands and large distances thereto. The threat of external intervention aimed at taking over island territory especially Gan island, with the assistance of mercenaries or fundamentalist militant groups, cannot be ruled out. Destabilisation by domestic groups, including those in exile is again a reality. The above concerns are accentuated due to lack of strong national defence, communication and logistics network. Maldives National Defence Force (MNDF) comprises of Marine Corps, Security Protection Group and Coast Guard. The MNDF, with its small size and with little serviceable equipment, is inadequate to prevent external aggression and is primarily tasked to reinforce the Maldives Police Service (MPS) and ensure security in the exclusive economic zone.[6]

Maritime Security

Maldives has limited natural resources and imports almost all its requirements. Its economy rests exclusively on fishing and tourism. Due to lack of economic infrastructure, it seeks foreign investment in both these industries. Being a small island nation with no military capability of its own, Maldives is vulnerable to outside interference. Like any other island nation, Maldives also needs to protect her trade routes and seabed resources around the islands. Control of the Indian Ocean by external maritime powers remains a cause of concern to Maldives. The external threat can manifest in the form of a mercenary attack, or by terrorist groups.

Environmental Vulnerability

Consequent to the grave environmental threats resulting from global warming, which experts feel could result in this nation being flooded out of existence 70 years hence, the Maldivian authorities are giving high priority to promoting "environment friendly tourism". Coral mining is banned, and certain marine species are protected in order to keep the atolls' reputation for good diving. They are focusing on sensitising the world population and governments to dangers of the global warming process.[7]

Economic Vulnerability

Maldivian Economy is based principally on tourism and fishing. It is economically vulnerable having limited natural resources and importing almost all its requirements. The Maldivian government initiated an economic reforms programme in 1989 and subsequently introduced regulations to allow more foreign investment. The dependence on tourism leaves the economy vulnerable, and the global economic downturn coupled with political instability has led to fall in tourists which have had an adverse impact on the economy.[8]

Internal Stability

Rising Islamic Fundamentalism.   Islamic fundamentalism has been on the rise in recent years. A fairly moderate Maldivian society, fuelled by ultra-conservative Salafist preachers from Pak and the Middle East and the spread of madrasas, is rapidly changing into one of religious intolerance and xenophobia. Islamic extremism began to be imported into Maldives in the late 1990s, with the advent of international 'religious terrorism', when Maldives was under the dictatorial regime of Maumoon Abdul Gayoom. In Feb 12, as protesters backed by mutinous police toppled president Mohamed Nasheed, a handful of men in Taliban-style intolerance, stormed the Chinese-built museum and destroyed its display of priceless artifacts from the nation's pre-Islamic era, dating back to the 12th century, thus erasing all evidence of its Buddhist past. Rise of Muslim fundamentalism,[9] influence of jihadis, as also any form of instability has major adverse implications for India's security.

Socio-Economic Divide.   The high unemployment rate (more than 11.6%[10]), predominantly tourism dependent economy (6,00,000 tourist arrivals against a total population of 3,69,000) and 15% of the population living below the national poverty line has widened the poor-rich divide.[11] The socio-economic conditions coupled with the arrival of clerics from West Asian countries/Pakistan and availability of internet, CDs on religion has led to rise in religious extremism.

Drug Abuse.   Drug abuse in Maldives has grown to disturbing levels. Male is home to a number of street gangs engaging in violent crime and competing to sell drugs. According to United Nations Children Fund (UNICEF)-2012 report, there are some 8,000 drug users in the country.[12]

Foreign Policy

Security and Protection of Small States.   Still affected by memories of the 1988 coup attempt; Male's foreign policy concentrates on mustering support of the international community towards evolving a mechanism to protect small states in the event of external threat. A Maldivian resolution to this effect was adopted without a vote by the United Nations General Assembly (UNGA) in Oct 89. Their position is that "the security and protection of small states must be accepted as an integral part of international security and peace".

Non Alignment Policy.[13]   Male has followed the stance of strict non-alignment even on issues of regional security, thereby, supporting the proposals to declare the Indian Ocean a Zone of Peace and South Asia a Nuclear Weapon-Free Zone.

Pursuance of Policy of Close Friendship with India.[14]   India has a clear edge and strategic advantage over other countries seeking influence in Maldives, as the people identify themselves more with India than with any other country, due to the close geographical proximity combined with ethno-religious similarities (akin to Malabar Muslims of Kerala) and significant contribution by the Indian diaspora, especially in the field of education and medical support. However, this relation is under strain due to the recent GMR imbroglio, rising Islamic fundamentalism and Maldives' growing relationship with China and Pakistan.

China-Maldives Relations.   The relations between China and Maldives have grown steadily over the years, due to sustained policy of China to strategically engage Maldives. China has positively developed its military relations with Maldives and hopes to enhance bilateral cooperation further, to safeguard regional peace and stability. Funds worth US $ 700 Million have been allocated by China for economic/technical projects and infrastructure development in the Maldives. The Chinese tourist footprint in the country too is significant with 3, 59,000 tourists visiting Maldives in 2014-15.[15]

Pak- Maldives Relations. The relations between both the countries have been cordial and friendly. The main binding factor is the common religious background. Maldivians are Salafist Sunni Muslims. Bilateral trade between the two is miniscule with only 0.38% of imports to Pakistan. However, there is deepening Military Cooperation between the two countries.[16] Maldives has shown interests in production of small arms ammunition, JF 17 ac, K8 security vehicles and BPJs. Additionally Pak is imparting training to Maldivian security personnel in intelligence and medical fields. Various military courses are being offered to MNDF.

US – Maldives Relations. The United States has friendly relations with Maldives and had publicly endorsed India's timely intervention on behalf of the Maldivian Government during the November 1988 coup attempt. Maldives has signed a trade and investment framework agreement with the US, providing to enhance bilateral trade and investment. The US and Maldives also enjoy a close military-to-military relationship including joint exercises and training opportunities for Maldivian officers at US service academies. The US recognises the importance of promoting security in the Indian Ocean, and US Naval vessels have regularly called at Maldives in recent years.[17] Maldives has extended strong support to US efforts to combat terrorism and terrorist financing.

India's Interests[18]

Security Interests

Maldives is positively inclined towards India and as such does not pose any threat to India. However, its geo-strategic location dominating some important SLOC in the Indian Ocean is of immense maritime and security interest to India. The dispersed nature of its islands and the difficulty in effectively patrolling/monitoring them implies that these could be used for purposes inimical to the security interests of India. This aspect needs to be continuously monitored. It is in India's overall strategic security interest to ensure Maldives continues its positive leanings towards India and is dissuaded from offering any bases or facilities to countries inimical to India's security interests. Post Tsunami, refusal to China's proposal to develop two of the Maldivian Islands is a move which has negated potential strategic disadvantage to India to some extent.

Preserving Strategic Space

On international issues, Maldives has traditionally been supportive of India and broadly coordinated its position with that of India in multilateral fora, such as the UN, the Commonwealth, the NAM and the SAARC. Maldives has extended full support for India's candidature for a permanent seat in the UN Security Council.

Ways and Means

Developing Leverages

India's interests can be protected by developing leverages, designed to build political goodwill and understanding, by maintaining close diplomatic, economic, technological and defence relations with Maldives.

India does not have any special treaty relationship with Maldives, however, its interests are based on a policy framework, designed to build political goodwill and understanding, without adopting a 'big brother' syndrome. Though Maldives perceives India as a staunch ally, it would not like to be seen as having formal treaty based relationship with India. We need to respect their sensitivities and nurture the special relationship which we share.

Economic and Commercial Relations

India and Maldives have wide ranging and growing economic ties. Bilateral trade which stood at Rs 377 crores in 2007-08 has risen to Rs 700 Crores in 2014-15.[19] With tourism and fishing as its only industries, Maldives imports a large number of essential commodities from India which includes agricultural produce, textiles, drugs, medicines, engineering and industrial products, cement etc. Investments by Indian companies have been increasing in sectors such as education, hospitality renewable energy, health and waste management and marine products. India has announced the provision of a $ 40 million line of credit for the housing sector and $100 million as soft loan for a comprehensive economic development package to Maldives.

Economic and Technical Cooperation

Under the Economic and Technical Cooperation Agreement, signed in February, 1986, a Joint Commission for Economic and Technical Cooperation was established between India and the Maldives. Co-chaired by External Affairs Minister and Maldivian Foreign Minister, the joint Commission meetings took place in 1990, 1992, 1995 and 2000. The meeting identified areas for strengthening bilateral economic cooperation. India has been offering assistance to Maldives development process.

Defence Cooperation Issues

India needs to continuously keep Maldives engaged through various defence cooperation initiatives to maintain its dependence on India. Since 1988 defence has been a major area of cooperation between India and Maldives. India has adopted a very flexible and accommodating approach to meet Maldivian requirements of defence training and equipment.

In April 2016, during the state visit of Maldives President Abdulla Yameen Abdul Gayoom to New Delhi a crucial action plan on defence cooperation has been signed.

New Delhi is viewing its relationship with Male from the strategic and security prism, and the new action plan has been developed in the wake of growing Chinese influence in the island country.

The action plan is an important component of the India-Maldives bilateral relationship and the shared strategic and security interests of the two countries in the Indian Ocean region. The Action Plan envisages an institutional mechanism at the level of the Defence Secretaries to further bilateral defence cooperation. The prompt implementation of a concrete action plan in the defence sector will strengthen the bilateral defence cooperation. Development of ports, continuous training, capacity building, supply of equipment and maritime surveillance will be its main elements.[20]

Apart from the above the Indian naval and coast-guard ships have been regularly visiting Maldives on goodwill as well as on OTR (Operational Turn Around) visits.

SRI LANKA

Introduction

Sri Lanka is located at the junction of crucial maritime trading routes in the Indian Ocean connecting Europe and the Middle East to China and rest of Asia. Its location makes it an ideal communication and monitoring centre and is an ideal location for setting up a Command and Communication centre for monitoring traffic and intelligence gathering in the IOR. Sri Lanka has a valuable asset in the form of a natural harbour at Trincomalee, which is enclosed by huge rocks and small islets. It provides natural shelter and is ideal for basing nuclear submarines due to depth of the harbour. Any power that controls this harbour has a great advantage from a naval and strategic perspective. Its location is thus important for projecting naval power into the Indian Ocean, and is thus, envied as a military positioning point for major powers with interests in the region.

While the struggle over balance of power has diminished in the post-Cold-War era; India retains strategic interests in Sri Lanka because of pragmatic security considerations. The three-decade long armed conflict between Sri Lankan Armed Forces and the LTTE came to an end in May 09. The end of the armed conflict saw over three lakh Tamilian civilians in Internally Displaced Persons (IDP) camps. India played a crucial diplomatic role in Sri Lanka's military victory over the LTTE[21], though India feels let down by the Sri Lankan Government, which allowed Sinhala triumphalism to dictate political discourse on the Tamil question, after its victory in 2009. India favours a negotiated political settlement, consistent with democracy, pluralism and respect for human rights acceptable to all communities, within the framework of a United Sri Lanka.

India's role in Sri Lanka assumes more significance now than ever before, with the end of the war and devolution of power sharing in limbo. While the LTTE is wiped out militarily and isolated internationally, issues like the existing militarisation in Jaffna[22], the war crime charges at UN and uncertainties with regard to long term political solution still dog Sri Lanka and would need India's cooperation and support. The call for India's greater engagement with Sri Lanka had resurfaced domestically with a demand from Tamil Nadu parties urging India to play a more proactive role with regard to rebuilding and sustaining peace in post-war Sri Lanka, and in ending assault on Indian fishermen in the Palk Strait. On the other hand, the fostering of ties by Sri Lanka with Pak and China push for more primed hands-on role from the point of view of India's long-term strategic interests. There is therefore, a need to have a re-look at India's policy options towards Sri Lanka, in light of the recent developments.[23] In the past two decades, India and Sri Lanka have successfully built friendly ties, which have expanded to include robust economic links.

Security Issues

Internal Stability- Reconciliation Process with Tamil Minority

After winning the Eelam war, the government's reconciliation process is going through at a slow pace which is alienating not only the Tamil support but also some of the goodwill generated in India, US and EU countries. The Sri Lankan Government needs to address the political process of devolution to Tamils, as the massive development and infrastructure projects have not won over many in Tamil population. The assertion of Sinhala triumphalism has encouraged xenophobia, which could lead to a backlash by minorities and is a cause of concern for the Sri Lankan Government.[24]

Threat from External Actors

Sri Lanka is strategically placed to exploit the geopolitical struggle unfolding in the Indian Ocean between China and India, with the US having its own agenda for retaining its influence. While Pakistan is playing for stakes in Sri Lanka with Chinese acquiescence, to queer the pitch for India, the Russians too are keenly observing the activities in the Indian Ocean. It is pertinent to mention that Sri Lanka has always tried to play a divisive role by inviting external actors in the affairs of the Indian Ocean and thus act against India's interests. An example of the attitude was the permission granted by the Sri Lankans, to allow the Pakistan Air Force to refuel on its soil, during the Bangladesh War.[25] India can draw satisfaction from the fact that in regard to Sri Lanka, its interests broadly converge with those of the US, since the Americans are as keen to ward off the Chinese challenge for hegemony in the Indian Ocean, as India is.

Indian Interests - Ways and Means

Building Strategic Partnership

It is in India's strategic interest to develop strong relations with Sri Lanka. It is essential that we prevent the non-regional and other influential powers from making economic/ military forays on this important neighbour. Strategic partnership needs to be developed by sharing information/ knowledge on issues of mutual interest, promoting security cooperation in the region, provide a medium to understand strategic thinking, in addition to opening channels for track II diplomacy. These would help address mutual security concerns and challenges; increasing all forms of economic and humanitarian aid would be required.

Economic Dependence

Sri Lanka has long been a priority destination for direct investment from India. Sri Lanka is one of India's largest trading partners in SAARC. India in turn is Sri Lanka's largest trade partner globally. Trade between the two countries grew particularly rapidly after the entry into force of the India-Sri Lanka Free Trade Agreement in March 2000. According to Sri Lankan Customs, bilateral trade in 2015 amounted to US $ 4.7 billion. Exports from India to Sri Lanka in 2015 were US$ 4.1 billion (up by 2.1%), while exports from Sri Lanka to India were US$ 645 million (up by 3.2%). India is among the top four investors in Sri Lanka with cumulative investments of over US$ 1 billion since 2003.[26]

The 'China-Card' or the 'Islamabad-Card' is not expected to alter the importance of India. However, India should do its best to bring about a trade balance, which is not averse to Sri Lanka and make the process sustainable. Sri Lanka's economy is significantly dependent on exports. A step in this direction will insulate the bilateral relations from the vagaries of Tamil Nadu politics. India could also help Sri Lanka in diversifying its exports, which is presently dependent on food and textiles. This will help open up opportunities for increasing the volume of exports from Sri Lanka to India with consequential impact on the mutual trade balance.

Devolution Issue

While India should continue to provide a high quantum of assistance to Sri Lanka for rehabilitation of its northern war-ravaged area, to ensure that the benefits accrue to the local inhabitants, pressurising the Sri Lankan Government on devolution of power to ethnic Tamils[27] albeit under the provisions of the Sri Lankan Constitution should be avoided beyond a point. A multi-party approach to such a sensitive issue may be a more desirable method, apart from suitable back channel dialogues and military diplomacy. While the issue of devolution cannot be put on the back-burner, the Indian Government has to adopt a multifaceted approach on cultural, economic and security fronts, for stability of bilateral relations, in the overall interests of India.

Countering Chinese and Pak Influence

China and Pak's strategically oriented influence on Sri Lanka's defence and economic activities are a cause of concern, but these should not be over-emphasised by India. It is unreasonable not to expect Sri Lanka, in her national interest, to take advantage of lucrative Chinese contracts in energy and other sectors or buying arms and ammunition from China/Pak, when India is reluctant to meet all of Sri Lanka's demands.

However, it is of concern to India, when the port of Hambantota in Sri Lanka is being developed by the Chinese. It forms an important pearl in China's 'String of Pearls' strategy aimed at increasing its economic and defence footprints in the IOR and provide added advantage in operational turn-around in the Bay of Bengal and Arabian Sea. It has dangerous portends on India's trade and effect its seaborne deployment, in addition to marginalisation of India's growing influence in Indian Ocean.

Emerging Threats

China has also emerged as one of the major arms supplier for, after India and the West repudiated to sell weapons to Colombo, for use in the war. In 2007, Colombo signed an arms deal with China worth US$37.6 million, for a wide variety of arms, ammunition, mortars and bombs.[28] Pak also took advantage of the vacuum created by India and has sold 22 Al-Khalid tanks and a wide range of ammunition to Sri Lanka.[29] While Pak and Chinese influence in Sri Lanka is not envisaged to threaten India's interest, the allocation of an oil exploration block in the Gulf of Mannar to China (a few miles from India's southern tip)[30] and reports of Pak's interest in bringing around Muslim population in Sri Lanka under its influence have serious security implication for India, in the long run.

Fishermen Issues

Given the proximity of the territorial waters of both countries, especially in the Palk Straits and the Gulf of Mannar, incidents of straying of fishermen and poaching are common. Both countries have agreed on certain practical arrangements to deal with the issue of bonafide fishermen of either side crossing the International Maritime Boundary Line (IMBL). Through these arrangements, it has been possible to deal with the issue of detention of fishermen in a humanitarian manner.[31]

Defence Cooperation Initiatives

India has and needs to further step up its defence cooperation with Sri Lanka based on the island nations strategic location, geo strategic importance and allied factors such as increasing inroads of Pak and China. There is absence of institutionalised defence cooperation mechanisms; however both the armed forces have close interaction in terms of provision of vacancies for training courses, conduct of joint training exercises etc. The 4th India-Sri Lanka joint training Exercise, 'Mitra Shakthi', designed to enhance understanding of transnational terrorism, inter-operability skills, conduct of joint tactical operations, sharing of each other's experiences was held at Sri Lanka in October 2016.[32]

Endnotes

1   (2014) "Maldives: Its Size, Strategic Importance and Vulnerability" ,[Online: web] Accessed 27 Mar 2017 URL: http://www.southasiaanalysis.org/node/1654

2   (2016) "Maldives Population",[Online: web] Accessed 27 Mar 2017 URL: http://www.worldometers.info/world-population/maldives-population/

3   (2016) "Indians in Maldives", [Online: web] Accessed 27 Mar 2017 URL: https://en.wikipedia.org/wiki/Indians_in_the_Maldives

4   (2013) "Abdulla Yameen sworn in as new Maldivian president",[Online: web] Accessed 27 Mar 2017 URL: http://timesofindia.indiatimes.com/world/south-asia/Abdulla-Yameen-sworn-in-as-new-Maldivian-president/articleshow/25953127.cms

5   (2013) "New Maldives president is former dictator's half-brother",[Online: web] Accessed 27 Mar 2017 URL: http://www.business-standard.com/article/news-ians/new-maldives-president-is-former-dictator-s-half-brother-profile-113111700291_1.html

6   (2017) "Maldives Military 2017",[Online: web] Accessed 27 Mar 2017 URL: http://www.theodora.com/wfbcurrent/maldives/maldives_military.html

7   (2014) "Environmental Changes in the Maldives: Current Issues for Management",[Online: web] Accessed 27 Mar 2017 URL: http://www.fao.org/docrep/X5623E/x5623e0r.htm

8   (2014) "Maldives Economy", [Online: web] Accessed 27 Mar 2017 URL:http://www.maldiveisle.com/economy.htm

9   (2013) "The perils of rising religious fundamentalism in the Maldives",[Online: web] Accessed 27 Mar 2017 URL: http://securityobserver.org/the-perils-of-rising-religious-fundamentalism-in-the-maldives/

10 (2014) "Maldives Unemployment Rate",[Online: web] Accessed 27 Mar 2017 URL:http://www.tradingeconomics.com/maldives/unemployment-rate

11 (2016) "Poverty in Maldives" ,[Online: web] Accessed 27 Mar 2017 URL: https://www.adb.org/countries/maldives/poverty

12 (2012) "National Drug Use Survey Maldives - 2011 / 2012",[Online: web] Accessed 27 Mar 2017 URL: https://www.unodc.org/documents/southasia/reports/National_Drug_Use_Survey_-_Report.pdf

13 (2016) "Maldives – Foreign Policy",[Online: web] Accessed 27 Mar 2017 URL: http://www.globalsecurity.org/military/world/indian-ocean/mv-forrel.htm

14 (2016) "India-Maldives Relations" ,[Online: web] Accessed 27 Mar 2017 URL: https://www.mea.gov.in/Portal/ForeignRelation/MALDIVES_23_02_2016.pdf

15 (2016) "The Receding Dragon: The decline in Chinese Tourists to the Maldives",[Online: web] Accessed 27 Mar 2017 URL: http://en.mihaaru.com/the-receding-dragon-the-decline-in-chinese-tourists-to-the-maldives/

16 (2016) "Pakistan, Maldives agree to increase defence cooperation",[Online: web] Accessed 27 Mar 2017 URL: http://fp.brecorder.com/2016/05/2016052548846/

17 (2016) U.S.-Maldives Relations", [Online: web] Accessed 27 Mar 2017 URL:https://www.state.gov/r/pa/ei/bgn/5476.htm

18 (2016) "India-Maldives Relations" ,[Online: web] Accessed 27 Mar 2017 URL: https://www.mea.gov.in/Portal/ForeignRelation/MALDIVES_23_02_2016.pdf

19 ibid

20 (2016) "India, Maldives sign six pacts, resolve to expand defence cooperation",[Online: web] Accessed 27 Mar 2017 URL: http://indianexpress.com/article/india/india-news-india/india-maldives-sign-six-pacts-resolve-to-expand-defence-cooperation/

21 Layton, Peter (2015) "How Sri Lanka Won the War- Lessons in strategy from an overlooked victory",[Online: web] Accessed 27 Mar 2017 URL:http://thediplomat.com/2015/04/how-sri-lanka-won-the-war/

22 (2016) "Militarisation is a problem in the Tamil areas in Lanka" ,[Online: web] Accessed 27 Mar 2017 URL: http://www.rediff.com/news/interview/militarisation-is-still-a-problem-in-tamil-areas-in-lanka/20160525.htm

23 (2016) "Engaging Post-LTTE Sri Lanka: India's Policy Options",[Online: web] Accessed 28 Mar 2017 URL: http://nias.res.in/publication/engaging-post-ltte-sri-lanka-indias-policy-options

24 Aliff, SM(2015) "Indo- Sri Lanka Relations after the LTTE: Problems & Prospects",[Online: web] Accessed 28 Mar 2017 URL: http://jeteraps.scholarlinkresearch.com/articles/Indo%20Sri%20Lanka%20Relations.pd

25 (2011) "Pak thanks Lanka for help in 1971 war",[Online: web] Accessed 28 Mar 2017 URL: http://www.hindustantimes.com/world/pak-thanks-lanka-for-help-in-1971-war/story-UpZWXd0fFX5eDPac0KMIYL.html

26 (2016) "India-Sri Lanka Bilateral Relations",[Online: web] Accessed 28 Mar 2017 URL: http://www.hcicolombo.org/pages.php?id=28

27 (2016) "Looking at devolution of power to Tamils",[Online: web] Accessed 28 Mar 2017 URL: http://www.thehindu.com/news/sri-lanka-looking-at-devolution-of-power-to-tamils-within-the-constitution-wickremesinghe/article7655608.ece

28 (2009) "China's aid revealed in Sri Lanka's victory parade",[Online: web] Accessed 28 Mar 2017 URL: http://www.thenational.ae/news/world/south-asia/chinas-aid-revealed-in-sri-lankas-victory-parade

29 (2011) "Redefining Sri Lanka - Pakistan Ties an Indian Perspective" ,[Online: web] Accessed 28 Mar 2017 URL: http://www.vifindia.org/article/2011/may/18/Redefining-Sri-Lanka%E2%80%93Pakistan-Ties-an-Indian-Perspective

30 (2007) "India & China get Exploration Blocks in Mannar Basin",[Online: web] Accessed 28 Mar 2017 URL: http://tamilnation.co/intframe/tamileelam/070920oil.htm

31 (2016) "India-Sri Lanka Bilateral Relations",[Online: web] Accessed 28 Mar 2017 URL: http://www.hcicolombo.org/pages.php?id=28

32 (2016) "4thIndia-Sri Lanka Joint Training Exercise, 'MitraShakthi' Begins", [Online: web] Accessed 28 Mar 2017 URL: http://www.army.lk/news/4th-india-sri-lanka-joint-training-exercise-%E2%80%98mitra-shakthi%E2%80%99-begins

Chapter 5

Himalayan Kingdoms of South Asia

"Gross National Happiness is more important than Gross National Product"

- Jigme Singye Wangchuk

BHUTAN

Introduction

Bhutan[1] is a land locked country having a population of 7.418 lakh living in an area of 46,600 sq km. Bhutan extends 300 km East-West and 170 km in the North-South direction. It shares a 470 km border with China to the North and North West and 605 km with India in the South, East and West. Bhutan is a constitutional monarchy, with the King as a titular head of the state. The country comprises of 20 districts, with over 75% of the populace following the teachings of Buddhist Lamaist, while 24% follow Hinduism. The country is largely an agrarian society and its economy is essentially based on agriculture, forestry and animal husbandry. However, since opening up of its economy and introducing economic reforms, Bhutan was ranked second in South Asia and 11th in the world by real GDP growth rate at 8.1% in 2012.[2] Bhutan's industrial sector is in a nascent state, however, recently Bhutan has set up cement, steel and ferro alloy industries which along with its hydropower potential will further provide impetus to its economy. Bhutan is a member of UN, G-77, WTO, SAARC, Asian Development Bank and World Bank. The alliances it has formed both in regional and international organisation bolsters Bhutan's influence in the region.

The geo strategic importance of Bhutan stems from the fact that it is a buffer state between India and China, the two nuclear armed powers with mutual distrust. Thus strategically located between the Tibetan plateau and Assam-Bengal plains, a stable and secure Bhutan contributes immensely to India's security concerns.

Security Dynamics

Territorial Disputes

Bhutan has 811 sq km boundary dispute with China, and despite 24 rounds of talks to resolve the issue, little progress has been achieved.[3] The disputed areas lie in West Bhutan – Chumbi Valley and North Bhutan. The border dispute is primarily due to the watershed not being clearly defined and claims and counter claims based on traditional grazing rights of the Tibetans and Bhutanese. In 1998, China and Bhutan signed an 'Agreement on Maintenance of Peace and Tranquillity along the Sino-Bhutanese Border'; however, Chinese continue incursions into Bhutan's territory and have undertaken infrastructure development / road construction activity along the border. Moreover, Tibetan grazers in the summer months graze their herds in these disputed areas, with detachments of PLA overlooking their security.

External Threats

Bhutan does not face any external threat except from China due to its unresolved boundary dispute and Bhutan's traditional affinities and inclination towards India.

External Challenges

Bhutan and Nepal relations have been strained since April 1990, with the Bhupalese issue being a major irritant in their relations. The Bhupalese are direct descendants of immigrants from Nepal, Bengal and Sikkim. They reside in Southern Bhutan and constitute 35% of the total population. With the 'Citizenship Act of 1958' amended in 1977,[4] being made more stringent in 1985 with the dual aim of weeding out personnel of doubtful citizenship and to discourage further immigration, large scale ethnic cleansing took place, resulting in over one lakh Bhupalese leaving Bhutan.

Bhutan's internal situation though calm has the portents of conflagrating due to the Bhupalese movement and strained relations with Nepal.

Internal Challenges

Transition to Democracy. Bhutan transited from an absolute to constitutional monarchy after its first multiparty elections in 2008. The democracy is still in its nascent stage and the transition though smooth and meticulous needs to be monitored closely.

Armed Struggle by Bhupalese. The unresolved Bhupalese issue has portents to destabilise Bhutan. The armed struggle by Bhupalese / Maoists with tacit support of Indian underground groups can impact domestic environment in Bhutan and cause a law and order problem within Bhutan.[5] Reportedly the Bhutan Communist Party (Marxist – Leninist- Maoist), Bhutan Tiger Force and the United Revolutionary Front of Bhutan are composed of the Bhupalese and were behind the spate of bombings in the run up to the elections in 2008.

Lack of Industrial Infrastructure. Bhutan has a weak industrial base, which impacts its economic development. Further, lack of infrastructure development due to the rugged nature of terrain and lack of access to sea ports has adversely impacted the economic development of Bhutan.

Foreign Policy

China – Bhutan. China-Bhutan relations have been traditionally tense and strained due to historical, cultural and religious ties with Tibet. Bhutan does not have any diplomatic ties with China post 1959, after the Dalai Lama fled to India. However, exchanges and visits at various levels have significantly increased in recent times, resulting in considerable improvement in their relationship.[6] Bhutan's China relationship is centred on resolution of its border dispute in an amicable manner, while keeping India's concerns in mind. China has shown keen interest in developing infrastructure in Bhutan and re-opening trade links. However, there has been no positive response from Bhutan on this issue.

Bhutan - Nepal. Bhutan-Nepal relations were established in 1983. The relations remained cordial till April 90, when Bhupalese of Nepalese origin sought refuge in Nepal. Nepal has expressed open support and sympathy towards their plight against Bhutanese repressive policies. The ongoing refugee issue is a major irritant in Nepal-Bhutan relations.[7]

Bhutan - Bangladesh. Bhutan was the second nation to recognise Bangladesh on attaining independence. It views Bangladesh as an access to the sea and the opportunity to be less dependent on India's land route for trade. Both nations are signatories of the 'Preferential Trading Agreement', which further strengthens bilateral ties.[8]

India – Bhutan.[9]

The basic framework of India-Bhutan bilateral relations is the 'Treaty of Friendship and Cooperation' signed in 1949 between the two countries, which was updated in February 2007. The special relationship between the two countries has been sustained by the tradition of regular visits and extensive exchange of views at the highest levels. Mutually beneficial economic linkages between India and Bhutan have been an important element in the bilateral relations. India continues to be the largest trade and development partner of Bhutan. For the 11th FYP (2013-18), India has committed Rs 45 billion, which is 68 per cent of the total external assistance. India has also extended to Bhutan a standby credit facility of Rs 1000 crores at a concessional interest rate of five per cent per annum for five years to help it to overcome the rupee liquidity crunch. The two countries have a free trade regime and duty free transit of Bhutanese merchandise for trade with third countries. The bilateral trade between the two countries in 2015 was Rs 8550 crores.[10] Hydropower is one of the main pillars of bilateral cooperation. Three hydro-electric projects totalling 1416 MW, are already exporting electricity to India.

As far as Defence Cooperation is concerned, defence ties date back to 1953 and encompass wide range of activities ranging from training, courses and supply of military hardware. 'Operation All Clear' in 2003 in which RBA flushed out the ULFA, NDFB and KLO militants from their camps in Southern Bhutan; reflects the deep understanding and cooperation between the two states.[11] On the international front, Bhutan has consistently sided with India on crucial issues in regional and international forums, reflecting the stable and genuine nature of the bilateral relations.

India and Bhutan have extremely warm and cordial relations with no major issues of divergence. However, Bhutan is sensitive to being seen as a

'Protectorate' of India. The 1949 'Treaty of Friendship' was revised in 2007 which clarifies Bhutan's status as an independent and sovereign nation with independent foreign policy.

India's Concerns- Ways and Means

Bhutan is a buffer state between the two Asian giants with inimical relations. For India a weak Bhutan as a buffer means a weak extended frontier with China. Therefore, India played a major role in bringing an end to Bhutan's erstwhile isolation. The re-negotiation of borders has been a focal point of Chinese foreign policy towards all its neighbours. In the case of Bhutan, however, this was probably its secondary objective. The ease with which the disputed areas were substantially narrowed down, and the actual areas that China truly wants, both point in this direction. Beijing's primary objective is to gain diplomatic and strategic leverage over India. China's looming presence in Bhutan might ultimately undermine its unique cultural heritage and its overall policy goal of 'Gross National Happiness'.

Though settlement of boundary issue is in Bhutan's National interest; any further deepening of ties of Bhutan with China has to be prevented. China's penchant to use aid and investment as a policy tool is well known. Therefore, India has to actively engage Bhutan to restrict Chinese presence in Bhutan and should continue to keep the existing channels of correspondence and briefings open to allay apprehensions of the Bhutanese leadership in this regard.

India should continue to aggressively invest in capacity and capability building of the Bhutanese Security Forces by stepping up assistance in equipment, training, logistics and intelligence. While IMTRAT continues to serve as an interface for training requirements, regular joint exercises should be conducted for confidence building and greater synergy.

NEPAL

Introduction

Nepal is one of the world's most impoverished regions in the world. It is bordered to the North by the Tibetan Autonomous Region of China and to the South, East, and West by the Indian states of Uttarakhand, Uttar Pradesh,

Bihar, West Bengal and Sikkim. Nepal is separated from Bangladesh by the narrow Indian Siliguri corridor. The unique geo-strategic location of Nepal has made it a playing ground between China and India, with both countries endeavouring to increase their sphere of influence over the landlocked country. However, Nepal's strategic importance stems not only from its geo-political location but also from its transformation into a new buffer zone between India and China in the 1950s. The bilateral relations of Nepal with both India and China have been friendly. However, despite Nepal being a Hindu nation and having extremely close religious, cultural, economic and people to people links with India, there is an environment of continued distrust between the two countries. This has been further aggravated by Nepal's Foreign Policy of balancing the competing influence of China and India.[12]

Security Challenges

Institutionalisation of Democracy and the Constitution

Nepal saw a successful transition to parliamentary democracy in 2013 after years of turmoil. Constituent Assembly Elections were held in Nepal on 19 November 2013. The vote was repeatedly delayed, having previously been planned for 22 November 2012 following the dissolution of the 1st Constituent Assembly on 27 May 2012, but it was put off by the Election Commission. The Nepali Congress emerged as the largest party in the 2nd Nepalese Constituent Assembly, winning 196 of the 575 elected seats. On 22 January 2014, after a delay of over two months, the interim Parliament was convened with 565 out of 601 members taking the oath of office in 11 different languages, proving once again that Nepal being a multi ethnic, multi lingual and multi-cultural country, the decision to have a federal constitution was the right choice of the people. On 10 February 2014, Mr Sushil Koirala of Nepali Congress was elected as the PM, clearing a major hurdle in the formation of a new government in the Himalayan nation. In August 2016 Pushpa Kamal Dahal was elected for a second stint as Prime Minister of Nepal. Prachanda became the 24th Prime Minister since Nepal's adoption of multi-party democracy in 1990 and the eighth since the abolition of the monarchy in 2008.[13]

Nepal replaced its Interim Constitution of 2007 with a new Constitution which came into effect on Sept 20, 2015. The Constitution was drafted by the Second Constituent Assembly following the failure of the First Constituent Assembly to produce a constitution in its mandated period. The constitution was endorsed by 90% of the total lawmakers. Out of 598 Constituent Assembly members, 538 voted in favour of the constitution while 60 voted against it, including few Terai based political parties refrained from the voting process. However, the promulgation of constitution saw large scale protests and blockades in eastern Terai by the Madhesi communities, ethnically and socially close to Indians just across the border, complaining of discrimination and lack of acceptance by the Nepalese state. Many in Nepal blamed India for patronising the Madhesi issue.[14]The government is reconciling with agitating Madhes based political parties, who have been calling for changes in constitutional provisions like citizenship, language, making constitution more inclusive and provincial demarcation. On 08 Jan 2017, Nepal government tabled a constitution amendment bill in parliament despite resistance from the opposition parties including the main opposition CPN-UML. The bill is one step forward to address the demands of the Madhesis.[15]

Nepal's democracy faces internal security challenges by a messy political legacy. While rapid political changes took place, economic growth, national resources and the policy environment remain crippled by structural weaknesses and disjointedness; extreme inequalities; increasing the crisis of capacity and credibility. There is need of transformational leadership followed by participative/democratic, authentic and strategic models.[16]

India - Nepal – China: Strategic Dynamics

Chinese Perspective

China's Concerns. China's economic growth and military modernisation in the last decade has been unprecedented and has become a cause of global concern despite China's endeavours for showcasing its rise as peaceful. Its sustenance of its economic growth is dependent upon its ability to not only sustain the current markets, for its consumer goods but to further develop new markets besides finding new options for infrastructure development across the globe. China's growth which has mostly been concentrated in its coastal regions, has led to a huge urban rural divide, which is amongst the highest in the world. A potential economic instability can lead to domestic turbulence which can be further aggravated due to the Tibetan issue and the present situation in the restive province of Xinjiang. China strongly believes that domestic instability leads to external intervention.

Nepal: An Ideal Destination. Therefore, Nepal's geostrategic location, its politico-economic condition (amongst the ten poorest countries in the world), poor state of development and literacy make it an ideal destination for China for its economic ventures. Moreover, China's economic hold over Nepal, home to some 20,000 Tibetan refugees, gives it the leverage to exert pressure over Nepal to prevent anti-China separatist activities by the Tibetans from Nepalese soil. The Nepalese armed forces regularly detain Tibetans carrying out any anti-China activity. Further, with Nepalese Army's manning of the borders on behest of China, the number of Tibetans crossing the border into Nepal has significantly reduced.

Spin Offs. China considers India, an emerging power, as a challenge to its global and regional aspirations. Its increasing presence in Nepal not only marginalises India's regional power status but affords it strategic advantages in the long term. It is therefore investing in strategically important infrastructure like airports and important highways to gain strategic foothold in Nepal and proximity to India.

India's Perspective

Marginalisation of India's Economic Interests in Nepal

India continues to remain Nepal's largest trade partner accounting for 66 percent of Nepalese total external trade. However, China's influence in Nepal's economy continues to grow by leaps and bounds with Beijing topping the list of nations who have pledged maximum FDI into the Himalayan nation. China accounted for as much as 68 per cent of all FDI pledged for Nepal in the first half of 2017 fiscal year. This is a massive jump from China's 40 per cent share of the total FDI pledged for Nepal by various countries in 2015-16. According to Nepal's Department of Industry, China accounted for $51.77 million out of a total of $76.39 million FDI pledged for Nepal in the first half of the current fiscal year. This has further cemented China's position as top contributor of FDI for Nepal.[17]

The rising Chinese economic presence and strategic influence in the country is emerging as a challenge for India. India feels that increasing economic footprint of China in Nepal is due to Nepal's intentions of creating an environment of competition between China and India even at the cost of India's sensitivities, despite shared religious and cultural background between the two countries.

Bilateral Relations

The 1950 Indo-Nepal Treaty of Peace and Friendship established a close Indo-Nepalese relationship on commerce, defence and foreign relations. It lays great importance on the two countries' shared common regional and cultural affinity as well as the special bilateral relations. However, off late the treaty is being increasingly resented in Nepal, which has begun seeing it as an encroachment of its sovereignty and an unwelcome extension of Indian influence. On 27 Jul 2014, during the visit of India's Foreign Minister to Nepal, both the countries issued a 'Joint Statement' committing themselves to 'Review the entire gamut of the Bilateral Relations' between the two countries.

Defence Relations

India and Nepal share a unique bonding when it comes to defence cooperation. There are approximately 35,000 Gurkha soldiers of Nepalese origin in Indian Army and approx 93,000 pensioners in Nepal. India has been playing a leading role in helping the Nepalese Army in its modernisation through provision of equipment and training. The Indian Army also provides total funded training vacancies to Nepalese Army personnel in various Indian Army training institutions. The two sides also conduct 'Exercise Suryakiran', a joint battalion level exercise, each year alternatively in Nepal and India.[18] However, despite the close cooperation between the two sides, Nepal developed close cordial relations with China and Pakistan between 1970 and 1988. Defence Cooperation between these countries during 2004 and 2006 further strengthened as a result of deterioration in relations with India, US and UK for repressing democracy. Nepal's growing proximity to China and Pakistan is viewed by India as against the spirit of Treaty of Peace and Friendship and is the main issue of divergence between the two countries.

Other Areas of Concern

Nepal is a safe haven for extremists and anti-India elements. Reportedly, there is a proliferation of Madrassas on the Indo-Nepal Border on the Nepalese side.[19] Moreover, the porous borders lend themselves to be exploited as transit route for terrorists, drug trafficking, induction of fake currency notes etc at the behest of Pakistan's ISI. India is also concerned about the progress of many development projects in Nepal which are delayed due to some or the other difference/controversy. Moreover, for the last several years no new joint venture project has come from India to Nepal. Even those joint ventures which are in operation in Nepal increasingly feel insecure.

China's India Strategy in Nepal. China has been trying to erase Nepalese dependency on India. With India sharing a 1,751 km open border with Nepal running through 20 districts of five Indian states, China's overstepping in Nepal has a real and concrete strategic impact on India's security. This needs to be viewed alongside Chinese increasing footprints in India's other neighbouring countries namely Pakistan, Bangladesh, Myanmar and Sri Lanka. India is wary of China's real intentions in Nepal as to whether its assistance is a gesture to a neighbour in need or is perhaps the result of a larger foreign policy aimed at Chinese expansionist designs in the region, to fulfil its long-term ambition to use Nepal as a corridor to enter the huge Indian markets and to pose a military threat in being. It is however, debatable as to whether the rail and road infrastructures can give China strategic conventional military advantages to move to the Indian heartland. But definitely these along with the economic and other Chinese packages are designed to weaken India's Influence in Nepal. If Chinese wave continues unabated in Nepal, India might face multiple security threats in future.

Nepal's Perspective

Nepal regards China as a reliable friend. Its domestic politics is showing enhanced inclination towards Beijing because China is helping the country reduce its considerable trade deficit. This has allowed Sino-Nepal relations to improve. Sino-Nepalese trade has grown 75 percent between 2009 and 2012. However, Nepalese exports are miniscule and barely account for one percent of the country's bilateral trade with China. To become a commercial nucleus, Nepal needs better infrastructure in terms of high mountain container facility, roads, hydroelectric projects etc for which the Chinese are providing assistance and technology. China is also considering the development of existing trading points in Nepal into dry ports to enhance the volumes of trade and commerce. Therefore, keeping into view growing role of China in South Asia in general and the benefits it can accrue; Nepal in March 2016 secured transit rights through China.[20] China is top most investor in Nepal today and Chinese investments in Nepal are growing although presently lower in comparison to the need and potential. On its part in return for the monetary benefits; Nepal does not shy away from either echoing the 'One China Policy' and ruthlessly cracking down on any kind of anti-China activities on its soil nor gets constrained by India's sensitivities.

Ways and Means

China has historically behaved as a domineering power in its dealings with its neighbours, especially when it feels that it cannot actively control development in its periphery which could lead to an eventual reduction of its sphere of influence in the neighbourhood. The nature of Chinese diplomacy in Nepal goes beyond the political domain. Its expanding interface with Nepal is being translated into regional influence and is helping China to promote its strategic and economic interests in South Asia while making inroads as a counterweight to India and equally safeguarding its core national interest of Tibet. It's economic and political presence in Nepal has so far worked successfully along these two lines.

Even though China is still far behind India in terms of overall investment in Nepal, it is likely to catch up soon. China's economic control over Nepal can make India vulnerable to Chinese pressures. India has to realise the implications of the fact that the mighty Himalayas are no more a border between Nepal and China.

India has to further realise that in the present political and economic environment in Nepal, wherein almost half the population is unemployed and more than half is illiterate, with more than 30 percent of the people living in abject poverty, Nepal surely has serious business to engage with China. Therefore, it is imperative that India seriously works towards regaining the 'Strategic Space' in Nepal, which it has lost out to China, by making Nepal a part of India's economic dynamism. Agreements such as the Bilateral Investment Promotion and Protection Agreement to smoothen and encourage the flow of Indian investments in Nepal; US $ 250 million credit line from EXIM bank of India at 1.75% interest with repayment in 20 years for financing infrastructure projects including highway, bridges, railway, irrigation, hydro-power etc; and use of Vishakhapatnam Port to facilitate Nepal's third-country trade are few such initiatives.

Apart from the above, India should be able to clearly articulate its concerns to Nepal and also the importance for Nepal to keep its national assets and potential growth in its hands rather than letting these be controlled by China for seeking short-term gains which could virtually mean a sell-out. Defending territorial sovereignty under international law is different from protecting economic rights under the tenets of market liberalisation. India at the same time should try and take a lead for trilateral economic engagement with China and Nepal to reduce existing competitions and pave path for implementation of mutually beneficial trade and commerce policies for overall regional development.

India needs to fine tune its relationship with Nepal to be more responsive to changing dynamics in the strategic environment, drawing upon the advantages it enjoys and try to overcome the latent anti-Indian sentiment. With relations improving between the two governments and amendment of the constitution taking a desired turn, India can be optimistic of improved bilateral relations between the two countries.

Endnotes

1 (2017) "Bhutan",[Online: web] Accessed 30 Mar 2017 URL:https://en.wikipedia.org/wiki/Bhutan

2 (2012) "Bhutan's economic growth rate at 8.1%" ,[Online: web] Accessed 30 Mar 2017 URL: www.bbs.bt/news/?p=15058

3 (2016) "China, Bhutan hold 24th round of boundary talks, aim to strengthen ties",[Online: web] Accessed 30 Mar 2017 URL:http://indianexpress.com/article/world/world-news/china-bhutan-hold-24th-round-of-boundary-talks-aim-to-strengthen-ties-2970199/

4 (2016) "Bhutanese Citizenship Act 1958" ,[Online: web] Accessed 30 Mar 2017 URL: https://en.wikipedia.org/wiki/Bhutanese_Citizenship_Act_1958

5   Katoch, Prakash (2013) "Dealing with Doklam",[Online: web] Accessed 30 Mar 2017 URL: http://www.claws.in/985/dealing-with-doklam-prakash-katoch.html

6   (2016) "China-Bhutan Relations" ,[Online: web] Accessed 30 Mar 2017 URL: http://www.globalsecurity.org/military/world/bhutan/forrel-prc.htm

7   (2016) "Bhutan-Nepal Relations" ,[Online: web] Accessed 30 Mar 2017 URL: http://thediplomat.com/tag/bhutan-nepal-relations/

8   (2012) "Bhutan and Bangladesh decided to renew bilateral trade agreement", [Online: web] Accessed 30 Mar 2017 URL: http://www.bbs.bt/news/?p=38843

9   (2014) India-Bhutan Relations,[Online: web] Accessed 30 Mar 2017 URL: https://mea.gov.in/Portal/ForeignRelation/Bhutan_April_2014_eng.pdf

10 (2015) "India-Bhutan Trade Relation",[Online: web] Accessed 30 Mar 2017 URL: https://www.indianembassythimphu.bt/pages.php?id=42

11 Banerjee, D (22\004)"Operation All Clear",[Online: web] Accessed 30 Mar 2017 URL: www.ipcs.org/pdf_file/issue/IB18-OperationAllClear.pd

12 Shah, Fahad (2016) "Nepal's Balancing Act- Walking the Tightrope Between China and India" ,[Online: web] Accessed 31 Mar 2017 URL: https://www.foreignaffairs.com/articles/china/2016-02-25/nepals-balancing-act

13 (2016)"Pushpa Kamal Dahal", [Online: web] Accessed 31 Mar 2017 URL: https://en.wikipedia.org/wiki/Pushpa_Kamal_Dahal#Second_term_as_prime_minister

14 (2015) "I will never forgive what India has done to me",[Online: web] Accessed 31 Mar 2017 URL: https://www.telegraphindia.com/1151025/jsp/7days/story_49480.jsp

15 (2017) "Nepal govt tables constitution amendment bill",[Online: web] Accessed 31 Mar 2017 URL: http://www.hindustantimes.com/world-news/nepal-govt-tables-constitution-amendment-bill/story-uPiEympiSvwy9R0cTXezfI.html

16 Thakur, Mohan Shrestha (2016) "Internal security issues: Ways to address them",[Online: web] Accessed 31 Mar 2017 URL:https://thehimalayantimes.com/opinion/internal-security-issues-ways-address/

17 (2017) "India watches warily as China further ramps up FDI into Nepal", [Online: web] Accessed 03Apr 2017 URL: http://timesofindia.indiatimes.com/india/india-watches-warily-as-china-further-ramps-up-fdi-into-nepal/articleshow/57008982.cms

18 (2016) "10th Indo-Nepal joint military exercise Surya Kiran commences", [Online: web] Accessed 31 Mar 2017 URL: http://currentaffairs.gktoday.in/10th-indo-nepal-joint-military-exercise-surya-kiran-commences-11201636797.

html http://currentaffairs.gktoday.in/10th-indo-nepal-joint-military-exercise-surya-kiran-commences-11201636797.html

19 Singh, Rajesh (2014) "India Seeks Nepal Help To Stem Isi-Funded Madrasas", [Online: web] Accessed 31 Mar 2017 URL:http://www.dailypioneer.com/todays-newspaper/india-seeks-nepal-help-to-stem-isi-funded-madrasas.html

20 (2016) "Nepal seals agreement on transit rights through China",[Online: web] Accessed 31 Mar 2017 URL:http://www.thehindu.com/news/international/nepal-inks-transit-treaty-with-china-to-have-first-rail-link/article8381195.ece

Chapter 6

Security Environment in Bangladesh & Myanmar

"The ideology of Islamic radicalisation and extremism crosses continents - we are all in this together. At stake are not just lives, it's our way of life. That's why this is a challenge we cannot avoid - and one, we must meet"

- David Cameron

Introduction

Myanmar is geographically the largest country in South East Asia. It shares land borders with India, China, Bangladesh, Laos and Thailand and has direct access to the Bay of Bengal and the Andaman Sea. Both Bangladesh and Myanmar share a 5000 kms porous land border and an uninterrupted coastline with India[1]. India views Myanmar as a gateway to the ASEAN countries and also as a buffer between India and China. Myanmar is therefore critical to the security of India's North Eastern borders. A rise in Islamic fundamentalism in Bangladesh and a backlash against the minority Muslim population in Myanmar has resulted in the resurgence of Islamic terror groups in the region. This has serious security implications for India.

Spread of Radical Islam in Bangladesh

Islamisation of Bangladesh

As per Lt Gen Chowdhury Hasan Sarwardy of Bangladesh Army; since independence, Bangladesh has experienced three kinds of terrorism. First is political violence by so called left wing terrorism. Next is an insurgency that emerged in early eighties, demanding autonomy for Chittagong Hill Districts. Lately militancy in the name of religion emerged in Bangladesh. Recently, activities of these extremist group included killing of few bloggers who criticized Islamic ideology, non-Muslim religions preachers, foreigners involved in development projects, law enforcing agency members etc.

However, many scholars feel that Bangladesh emerged as a secular nation post its Liberation in 1971, but soon turned into an Islamic State. This gave rise to Muslim Fundamentalist Groups, facilitating the resurgence of terror organisations. However, off late, Bangladesh is considering dropping Islam as state religion. Dr Abdur Razzak, a leading member of Bangladesh's ruling Awami League party has proposed that religion be withdrawn from the country's constitution during a discussion at the National Press Club in the capital Dhaka stating that "The force of secularism is within the people of Bangladesh and that there is no such thing as a 'minority' in our country"[2].Some of the key Islamic radical groups in Bangladesh are discussed in the succeeding paras.

Jamaat-e-Islami (Jel)

The Jel[3] has its roots in Pakistan sponsored Al Badar formed prior to the Liberation of Bangladesh in 1971. Post 1971, AI Badar transformed into Jel and entered the mainstream as an ally of the Bangladesh Nationalist Party. The Jamaat draws its strength from the rural belt and aims to establish an Islamic State, based on Sharia. The International Crimes Tribunals have awarded death penalties to senior leaders of Jamaat. It was debarred from contesting General Elections in August 2013.

Hifazat-e-Islam (Hel)

The Hel[4] is a conglomerate of a number of radical Islamist organisations. It is headed by Maulana Ahmad Shafi. The Hel is supported by the 'Quami Madrassas' and wields considerable influence over the semi-urban and rural populace. While Hifazat does not have direct links to terror groups, education imparted in the Madrassas under its control remains a cause of concern. Pakistan had undergone a similar transition with the Zia regime fomenting a radical strain of Islam. Mr Tariq Karim, the Bangladesh High Commissioner to India said (IIC, Delhi, 24 Mar 14) that the Hel was poised to be the next Taliban.

Islami Chhatra Shibir (ICS)

Formed as Islamic Chhatra Sangha, student wing of the Jamaat-e-Islami in 1941 and its members contributed heavily to the Al Badar during the 1971 Liberation War. It was renamed Islami Chhatra Shibir in 1977[5]. The ICS has been portrayed as one of the world's 10 most active non-state armed groups in 2013. In 2013, the ICS cadre is documented to have engaged in rampant acts of arson and violence against law enforcement agencies/ establishment & ICS cadres targeted the minority Hindu and Buddhist communities along with Awami League functionaries in the run-up to the General Elections 2014. Through Jamaat, ICS maintains its links with Pakistan's ISI.

Terror Groups in Bangladesh

The presentment threat of terrorism in Bangladesh has created concerns both in the country and abroad. Presently there are close to 40 militant and fundamentalist organisations which are active in Bangladesh. Some of the main terrorist groups in Bangladesh are discussed in the succeeding paras.

Harkat-Ul-Jihad-al-Islami Bangladesh (HuJI-B)

The origin of the HuJI[6] is rooted in the Soviet-Afghan War. A large number of volunteers had gone to Afghanistan to fight alongside the Mujahideen in the war against the former Soviet Union. A large number of these Mujahideen returned to Bangladesh during the BNP regime of Begum Khaleda Zia (1991-96) and are now spearheading the fundamentalist movement in the country. While the HuJI was raised in Pakistan, its affiliate in Bangladesh, called HuJI-B, was raised in 1992. HuJI maintains active contact with the Al Qaeda and the Taliban; its founding leader in Bangladesh, Fazlur Rehman Khalil, was one of the six signatories of Osama bin Laden's first 'Declaration of Holy War' against the United States.

Lashkar-e-Taiba (LeT)

The LeT has a well-established network in Bangladesh[7]. Three of its cadres were arrested from a Madrassa in Chittagong in November 2009. They were planning to bomb the Indian, American and British embassies in Dhaka. Pakistan based LeT operatives, along with activists of Falah-e-Insaniyat (an NGO), had visited Myanmarese refugee camps in Bangladesh and also those along the Bangladesh – Myanmar border, in the aftermath of the Rohingya exodus in 2012.

Jamaat-Ul-Mujahideen, Bangladesh (JMB)

Formed in 1998, the JMB is another name for the radical Islamist group, the Jagrata Muslim Janata Bangladesh (JMJB)[8]. The JMB was banned by the government of Bangladesh in Feb 2005. They however, asserted their presence by carrying out 500 blasts in different locations across Bangladesh in Aug 2005. Many members of the JMB and JMJB have been cadres of the Islami Chhatra Shibir.

Al Qaeda- Presence in Bangladesh

Al Qaeda taking advantage of growing Islamist militancy in Bangladesh is co-opted or affiliated with home-grown jihadist groups. It has formed a branch -- al Qaeda in the Indian Subcontinent - which includes Bangladesh. Earlier there was no concrete proof of Al Qaeda's presence in Bangladesh; however, under mentioned events in the recent past are indicative of Al Qaeda's (AQ) growing interest in the region.

- *Massacre Behind a Wall of Silence.* AQ's media arm, Al Sahab recently released a video on Bangladesh titled 'Bangladesh-Massacre Behind a Wall of Silence', with a voice-over by AQ Amir Ayman al Zawahire. The video shows the Bangladesh SF in poor light and mentions Myanmar and India several times. It alludes to the close alliance of US and India in subjugating Islam in South Asia and threatens India.

- *UN Report Feb 2014.* The UN Security Council Al Qaeda Sanction Committee report dated 14 Feb 2014 asserts that AQ network is active in Bangladesh[9]. The Committee indicated that two NGOs, Al-Herminie and Global Relief Foundation, working in Bangladesh are involved with AQ. The NGOs have provided financial and technological help to the network, including Osama bin Laden in the past.

Al Qaeda appears to be interested in maintaining and tightening its grip on Afghanistan, Kashmir and Arakan (Rakhine state, Myanmar). As Bangladesh shares a long and porous border with Myanmar, it is not difficult to recruit extremists and direct them to Myanmar to fight against "those who oppress Muslims." As such, the Bangladesh-Myanmar border is highly vulnerable to exploitation by terrorists, especially AQIS. There is also half a million Rohingyas (refugees and illegal immigrants) in Bangladesh who view the fight against Myanmar military as an existential struggle. Travelling to Syria and Iraq is becoming increasingly difficult due to the anti-IS military offensives there. Therefore, these new fronts, particularly western Myanmar, are potential destinations for Bangladeshi jihadists. If mismanaged, the Rohingya militancy will escalate, as societal frustrations fuse with narratives fuelled by religious fundamentalism. The otherwise dormant AQIS in recent months has shown signs of revival, particularly in the social media. It is possibly trying to exploit the space left by IS due its military setbacks in its heartland in Iraq and Syria. AQIS' revival, at least on social media, demonstrates that the group is attempting to keep its old network in South Asia intact[10].

ISIL in Bangladesh

On the night of 1 July 2016, five militants took hostages and opened fire on the Holey Artisan Bakery in Dhaka, Bangladesh. 29 people were killed, including 20 hostages (18 foreigners and 2 locals), 2 police officers, 5 gunmen, and 2 bakery staff. According to Bangladesh's Inspector General of Police, all the attackers were Bangladeshi citizens. Islamic State of Iraq and the Levant (ISIL) claimed responsibility for the incident and released photographs of the gunmen; and dispelled any doubts that it was behind the terror attack. In doing so, the group provided another example of its growing footprint in Asia -- and opened up another theatre in its contest with al Qaeda[11].

However, the home minister of Bangladesh, Asaduzzaman Khan, stated that the perpetrators belonged to Jamaat-ul-Mujahideen and were not affiliated with ISIL[12]. The AKM Shahidul Hoque, inspector general of police further stated that the propaganda of ISIL presence in Bangladesh was baseless and that the militants were actually homegrown who might have been embodied the IS philosophy and ideology; but have no link with the IS[13].

However, there are concerns about IS' re-emergence in view of its continued online activities and recruitment of members. Reportedly two or three youth go missing almost every month in various parts of the country and some of these cases even go unreported. Local security officials consider this trend alarming because in the past such disappearances frequently occurred prior to an attack in the country by members of a terrorist cell. It is highly likely that some overseas Bangladeshi IS supporters, including Bangladeshi fighters in Syria, are actively recruiting Bangladeshi residents and the diaspora community. According to Bangladesh's counter-terrorism professionals, IS has changed its recruitment strategy and now runs a network of recruiters who act as intermediaries/liaisons to hire new recruits for IS local cells in Bangladesh. Presently, the Bangladeshi IS recruiters appear to be more sophisticated and better resourced as they have access to and are active on various social media platforms, including Facebook. Several factors indicate that IS in Bangladesh still has access to finances and explosives. In this respect, the group's cross-border linkage in India remains of particular concern. According to the confession of a high-value IS detainee in Bangladesh, the group has sent at least two of its operatives to India for advanced training in manufacturing Improvised Explosive Device (IED)[14]. Reportedly Bangladeshi citizens are being recruited overseas too particularly in Malaysia.

Ansar al Islam

Bangladesh's law enforcement agencies have said that Ansar al Islam has a deeper reach in the country than IS. Ansar al Islam is affiliated with the Al Qaeda in the Indian Subcontinent (AQIS), and operates on behalf of the latter in Bangladesh. Members of Ansar al Islam were responsible for the killings of more than a dozen Bangladeshi bloggers and activists since 2013, and the authorities have not been able to make much progress in neutralising its threat. There are also indications that Ansar al Islam operatives may have a strong link to Malaysia and some of its members have become pro-IS.

The group's online presence and continued propaganda remains a major concern. There are clear indications that the group is trying to target the NGOs promoting tolerance in the country. For instance, on 24 February 2017, Ansar al Islam uploaded an audio message condemning an NGO for promoting moderation among the Qawmi madrassa students and alerted the students not to participate in the campaign. It is highly likely that the group has been able to recruit some madrassa-educated online activists and use them for conducting smear campaign against the NGOs. According to

Bangladesh's law enforcement agencies, Ansar al Islam continues to hire new recruits and is possibly working closely with other terrorist groups in the country, in particular JMB. Additionally, the authorities have also expressed concern over Ansar al Islam's efforts to boost its IED capabilities and hence its capacity to conduct deadlier attacks[15].

Anti-Muslim Trends in Myanmar

Anti-Muslim Sentiment

Myanmar has a minority Muslim population which is concentrated around Mandalay, Central Myanmar and the Rakhine State, coastal Myanmar, bordering Bangladesh. A Census conducted in 1982 pegged their population at four percent; a fact disputed by many who suggest that the population was infact at ten percent and that the then Military 'Junta' had released a more palatable figure. The indigenous majority Myanmarese considers the Muslims outsiders and historical enmity exists between the two communities.

Wirathu's 969 Movement

Wirathu, a monk having a wide following among Buddhists in Myanmar, has spearheaded an open confrontation with the Muslims. He has been vocal in inciting the Buddhist majority against the Muslims and has justified use of force and violence as a means to protect Buddhism. The violence in Mandalay has been a direct consequence of the wrath spewed by Wirathu. The 969 Movement is opposed to the expansion of Islam into predominant Buddhist Myanmar. The three digits symbolise the virtues of Buddha, Buddhist practices and the Buddhist community[16]. Wirathu is a strong proponent of this Movement who wants that the Muslims in Myanmar should adopt Myanmarese culture and avoid wearing Muslim attire.

The Rohingya Issue

Genesis

The Rohingyas (Sunnis) are stateless people, with successive Myanmarese Government denying them citizenship. Social, cultural and religious differences have been the cause of historical enmity between the Rohingyas and the Myanmarese.

Violence against Rohingyas

The rape and murder of a Rakhine Buddhist woman and subsequent events in end May 2012, led to violent ethnic clashes in the Rakhine State[17]. The figures officially released by the government cited 78 dead, 87 injured, thousands of homes destroyed and more than 52,000 displaced. However, those released by the Burmese Rohingya Organisation (based in UK) cited 650 killed, 1200 missing and more than 80,000 displaced, which appear to be realistic given the levels of violence.

Rohingya Terror Groups

There are inputs regarding an increase in the activities of the Rohingya Solidarity Organisation, based in Bangladesh. Attempts have been made by Islamic terror groups to recruit the Rohingyas. Soon after the riots in 2012, LeT using its trained Rohingya terrorists, formed an organisation known as Difa-e-Mussalman Arakan-Burma with a view to unite the disgruntled Rohingyas to oppose the ruling regime in Myanmar.

Al Qaeda's Support for Rohingyas

Post the Rakhine State violence of Jun / Oct 2012, Al Qaeda came out in support of the Rohingyas. The video 'Bangladesh-Massacre Behind a Wall of Silence' also targeted and spread negative propaganda against the government of Myanmar for the persecution of the Muslims. It also derided Aung San Suu Kyi for accepting the Nobel peace award.

HuJI (Arakan) (HuJI-A)

The HuJI-A, which is based in Karachi, has sworn to avenge the injustice meted out to the 'Muslim Brethren' in Myanmar. It has direct links with the Jamaat-Ud- Dawa Amir Hafiz Sayeed. JuD is the front organisation of the LeT. HuJI-A chief, Maulvi Abdul Qudus Burmi is known to share a personal rapport with Hafiz Sayeed[18].

Current Developments

Attack on Chief Minister of Mandalay

U Ye Myint, the Chief Minister of Mandalay, escaped unhurt in a landmine blast targeting his convoy on 31 Jan 2014. The landmine is suspected to have been planted by cadres of Chiang Mai (Thailand) based Muslim Liberation Organisation of Burma (MLOB). The attack was possibly in retaliation to the anti- Muslim riots that had broken out in Mandalay in Mar 2013, for which the Chief Minister was accused of inaction. In addition to the Rohingya Solidarity Organisation (RSO), Tehrik-e- Azadi Arakaan is also trying to make inroads among disgruntled Myanmar Muslims to carry out subversive activities.

Support from Pakistan

Though not confirmed, there are reports that, there are communications from Islamabad to the Pakistan High Commission in Dhaka directing the Commission to facilitate radical Islamic activity. While the activity of the ISI is a known fact, this development indicates systemic involvement at the highest level of governance in Pakistan.

Myanmar National Census

There is widespread anger and opposition to the inclusion of Rohingyas, even under the sub head Bengalis in the Census – 2014. There are indicators that the census would reveal the actual size of the Muslim population, which is much larger than the officially stated figure of four percent.

Attack on Border Outposts

On 09 Oct 2016, nine policemen were killed in a coordinated attack on three border posts in western Myanmar by members of the Rohingya ethnic group. Violence flared up in Rakhine province subsequently drawing an allegedly brutal reprisal from government forces. The primary terror group involved in Rakhine appears to be the Harakah al-Yaqin (Movement of Certainty), which the Myanmar government refers to as the Aqa Mul Mujahidin.

The organisation is led by a committee of around 20 senior leaders based in Saudi Arabia. According to a report by International Crisis Group (ICG), all are Rohingya émigrés or have Rohingya heritage. They are well connected in Bangladesh, Pakistan, and possibly India. The Harakah al-Yaqin itself may have been born out of the jockeying for power between the ISIL and Al-Qaeda in the Indian subcontinent. The recent involvement of foreign jihadi groups in the conflict between Myanmar's majority Buddhist population and the embattled Rohingya minority could mean further instability on India's eastern and northeastern flanks[19].

Terror Attacks and Support within India

Recent Incidents

A number of radical Islamic terror organisations have taken root in India in the past decade or so. The support to non-state actor operations from Pakistan and Bangladesh has resulted in terror attacks across India. Some recent incidents which reflect the spread of Islamic Terrorist Organisation in India are discussed in the succeeding paras.

- *Bodh Gaya Blast*. The bombings in Bodh Gaya, Bihar on 07 Jul 2013 may have been the handiwork of fundamentalist Muslim organisations, as fallout of the prosecution of Rohingyas. Muslims in Mumbai also took out a protest march last year against riots in Myanmar. LeT released a video in support of the Rohingyas culminating with clips of Bodh Gaya blasts. This lent credence to the theory that the attacks were in retaliation to the persecution of Rohingyas in Myanmar.

- *Arrest of Abdul Karim Tunda*. This LeT operative was arrested in Aug 2013 from the Indo- Nepal border. Having received extensive explosives training in Pakistan, Tunda is known to have established strong links with ISI, Jaish-e-Mohammed, Indian Mujahideen and Babbar Khalsa. He is also known to have established contact with Rohingya operatives in Bangladesh as well as in Karachi. Tunda has been in touch with JuD Hafiz Saeed, Maulana Masood Azhar, Zaki-ur-Rehman Lakhvi and also Dawood Ibrahim. Azam Cheema, the intelligence Chief of LeT and the mastermind of the 2008 Mumbai attacks has been a close associate of Tunda.

- ***Yasin Bhatkal's Bangladesh Linkage.*** The founder of Indian Mujahideen (IM), Mohd Ahmed Sidibappa @ Yasin Bhatkal was arrested in Aug 2013 at the Indo-Nepal border, in Bihar. He had received extensive training in handling arms and explosives in Pakistan in 2006. Bhatkal was supplied with explosives smuggled across from Bangladesh. Bhatkal has been accused of carrying out blasts at the German Bakery in Pune and the Bangalore Stadium in 2010.

- ***Arrest of IM Operative in Dhaka.*** Indian Mujahideen's (IM) Pakistani operative Zia-ur Rehman alias Waqas had been hiding in Bangladesh and was supposed to leave for Pakistan via Nepal when he was apprehended by RAW on 11 Apr 2014. The ISI handlers of Waqas in Pakistan were worried that he had been exposed and needed to bring him to Pakistan. Accordingly, ISI got passport made for Waqas. However, when he reached the airport, Bangladesh's immigration officials discovered that there was no entry stamp on his passport. The Indian agents managed to spirit him away to India without leaving any footprints. Waqas proved his utility by furnishing details of IM cells with whom he had collaborated. This further led to the arrest of another IM Commander Tehseen from Nepal.

HuJI Influence on North East Insurgent Groups

HuJI has strong links with the Students Islamic Movement of India (SIMI), LeT and Jaish-e-Mohammed (JeM)[20]. It carried out the 2006 attack on the Sankatmochan Temple and the Varanasi Railway Station in collaboration with the JeM and SIMI. HuJI and JeM collaborated in the Dec 2005 attack at the Indian Institute of Science (IISc), Bangalore. HuJI also maintains links with militant groups operating in the North East. The HuJI-B, is a direct offshoot of the same parent organisation.

Implications for India

The spawn of terror organisations in Bangladesh and Myanmar and the events highlighted above have serious security implications as covered in succeeding paragraphs.

Influx of Rohinyga Muslims

The ethnic violence in Myanmar has led to an illegal influx of Rohinygas into India largely through Bangladesh. They live in refugee clusters in Delhi, UP, Maharashtra and NE states. Reports indicate that pan-Islamic groups are radicalising this community to seek retribution. LeT leader Hafeez Saeed, issued a statement in Jun 13 falsely accusing India of assisting the Myanmar regime in prosecution of Rohingyas.

Demographic Impact

A steady influx of illegal immigrants into our North Eastern states from Bangladesh has resulted in a demographic shift. This is also apparent in all districts of West Bengal and Assam bordering Bangladesh. The influx of these illegal immigrants is turning these districts into Muslim- majority region. The shift from minority is likely to facilitate support to Islamic/ Jihadi terror groups operating from across the border in Bangladesh. It will then only be a matter of time when a demand for merger with Bangladesh may be made.

Mushrooming Madrassas in Siliguri Corridor

There has been a rapid increase in the number of Mosques and Madrassas in the border areas. In 2008, they numbered around 1466 of which 810 were registered. Along the Indo-Nepal border, there are 343 mosques and 367 madrassas in districts on the Indian side.[21]Given the level of literacy and religious beliefs among immigrant Muslims, they are susceptible to Islamic fundamentalism fuelled by religious institutions. There are suspicions that many mosques in West Bengal might be safe havens for radical elements and even arms. These are worrisome possibilities, given the changing demography in states like Bengal and Assam. Concerns are particularly acute in case of the Siliguri corridor, which is a strategic link for NE region with the rest of India.

Security of Andaman & Nicobar Islands

The number of illegal Rohingya people who have started landing on the shores of the A &N Islands needs to be taken into cognizance. The large spread of the Archipelago does not permit round the clock surveillance, and hence, it is not possible to check their influx into the Island chain.

There have been reports of a possible terror strike, akin to the 2008 Mumbai attack, on the A&N Islands in the recent past. Aceh Province, Indonesia is in close proximity to the Nicobar Islands. The spread of radical jihadi groups in Indonesia, coupled with the extant reality in Rakhine State of Myanmar is an emerging security concern.

Pan Bangladesh – Myanmar Terror Organisations

The presence of Rohingyas in large numbers in Chittagong, Bangladesh and Rakhine State, Myanmar is a cause of concern. The Rohingyas Solidarity Organisation is likely to receive an impetus, in terms of financial and moral support from the AI Qaeda and other fundamentalist organisations. ISI, through the LeT, has already tapped into the Rohingya community for recruitment and terror training. The porous land borders between India, Bangladesh and Myanmar present an opportunity for easy infiltration. A repeat of the Bodh Gaya blast, targeting the Buddhist community, is well within the capability of these groups.

Links with NE Insurgents

Despite ideological differences, the Indian Insurgent Groups operating in NE India have some linkages with the Muslim Fundamentalist Organisations. The linkages of the ULFA (I), KLO, NSCN (IM) with ISI, Pakistan are well established. The Jihadi terror groups in Bangladesh and Myanmar, which have direct links with the ISI, can facilitate the activities of these Indian Insurgent Groups (IIG) in NE India. The HuJI is known to have assisted ULFA in running camps in the Chittagong Hill Tracks in Bangladesh along the border of Tripura, prior to the crackdown by the Awami League government in 2010.

The China Factor

Coupled with the ongoing radicalisation in the region is the challenge of reducing China's increasing footprint in the area. Besides Chinese growing assertiveness in the region, concerted efforts are being made by them to develop closer relations in our neighbourhood-Bangladesh, Bhutan and Myanmar. China is assisting these countries in capacity building and investing heavily in multifaceted fields. Thus leaning their dependency towards itself, this would essentially reduce dependency on India which would be inimical to India's interest.

Fractured Elections in Bangladesh

The year 2014 saw India decisively supporting Sheikh Hasina's victory in the general elections which the sceptical US felt was not indicative of a popular support and that the mandate was fractured[22]. This led to emergence of anti-India rhetoric by the hardliners. It has also weakened the pro-India Government of Sheikh Hasina. Developments in Bangladesh are compounding the challenges before India's foreign policy establishment. The recent modernisation of armed forces being undertaken by Bangladesh is an example of aggressive posturing by them post China's inroads into the country. Why else would it buy 44 modern MBT-2000 tanks and what could be the threat when it has borders only with India and Myanmar?

Languishing CBMs

There has been a latent paralysis in pro-activeness to establish CBMs with these countries due to domestic compulsions and religious under pinning's as has been in the past. The Teesta water sharing accord between the two countries needs an early fructification.

However, it is pertinent to mention here that India has gone the extra mile in settling the maritime boundary with Bangladesh as well as the exchange of enclaves where India meticulously abided by the international law. These gestures have immensely contributed to the betterment of bilateral relations between the two countries.

Economic Corridors and Disruptions

The region is witnessing rejuvenated endeavour to complete its connectivity corridors in the real earnest. The 2800 Km BCIM economic corridor is nearly complete. BBIN initiative too is gathering momentum. However, the fructification of these is possible only when the sub regional peace and stability is assured.

Way Ahead

Bangladesh's on-going counter-terrorism efforts have been somewhat effective in reducing the threat of formidable attacks, its counter-terrorism policy in the overall context at the micro and macro level needs a relook. The focus of CT agencies remains in Dhaka while there is inadequate coverage of the more vulnerable northern and south-eastern regions of Bangladesh. There is an urgent need for more coordination and information sharing among the various security agencies in the country. Bangladesh also needs to generate a counter narrative by exploiting the media to create social awareness and resistance against extremism and terrorism. There are efforts in this direction but the progress is slow and the outcome remains to be seen. In recent months, there have been some concerns about the government's appeasement of an Islamist vigilante group known as Hefajat-e-Islam, which is a pressure group of madrasah (religious schools) teachers and students. The government has changed the content of some school textbooks by 'Islamising' them; a not so encouraging move as it may be counterproductive, especially at a time when the country is attempting to eradicate extremism[23].

A new threat landscape is emerging in Bangladesh, which will be more complex than ever before. It is marked by multiple groups, which are operating either on IS or AQIS platform. At times, these groups may also overlap and collaborate with each other. It is highly likely that both IS and AQIS will try to recruit from the 70,000 Rohingyas who have recently crossed over to Bangladesh to escape persecution in Myanmar. Prevention of exploitation of Rohingya refugees by terrorists will remain a key challenge for the government.

Conclusion

The targeting of Rohingya Muslims and the increasing strife between Buddhists and Muslims, two large religions in Asia, has disturbing implications for the region and for India. The LeT, assisted by the ISI, is believed to be recruiting Rohingyas, to seek revenge against the Buddhists as also stir trouble in Bangladesh, Myanmar and India. Reports also indicate that terrorist training camps are being run by the Bangladesh based Rohingya Solidarity Organisation, on the Bangladesh-Myanmar border, with funding from Saudi Arabia. The Bangladesh-Myanmar border seems to be turning into the next Af-Pak, as a centre for global jihad, and US and other Western security agencies have also stepped up monitoring of the area.

The resurgence of Islamic Terror Groups in the strategic neighbourhood of India has severe security ramifications. India has borne the brunt of mindless terror attacks, which Pakistan has attributed to non-state actors. The terror outfits, which had initially operated from across the border, have found internal support. The home grown terror groups have been deftly cultivated by operatives from Pakistan. The unhindered spread of the terror groups towards our Eastern Frontier needs speculation as to its long term implication. India can ill afford to deny the stark reality of being located in a region festering with Jihadi terrorist organisations. It is imperative that corrective action at the highest levels be instituted to ensure peace in India's strategic neighbourhood.

Endnotes

1   (2017) "Myanmar", [Online:web] Accessed 21 Mar 2017 URL: https://en.wikipedia.org/wiki/Myanmar

2   Samuels, Gabriel (2016) "Bangladesh considering dropping Islam as state religion",[Online:web] Accessed 21 Mar 2017 URL: http://www.independent.co.uk/news/world/asia/bangladesh-islam-state-religion-government-considers-dropping-a7418366.html

3   (2017) "Bangladesh Jamaat-e-Islami" ,[Online: web] Accessed 21 Mar 2017 URL: https://en.wikipedia.org/wiki/Bangladesh_Jamaat-e-Islami

4   (2013) "Bangladesh's radical Muslims uniting behind Hefazat-e-Islam",[Online: web] Accessed 21 Mar 2017 URL: https://www.theguardian.com/world/2013/jul/30/bangladesh-hefazat-e-islam-shah-ahmad-shafi

5   (2014) "Islami Chhatra Shibir", [Online: web] Accessed 21 Mar 2017 URL:https://www.trackingterrorism.org/group/islami-chhatra-shibir

6   (2017) "Harkat-ul-Jihad-al Islami Bangladesh (HuJI-B) Terrorist Group, Bangladesh", [Online: web] Accessed 21 Mar 2017 URL: http://www.satp.org/satporgtp/countries/bangladesh/terroristoutfits/Huj.htm

7   Montero, David (2010) "Pakistani militants expand abroad, starting in Bangladesh",[Online: web] Accessed 21 Mar 2017 URL: http://www.csmonitor.

com/World/Asia-South-Central/2010/0805/Pakistani-militants-expand-abroad-starting-in-Bangladesh

8 (2014) "Jama'at ul Mujahideen Bangladesh (JMB)" ,[Online: web] Accessed 21 Mar 2017 URL: https://www.trackingterrorism.org/group/jamaat-ul-mujahideen-bangladesh-jmb

9 (2016) "Security Council Committee Pursuant To Resolutions 1267 (1999) 1989 (2011) And 2253 (2015) Concerning Isil (Da'esh) Al-Qaida And Associated Individuals Groups Undertakings And Entities" ,[Online: web] Accessed 23 Mar 2017 URL: https://www.un.org/sc/suborg/en/sanctions/1267/monitoring-team/reports

10 Bashar, Iftekharul (2017) "Counter Terrorist - Trends and Analyses", [Online: web] Accessed 25 Mar 2017 URL: https://www.rsis.edu.sg/wp-content/uploads/2017/03/CTTA-March-2017.pdf

11 Lister, Tim (2016) "ISIS attack in Bangladesh shows broad reach as 'caliphate' feels pressure" ,[Online: web] Accessed 23 Mar 2017 URL: http://edition.cnn.com/2016/07/03/asia/bangladesh-isis-al-qaeda/

12 (2016) "July 2016 Dhaka attack",[Online: web] Accessed 23 Mar 2017 URL: https://en.wikipedia.org/wiki/July_2016_Dhaka_attack

13 (2017) "Police boss refutes IS existence in Bangladesh",[Online: web] Accessed 23 Mar 2017 URL: http://www.thedailystar.net/city/police-boss-refutes-existence-1375225

14 Bashar, Iftekharul (2017) "Counter Terrorist - Trends and Analyses",[Online: web] Accessed 25 Mar 2017 URL: https://www.rsis.edu.sg/wp-content/uploads/2017/03/CTTA-March-2017.pdf

15 ibid

16 Thompson, Nathan (2013) "The 969 Movement and Burmese Anti-Muslim Nationalism in Context",[Online: web] Accessed 23 Mar 2017 URL: http://www.buddhistpeacefellowship.org/the-969-movement-and-burmese-anti-muslim-nationalism-in-context/

17 (2013) "Burma: End 'Ethnic Cleansing' of Rohingya Muslims",[Online: web] Accessed 25 Mar 2017 URL: https://www.hrw.org/news/2013/04/22/burma-end-ethnic-cleansing-rohingya-muslims

18 (2015) "Harkat-ul-Jihad-al-Islami Arakan (Burma)" ,[Online: web] Accessed 25 Mar 2017 URL: https://www.trackingterrorism.org/group/harkat-ul-jihad-al-islami-arakan-burma

19 (2016) "A new terror group has emerged in Myanmar—and India should be worried", [Online: web] Accessed 27 Mar 2017 URL: https://qz.com/866665/

rohingya-crisis-a-new-terror-group-has-emerged-in-myanmar-and-india-should-be-worried/

20 Singh, Amarjeet (2009) "Unholy alliance in North-East India",[Online: web] Accessed 27 Mar 2017 URL: http://www.idsa.in/idsastrategiccomments/ UnholyallianceinNorthEastIndia_MASingh_190209

21 (2002) "Mushrooming Madrasas A Menace to Nation",[Online: web] Accessed 27 Mar 2017 URL: www.hvk.org/2002/0502/64.html

22 Purohit, Devadeep (2014) "For Hasina, India swims against tide- Delhi stands by ally despite 'sham' polls"https://www.telegraphindia.com/1140107/jsp/ frontpage/story_17760386.jsp#.WNJFc2-GPcc

23 Bashar, Iftekharul (2017) "Counter Terrorist - Trends and Analyses",[Online: web] Accessed 25 Mar 2017 URL: https://www.rsis.edu.sg/wp-content/ uploads/2017/03/CTTA-March-2017.pdf

Chapter 7

China Factor in South Asia

"Begin by seizing something which your opponent holds dear; then he will be amenable to your will"

- Sun Tzu

Pakistan-China Strategic Nexus: An Overview

Symbiotic Relationship

"Pakistanis love China for what it can do for them, while China loves Pakistanis despite what they do to themselves".[1] China and Pakistan have long been strategic allies. Their collaboration and cooperation in all spheres has been comprehensive and has stood the test of time. Pakistan and China have vexed territorial and ideological disputes with India. Both have rallied against India bilaterally and at the international fora to stymie India's politico-diplomatic and security interests and this trend has shown a marked increase in the recent past. Founded on a shared enmity with India, China's backing to Pakistan has gone so deep that it was willing to offer the ultimate gift from one state to another: the materials that Pakistan's nuclear scientists needed to build the bomb. Pakistan acted as China's backdoor during its years of diplomatic isolation, the bridge between Nixon and Mao, and the front-line in Beijing's struggles with the Soviet Union during the late stages of the Cold War.

Pakistan now is a central part of China's transition from a regional power to a global one. The country lies at the heart of Beijing's plans for a network of ports, pipelines, roads and railways connecting the oil and gas fields of the Middle East to the mega-cities of East Asia. Its coastline is becoming a crucial staging post for China's take-off as a naval power, extending its reach from the Indian Ocean to the Persian Gulf and the Mediterranean Sea. Penetration by Pakistan's intelligence services into the darkest corners of global jihadi networks are a vital asset to China as it navigates its growing interests in the Islamic world, and seeks to choke off support for the militant activities that pose one of the gravest threats to China's internal stability.[2]

Pakistan is perceived by China to be its gateway to the Islamic bloc of countries. It helps to trap India within South Asia rather than permit it to emerge as a challenger to China. Pakistan also fulfils the Chinese aspirations to gain a land route to the Indian Ocean obviating its Malacca dilemma. Through Pakistan, China also attempts to gain influence in the Af-Pak region and monitor the extra regional presence in Afghanistan. At the same time China wants influence to limit Pak role in any possible support to ETIM. Pakistan also helped China gain access to US as a backdoor intermediary during the early turbulent years of its existence. Pakistan also provided China access to some Western weaponry and equipment which could then be copied by its manufacturers. On the other hand Pakistan has found an all-weather ally in China which supports it in all forums. China creates the two front dilemma for India reducing Indian threat to Pakistan. China has been generous in transfer of technology as also direct military aid. However, its most significant help is in the field of nuclear and missile technology, which Pakistan may not have been able to master on its own. China has also repeatedly come to rescue of Pakistan in terms of economic aid.

However, the extent of Chinese economic support to Pakistan is debatable and in terms of trade, it may well be China which benefitted more. China also vetoes any resolution in Security Council which goes against Pakistan. Hafiz Saeed being a case in point. The recent precondition of accepting Pakistan also, in case of Indian entry to the NSG underscores the level of Chinese support to Pakistan. There is a subtle alignment of Pakistan and China on Kashmir issue, the latter having emerged as a de facto stakeholder in Pakistani rhetoric on J&K.

Initial Relations

India was amongst the first countries to grant recognition to PRC in 1949. Nehru repeatedly extended a hand of friendship to China. China on the other hand viewed this relationship differently. China perceived India to be the most powerful country in South Asia, which may challenge China's rise subsequently. The Chinese therefore followed a policy of containment right from the beginning. Chinese priority was a complete control over its frontier territories of Tibet and Xinjiang. In fact much of China's strategic thinking was shaped by Mao - who believed that a rising nation must continue to push against its frontiers. This thinking was partly shaped by his experiences of the Century of Humiliation as also the Chinese civil war. Tibet as also the Southern boundary of Tibet constituted one such frontier. Therefore China was not content only with the annexation of Tibet - it also wanted to push further southwards.

However, China was yet weak militarily and did not want to be openly hostile towards India. They thus needed the benign Sino-Indian agreement of 1954. India at that time remained oblivious of this Chinese design. In fact, consequent to Chinese occupation of Tibet, India accepted that Tibet is a part of China. This state was possibly driven by beliefs of the then Prime Minister Nehru as also the Indian ambassador to China, Mr Panniker. They both believed China to be a long term Indian ally. Surprisingly, in the initial years the Pakistani leadership was not as well disposed towards China as they clearly were worried about Chinese territorial ambitions. The Pak tilt in this period was decidedly towards the US. Post the Chinese annexation of Tibet, the CIA covert operations to train the Tibetan guerrilla force for an uprising in Tibet against the PLA were directed from Peshawar.

India on the other hand provided the sustenance for PLA in Tibet in terms of food grains. During the visit of Ayub Khan to India on 24 Apr 1959, he proposed for a joint strategy for defense against China which was refused by Nehru. Strangely, the Karakoram highway (KKH) was started by the Chinese in 1959. The road was opened to public in 1979 - as USSR invaded Afghanistan. KKH was thus a major milestone in the evolving strategic alliance between China and Pakistan.

Post 1962 Sino-Indian Conflict

1962 proved Pakistan correct with respect to the Chinese threat from the North. This proved to be the turning point in Sino-Pak relations. The shift was accentuated by three factors. First, by this stage Sino-Soviet friendship was falling apart and China needed new friends. Second, by befriending Pakistan the Chinese hoped to counter-veil India as also grow closer to

US. Pakistan, also realized that it cannot wish away China being their neighbour. Third, and the last reason, was that the Indian defeat in 1962, brought to fore the urgency of settling the border issue with China. Post 1962, Pakistan went on to normalise its relations with China and after ceding of the Shaksgam valley resolved its border problems with China in 1963. China similarly understood and condoned Pakistan's reasons for joining SEATO / CENTO.

Pakistan thus shifted its position from being sceptical about China to becoming its ally. In fact, by settling and demarcating the border with China, Pakistan also somewhat legitimised its illegal occupation of PoK and the Northern areas. Thus seeds of Chinese intervention in the J&K dispute were sown at this stage. Chinese were cautious about making any statement on J&K till 1962 as they were concerned that India may similarly comment about Tibet. However, in 1964, they made statements about ill treatment of Muslims in J&K, signalling their support for Pak position. Role of Pakistan as an intermediary between China and US was established in late sixties and early seventies. This process was taken further during the Nixon era when Pakistan facilitated a number of high level secret negotiations between China and the US, finally resulting in US recognition of China as a permanent member of the Security Council in 1972.

Post 1962, Pakistan perceived that China could now militarily support them against a common foe in India. This hope was belied in 1965 war wherein, China provided only verbal support to Pakistan. Zhou Enlai then asked Pakistan to be prepared to wage a long drawn guerrilla war against India. Similarly, even in 1971 in spite of all the help that Pakistan was providing to China, the latter refused to bail out Pakistan militarily. The reasons for such Chinese behavior may well have been their internal political compulsions as also the fact that the Chinese armed forces were not very strong. China was also actively seeking the permanent seat in UN Security Council in 1971, which it would not have risked by unprovoked military action against India. Even during the Kargil war, Pakistan was heavily banking on the Chinese support which did not really materialise except for a few isolated statements.

Strategic Engagement: 1971-1990 and Beyond

This period was defined by the Soviet expansion in Afghanistan and the peak of cold war. Presence of Soviet troops in Afghanistan made Pakistan a frontline state for both the US and China. China funneled arms to the Afghan mujahedeen through Pakistan.[3]China truly became strategic ally of Pakistan extending to it military hardware, monetary support as also the ultimate gift of nuclear and missile technology. While the US-China-Pakistan relations waned during the Cold War, the Sino-Pak strategic partnership remained stable. Chinese support to Pakistan after its nuclear explosion was indicative of the degree of friendship and alliance between the two countries. However, like before Chinese support to Pakistan remained nuanced during the Kargil war.

Pakistan and China signed 'Free Trade Agreement in 2003' and the 'Treaty of Friendship, Cooperation and Good Neighbourly Relations in 2005', further cementing the relations between the two countries. In this treaty China reaffirmed the status of Pakistan as a strategic ally, whereas Pakistan restated its 'One China' stance. There is growing salience of Pakistan in China's strategic calculus, as Pakistan provides it access to the Indian Ocean Region. The coastline of Pakistan today offers the opportunity to China to give a strategic reach to the PLAN. China also has problems in the province of Xinjiang. It is 1/6th of China's land mass; however, it is important due to being home to its Nuclear Industry, being the largest gas producer and 2nd largest oil producer. Its network of communications enables China to access wealth of Central Asia. China believes that Pakistan plays an important role in Xinjiang. China projects Pakistan as a friendly Islamic country which gives access to China to the larger Muslim/ Islamic community and does not criticise China's iron hand policy on Muslims in Xinjiang.

Defence and Nuclear Cooperation

China and Pakistan defence cooperation forms the bedrock of their relationship. Their shared enmity and border disputes with India act as a strategic glue which holds their defence relations. For China, strengthening Pakistan's military capabilities allows it to keep Indian tied down in South Asia and hampers India's ambitions of rising as a global power. For Pakistan, China is an all-weather friend which gives it critical military technology to keep it at par with Indian defence preparations. Former Pakistani Ambassador to the US, Mr Husain Haqqani said in 2006 while describing China – Pak relations "For China, Pakistan is a low-cost secondary deterrent to India, For Pakistan, China is a high-value guarantor of security against India".[4]

Since 1962, China has been a steady source of military equipment to the Pakistani Army, helping establish ammunition factories, providing technological assistance and modernizing existing facilities. Between 2011 and 2016, Pakistan has been the biggest client of Chinese arms, receiving 35 per cent of China's arms exports.[5] China and Pakistan are involved in several projects to enhance military and weaponry systems, which include the development of the 'Chinese tailor made for Pakistan' JF-17 Thunder fighter aircraft, K-8 Karakorum advance training aircraft, a training aircraft for the Pakistan Air Force based on the Chinese domestic Hongdu L-15, space technology, AWACS systems, Al-Khalid tanks, which China granted license production and made modifications based on the initial Chinese Type 90 and/or MBT-2000.

China has also helped Pakistan in launching communication satellite PAKSAT 1R. They will also launch a satellite in June 2018 to carry out planning and execution of development projects under the China-Pakistan Economic Corridor (CPEC) more scientifically.[6]China is also providing GPS coverage to Pakistan and training Pakistani astronauts for space flights on board Chinese space crafts. The Chinese have designed advanced weapons for Pakistan, making it a strong military power in the Asian region. The two armies regularly conduct joint military exercises as well.

The Pakistan Ordnance Factories – a group of different arms industries –established with Chinese assistance manufactures and sells weapons to some 40 countries earning some $20 million annually. Similarly, Pakistan's nuclear industry – both civilian and military – owe entirely to Chinese assistance – financial and technological. Pakistani nuclear scientist, AQ Khan used Chinese designs in his nuclear designs while the Chinese did a massive training of Pakistani scientists by giving them lectures in China. American experts believe that during Benazir Bhutto's term in office, China tested Pakistan's first bomb in 1990.[7] Pakistan's Missile development programme is totally due to Chinese assistance, whether it is the Ghaznavi (Hatf-3) which is a scaled version of Chinese M11 missile technology or the Shaheen series based on Chinese two stage solid propellant missile M-18. Even the Babur Cruise Missile, has been produced by reverse engineering the American Tomahawk cruise missile by the Chinese. Further Pakistani Surface to Air Missile-Anza is the Pakistani version of PRC supplied

SAM and Pakistan Aeronautical Complex at Kamra was established with Chinese assistance in 1980.

After China joined NSG in 2004, its cooperation with Pakistan has continued under the so-called grandfather clause. China maintains that its deals on nuclear cooperation with Pakistan had been agreed on before it joined NSG in 2004 and hence, it can go ahead with them. It is important to note that the Karakoram Highway has been used to transport nuclear missiles and suspected fissile material from China to Pakistan.[8]

There is a diplomatic side as well to the China-Pakistan nexus. China has been shielding Pakistan based terrorists like Hafiz Saeed and 26/11 terrorist attack mastermind Zaki Ur Rehman Lakhvi against the UN sanctions. In addition, China lobbied for and got Pakistan included as a full time member in Shanghai Cooperation Organisation and wants it to be included in Nuclear Suppliers Group as well, mainly to balance inclusion of India in these forums. China also has been strengthening its relations with Pakistan to respond to growing closeness between the US and India. Two instances are enough to prove it. One, after the Indo-US nuclear deal was signed, China responded by signing a similar nuclear deal with Pakistan. Recently, China-Pakistan have signed a defense agreement in response to India-US logistics agreement. China-Pakistan defence relations will further grow in the future. Pakistan will acquire at least eight modified diesel-electric attack submarines from China by 2028 in a nearly $ 5 billion agreement. Given such a strategic nature of China Pakistan ties, the CPEC will further add to their existing relationship.

CPEC – A New Strategic Dimension in Sino-Pak Nexus

The China Dream[9] (*Zhōngguómèng*) is a term popularised after 2013 within Chinese socialist thought that describes a set of personal and national ideals in the People's Republic of China and the Communist Party of China. It is used by journalists, government officials, and activists to describe the role of the individual in Chinese society as well as the goals of the "Chinese nation". The Belt and Road Initiative (OBOR)[10] was accordingly launched with great fanfare as part of this China dream. OBOR has over a period of time become the signature initiative of Xi Jinping. He has attached certain personal credibility to its success. The strategy behind the Belt and Road Initiative is to diversify transit lines, thereby mitigating China's vulnerability to external economic disruption and reinvigorating China's slowing economy.

China's ideal would be to link its inland cities to global markets with a diversified network of transit routes and energy pipelines, many of which would take inland routes and serve as alternatives to existing sea-lanes. Aside from its long-term value as a contingency plan for Chinese trade, the Belt and Road strategy serves China's goal of alleviating its economic slowdown and correcting its internal geographic disparities. By official figures, China's economy is expected to grow at about 7 percent a year, though in reality, growth is likely to become substantially slower. To handle the slowdown, China aims to shift its industry away from the coast to the relatively underdeveloped inland provinces. Meanwhile, it seeks to produce higher value-added goods in coastal regions and expand coastal consumer bases to absorb manufactured goods from the newly industrialized interior. The Belt and Road Initiative will aid in this process by constructing physical links between China's inland industry and new markets. Belt and Road infrastructure projects may give China a way to offload some of its growing surpluses in construction materials and rural labor. Although it may not be economically or politically feasible to tap into these surpluses for every project, overall the initiative will help alleviate some of China's overcapacity problems.[11]

CPEC is a part of the OBOR initiative. CPEC is somewhat different from other alignments of OBOR, in that the alignment is over extremely difficult terrain and through disputed territory. Both nations have chosen to push for it in spite of obvious legal as well as physical hurdles. Clearly CPEC fulfils geo-economics as well as geostrategic needs of both nations. For China, the CPEC would be shortest route to the West Asian markets and would alleviate its Malacca Dilemma as China can import energy and carry out its trade with Africa and West Asia avoiding the US dominated Sea Lines of Communications in the Indian Ocean.

Gwadar is the culmination point of CPEC where the OBOR and the Maritime Silk Routes converge. Gwadar is located at a strategic place and control over Gwadar provides enhanced expeditionary capabilities to the Chinese Navy. Gwadar in times to come is likely to become a strategic naval base for PLAN. The relationship based on the shared common animosity towards India further gains from CPEC as it enhances the physical connectivity between the two nations. Moreover, Pakistan's economy desperately needs the infusion of this FDI for its infrastructure primarily in its power sector. The CPEC will also mark Pakistan's movement away from the US in its foreign policy and would be a symbol of close Pakistan-China relationship.

CPEC - Security Dimension

Pakistan is in the throes of serious security challenges. It is grappling with serious ethno-religious divide, sectarian violence, separatisms and Jihadi terrorism. Its internal security threats are closely linked with the external security challenges due to unsettled issue of Durand line which is contested by Afghanistan and volatile Line of Control (LoC)/Actual Ground Position Line (AGPL) in Jammu & Kashmir, including Siachen Glacier.

There is a simmering discontentment in Gilgit- Baltistan against Pakistani occupation and policies, in Pakistan Occupied Kashmir against Pakistan authoritarianism, in Baluchistan for autonomy, Sindh is in the grip of sectarian violence and Punjab is vulnerable to terrorist strikes by Tehrik-e-Taliban Pakistan and other anti- establishment terrorists groups. Pakistan is also the fountainhead of radical Islamic movement unleashed by the East Turkestan Islamic Movement (ETIM) in the restive Xinjiang province of China. The threat of ETIM terrorists is so strong that the Pakistan military Chief, General Rahil Sharif had to assure China that Pakistan will firmly crackdown on terrorist forces like the ETIM and protect the security of CEPC.[12]

Therefore, right from Xinjiang to Gwadar, the CPEC runs through areas which are highly susceptible to violence. The corridor in Gilgit-Baltistan runs close to the LoC. In view of the disputed nature of this territory and possibility of exchange of fire and forward posturing of troops, the CPEC runs the risk of disruption. The strategic and military objectives of China and Pakistan converge in Ladakh. Construction of Karakoram Highway (KKH) and its further upgradation in Gilgit Baltistan has major implications on the politico-diplomatic and security interests of India.

CPEC and Twin Threats from Pakistan and China

China's[13] defence white paper of 2015 has stipulated that PLA should be able to protect the Chinese interests anywhere in the globe as also be able to shape the international environment. The main strategic objectives of the PLA are to "safeguard China's national sovereignty, national security, and territorial integrity and support China's peaceful development." The white paper provides a clear confirmation that the PLA will continue to expand its range of operations and capabilities. Concomitantly, President Xi Jinping announced major reforms for PLA on September 3, 2015. Of particular interest for India is the West Zone, which merges the erstwhile Lanzhou and Chengdu MRs. Comprising more than half of China's land area, 22 percent of its population and more than one-third of China's land-based military, the newly constituted West Zone represents a strengthened military formation.

The merger of the Lanzhou and Chengdu MRs will improve joint planning, coordination and operations. Incorporation of the Qinghai region in the West Zone will facilitate the rapid induction and deployment of high altitude acclimatised and trained troops into Tibet and across Ladakh. Establishment of the West Zone also reveals China's increased and abiding military interest in the region in addition to facilitating focus on "threats in Xinjiang and Tibet as well as Afghanistan. Equally pertinent is the appointment of General Zhao Zongqi, till recently Jinan MR Commander, as Commander of the new West Zone. His credentials indicate he was handpicked for this post. The China's military strategy to achieve its strategic missions is active defense and local wars under "informationised" conditions. "Active defence" means that China is willing to counter threats pre-emptively, even outside China's sovereign territory. It also lays down the concept of prosecuting War Zone Campaigns which envisages achieving the end-state with minimum effort and at the lowest level of the escalatory matrix / operational continuum.[14] This runs from the Domination-cum-Deterrence (DCD) phase to Gaining Initiative by Striking First (GISF), concluding in the Quick Battle Quick Resolution (QBQR) phase, through measured application of military force.

The above developments indicate that China is better poised to achieve its military objectives in Ladakh in a two front collusive war with India.

Conduct of Joint Military Campaign against India

Gilgit–Gwadar has brought about a paradigm shift of monumental proportions in the entire strategic calculus about J&K. The presence of Chinese personnel has added to the complexity of the security dynamics in the region and so have the reports that Pakistan is actively considering a proposal to lease the region to Beijing for 50 years.Moreover, the law now permits PLA to be deployed outside the national boundaries for protection of Chinese assets in OBOR.[15] A study of the geo-strategic importance of the region comprising of Gilgit, Baltisatan, Saltoro Ridge, Shaksgam Valley and Aksai Chin will highlight the enormity of the military threat that India faces in an eventuality of a two front collusive war. Gilgit-Baltistan located to the immediate west of Saltoro Ridge is part of PoK with majority Shia population. The Shaksgam Valley immediately to the North of Saltoro Ridge has already been ceded to China by Pakistan illegally. Xinjiang lies to the immediate North of Shaksgam. Aksai Chin which is occupied by China lies to the South East of Shaksgam Valley.

The Nurba Valley and Ladakh leading to J&K are hemmed in on three sides by Baltistan, Shaksgam Valley and Aksai Chin. If the proposal to lease the Gilgit – Baltistan area goes through; all the three areas right up to Xinjiang will be under Chinese control. Saltoro ridge acts as a separator between Pakistan (Baltistan – Gilgit) and China. Its capture will jeopardize the security of Nubra Valley and Ladakh which will have an adverse effect on the security of entire J&K.

In the event of India-Pakistan war, China would support Pakistan with unrestrained war material, its assets in space, cyber, electromagnetic domain, its plethora of cruise missiles and unmanned vehicles, and by keeping the pressure on Chinese front with threat of troop's insertion by vertical envelopment. Thus, at the theatre level, China, without showing its hand, would open the third front.

Supply of Military Hardware

Pakistan came to rely on China for weapons and military equipment almost immediately after losing the Indo-Pak War in 1965. SIPRI has reported that just over half of Pakistan's weapons imports from 2010 to 2014 came from China and 30 per cent from the US. To a noteworthy degree, the Sino-Pakistan friendship has in terms of conventional arms been of greatest benefits to the two air forces. However, in a significant arms sale, China announced the sale of eight Type 039B/041 Yuan Class submarine to Pakistan in April 2015.[16] Military arms supply is the cornerstone of the deepening nexus and is aimed directly at blunting the edge that India enjoys in conventional war waging capabilities against Pakistan.

Activities of Concern and to be Watched

Security of CPEC

A day after Xi Jinping's visit, the Inter Services Public Relations wing of Pakistan Army came out with a tweet that Pakistan would raise a Special Security Division for CPEC which would comprise of 9 Army Battalions and 6 Wings of Civil armed forces and such division would be commanded by a Major General.[17] By February 2016, the news of the establishment of a special security division (SSD) commanded by Major General Abid Rafique in Rawalpindi army headquarters, came to light. An ISPR press release noted that Army Chief General Raheel Sharif visited the SSD and "emphasized the need to ensure a peaceful environment to be able to push all the planned developmental projects". He also said that the army was "totally aware of all campaigns against the Corridor and vowed that the security forces are ready to pay any price to turn this long cherished dream into reality".[18]

Two months later participating in a seminar on the "Development of Balochistan and Economic Corridor in Gwadar", he informed the audience that a 15,000-strong dedicated force is already in place under the ambit of Special Security Division for the CPEC".[19]He went on to claim "This year, we will move cargo from heartland China to Gwadar and beyond, fulfilling our dream". There were other reports of China planning to raise a special force and station it in Pakistan to protect its workers, which could reach a figure of bout 30,000 as the projects get implemented in full swing.[20]

Against the backdrop on May 16, 2016, the army chief, Raheel Sharif, visited Beijing and assured provision of full security to projects under CPEC. However, soon afterwards on May 30, 2016, there was a road-bomb attack on a Chinese engineer and his driver injuring both of them in Karachi. The attack was claimed by Sindhi nationalists and a note written in Sindhi recovered from the place of attack said "As a rising imperialist power and supporter of Pakistan's cause we consider China equivalent to Punjab", and "We will oppose every anti-Sindh project including the China-Pakistan economic corridor".[21] However, security concerns remain, despite reports of surrender by Baloch rebels and success of operation Zarb-e-Azb against the Pakistani Taliban.

Joint Patrolling

In a first, PLA and Pakistan's border police force carried out a joint patrol along their shared boder.[22] While China has been patrolling the region since 2014, this is the first time that the two armies have carried out a joint patrol in the region. It is interesting to note that the area of the patrol, identified as the "China-Pakistan border", is the frontier region of Pakistan occupied Kashmir – an area claimed by India as an integral part of its territory.

Joint Military Exercises

The PLA is presently focused on developing the capability to execute large scale, complex joint operations. This includes greater realism during exercise, improved core service capabilities, strengthening strategic campaign training and execution of long-distance manoeuvres and mobility operations. Exercises in western China focused on high altitude operations, with special emphasis on using space-based reconnaissance.[23] China and Pakistan have a long history of conducting joint military exercises. The two militaries seem to have achieved high degree of inter-operability, joint planning and intelligence sharing.

Sino-India Relations

India shares 3488 km of land borders with China, large portions of which are under dispute. The situation along the LAC with China has generally been peaceful despite the off and on incursions, as a result of the CBMs in vogue. While there are other issues of concern that may pose threat to our security, the existing reality of disputed borders with China will continue to be the main threat.

Issues of Divergence / Concern

Un-resolved Boundary Dispute

India and China have an unresolved boundary dispute. China continues to occupy approx 38,000 sq km of Indian territory in Aksai Chin and claims approximately 90,000 sq km in Arunachal Pradesh. Also, Pakistan has illegally ceded an additional 5,180 sq km to China. China has resolved its boundary issues with all other neighbours other than India and Bhutan. It is believed that China is deliberately going slow on the negotiations or wishes to keep the issue unresolved by carrying out intrusions, in order to assist its long-time ally Pakistan, by keeping India's second front open.

Modernisation of the PLA

Unprecedented modernisation and transformation of PLA is underway. This includes structural changes in Higher Defence Organisation, creation of Joint Theatre Commands, changes in strategic capability, missiles, space and cyber programme. These are a cause of immediate concern for India when seen alongside the infrastructure development in TAR and other disputed areas to include road, rail, airheads and communications.[24]

Control over Critical Resources

Control over critical resources remains another area of mutual suspicion between the two countries. Whereas, China perceives India to possess the capability to disrupt its SLOC through the Indian Ocean Region, India doubts Chinese intentions as an upper riparian state whenever it builds a dam/barrage close to the border.

Regional Assertiveness

China's increasing assertiveness in the South and East China is a cause of concern. It not only creates an environment of mistrust but challenges India's standing in the region, as the littoral countries expect India to assume a pivotal role in the region to counter China's apparent hegemonic intentions.

Alliances/Alignments

Pakistan. China had assumed a neutral stance on Kashmir during previous Indo-Pak conflicts; however, its full-fledged sp to Pak behind the scenes must be factored into our calculations in any future India-Pak conflict. The permanent presence of PLA personnel in the areas of Gilgit – Baltistan and the proposed construction of CPEC which shall pass through disputed areas between India and Pakistan has sovereignty issues and challenges India's sensitivities. Further it shall reduce, to some extent China's 'Malacca Dilemma', a strategic leverage with India.

Nepal. Chinese increasing footprints in Nepal especially in the field of trade and commerce aimed at carving out a sphere of influence for itself, challenges the traditional relations which India enjoys with Nepal. These can lead to tensions and potential conflict.

Bhutan. Relations between China and India may deteriorate in the event of Bhutan agreeing to realign its boundaries with China in areas of strategic importance to either side, especially in the area of Chumbi Valley and the vicinity of the Siliguri corridor.

Bangladesh. Defence cooperation between Bangladesh and China is on the rise. Sino-Bangladesh relations may get further enhanced if Chittagong Port forms part of the Chinese 'String of Pearls' strategy.

Myanmar. The setting in of democracy in Myanmar is not to the liking of China and has obvious implications on Sino – Indian relations. China needs Myanmar to have an opening into the Bay of Bengal through the Sittwe Port for the landlocked provinces of Yunnan and Sinchuan.

Sri Lanka. The Chinese construction of the Port of Hambantota and supply of almost eighty percent of the defence equipment to the Sri Lankan Defence Forces can translate into strategic connotations.

Maldives. China has expressed its desire to establish a listening post at Moroa Island, 14 Km Southeast of Male, giving it strategic advantages by enabling it to effectively monitor its vulnerable SLsOC.

US, Japan and Countries of SE Asia. China considers India as the 'Lynchpin' in the 'US Pivot to Asia' strategy. The growing closeness of India with US, Japan and the countries of SE Asia is considered by China as a collective effort towards its containment, which may exacerbate India-China tensions.

Political/Economic Rivalry

Resources. China, considered to be the manufacturing hub of the world, will continue to seek raw materials and multifarious energy sources. While India has the potential to provide the former, the bid for energy sources will always pit one against the other.

Markets. China's booming economy will always look for increasing its share in the world markets such as the US, ASEAN and now CARs. India also strives to maintain its trade balance and aims to increase its share in areas of mutual interest such as textiles, thereby leading to an increased competition between the two. India is skeptical of the implications of China's OBOR initiative. It feels that apart from creating undesirable competition it has strategic connotations as well.

Regional Leadership. China has strived to curb India's ambition to play a greater role in the SCO and the ARF; India on its part remains suspicious of China's role in SAARC.

Global Role. China is unlikely to allow India to gain its rightful position as a permanent member of the UN Security Council, or indeed support any meaningful expansion of India's role as a globally effective power.

Issues of Convergence

Ancient Civilizations. India and China are ancient civilizations with rich cultural heritage. Both the countries have a large population base; together constituting $1/3^{rd}$ of the world population with common aspirations and challenges.

Maintenance of Peace and Tranquility. The two countries have committed themselves to resolve all outstanding and contentious issues through Peaceful means and Institutionalized Dialogue Mechanisms. The disputed but peaceful borders between the two countries reflect upon the maturity of the two countries and commitment towards maintenance of regional peace and stability.

High Level Visits. Regular high level visits symbolize our emerging relations. President Xi paid a state visit to India from Sep 17-19, 2014 and PM Modi visited China from May 14-16, 2015. The visit was rich in symbolism and substance and it opened up a new chapter in India-China relations.

Trade and Commerce. Trade and economic relationship between the two countries has seen rapid progress in the last few years. India-China bilateral trade which was as low as US $ 2.92 billion in 2000 reached US$ 70.73 billion in 2015-16. The trade deficit in favour of China stood at US $ 53 billion in 2015-16.[25]

Cultural Relations. In 1955, the first Indian cultural delegation headed by then Deputy Minister of External Affairs visited China. Since 1988 both countries are bringing their people together through structured 'Cultural Exchange Programmes'. The momentum has been set and the pace can only increase in the 21st century.

Education Exchange Programme. India and China signed the 'Education Exchange Programme' in 2006, which is an umbrella agreement for education cooperation between the two countries. Under this agreement, government scholarships are awarded to 25 students by both sides in recognized institutions of higher learning in each other's country. The cooperation in the education sector between the two sides has resulted in an increase in the number of Indian students in China. As on 2014, there were 10491 Indian students studying in various Universities in China in various disciplines. Similarly, around 2000 Chinese students are studying in various educational institutions in India.

Cooperation in Multilateral Forums. India and China meaningfully cooperate with each other in Multilateral forums like BRICS, BCIM forum etc, where they are playing an increasingly important role.

Shared Security Concerns. The two countries have shared security concerns as well, like the emerging situation in W Asia and Afghanistan. Both the countries are also committed towards global war on terrorism.

Defence Cooperation. Bilateral defence interaction between India and China has been growing steadily. Ships of the Navies of both countries have made regular port calls; enhancing bilateral defence cooperation. India and China hold an 'Annual Defence Dialogue' to discuss security and defence cooperation issues between the two countries. There have been regular high level exchanges at the level of Defence Ministers and Service Chiefs, functional level exchanges and military education exchange between India and China. The 6th Joint Indo-China Military Exercise 'Hand in Hand' was held in November 2016 at Pune[26] and Joint Tac Ex in E Ladakh(Disaster relief) on 06 Feb 16.

Chinese Increasing Footprints in South Asia- String of Pearls Strategy

Introduction

The 'string of pearls' strategy, is reportedly a term coined by US strategic planners, to describe the actions initiated by China to strategically encircle or militarily contain potential adversaries by building strategic relationships, and/or establishing control over key geo-strategic points (pearls) in the vicinity of such countries, or their interests. Obviously, the objective of such a purported strategy, involving establishment of a series of well sited strategic footprints, would be the achievement of national interests in the military or the politico-economic realm.

It is in this context that Gwadar port on the Makran coast in Pakistan has been described as "the Western most pearl in a string which stretches along the sea lanes from the Persian Gulf to the South China Sea, to protect China's energy interests and other security objectives". China's other actions in Asia in the recent past include building naval bases and airfields in Myanmar, a port each in Bangladesh and Sri Lanka, strengthening military ties with Pakistan, Iran, Saudi Arabia, Africa, the Central Asian Republics, Nepal, Bangladesh, Sri Lanka and Cambodia, as also an ambitious plan to build a 20 billion dollar canal in Thailand to bypass the Straits of Malacca. It is not surprising thus that these activities have raised concerns in various countries, for a number of credible reasons.

For China, Gwadar's strategic value stems from its proximity to the Straits of Hormuz and the strong US naval presence in the Persian Gulf region, which enables the latter to choke off China's energy supplies, about 60 % of which come from West Asian sources. Relatedly, Gwadar provides China with a 'listening post', from where it can monitor US and other naval activity in the Persian Gulf, Arabian Sea and the Indian Ocean. It could also be argued, from China's point of view, that its involvement in developing facilities in various countries are purely benign in intention as they are only a consequence of commercial processes where Chinese companies have successfully gained contracts based on the strength of their past achievements. However, others may argue that, only the politically naïve would accept such an argument, as the pattern of such engagements by China decidedly have a strategic 'ring' to it – they have resulted not only in China gaining access to blue water ports in the Indian Ocean, Arabian Sea, the Bay of Bengal and the South China Sea, but have also provided China the capability to interfere with/ interdict maritime activity in these waters, in case of a conflict situation developing in the future.

A number of related questions come to the fore, when analysing China's strategic footprints in the regional and global arena. Are these 'footprints' purely a consequence of commercial interests or are they aimed at furthering or achieving military interests? If China is indeed following a well deliberated 'string of pearls strategy', how will China leverage the 'pearls' in the future? Are the 'pearls' aimed at containing specific countries, or is it just part of a broader response to a similar strategy that the US appears to be playing against China? What are the possible future manifestations, especially in South Asia with regard to new 'pearls' that, in China's perception, would need to secure in the future?

China's Footprints in South Asia

Over the last two decades or so, China has established close relationships with a number of countries in South Asia and has also developed crucial infrastructure facilities in some of these. There is a need to look at these 'footprints' closely as these have major implications on the stability of South Asia.

Pakistan

Sino – Pak nexus has been dealt in detail in the preceding paras. However, the same as part of its string of pearls policy in South Asia is summarised in brief. CPEC has changed the complexion of emerging competitions in the region. Establishment of 'Gwadar Naval Port' in the Western Makran coast of Pakistan is just a small manifestation of the much larger relationship, which encompasses cooperation on a whole range of issues including supply of military equipment and nuclear weapon technology, as also close cooperation in the realm of foreign policy. Gwadar which is just 72 kms from Iran and 400 kms from the Strait of Hormuz, addresses major strategic concerns of China. The construction of port facilities by China at Gwadar and establishment of the 'monitoring post' have resulted in it being called, in certain circles, as the 'Chinese Gibraltar'. Presence of Chinese Naval ships and submarines at Gwadar is a cause of concern especially for India[27].

Myanmar

Myanmar[28] is a geo-strategic factor in the Asian political dynamics. It is located at the tri-junction of South Asia, Southeast Asia and East Asia, thereby, historically serving as a trade corridor. Most importantly, it also maps as a critical juncture between India and China, where it shares common borders with the two rising Asian giants - with a 1,643 kilometre border with India and 2,185 kilometre border with China. It acts as a land bridge for both the countries - for India's Northeastern states and Southern provinces of China. This geostrategic location has made Myanmar a strategic convergence point between India and China, through which they can expand their connectivity and cooperative links. In this context, India's concerns over Myanmar emerges from rising Chinese footprints in India's 'Look East' - whereby similar to Pakistan, Myanmar is perceived to be a Chinese proxy for balancing India in the region. While for China, Myanmar acts as a gateway to India's sphere of influence - the Bay of Bengal and the Andaman and Nicobar Islands. These factors contribute to India's rising security concerns as China's strategic interests in Myanmar pose serious threats to India's maritime and economic interests in the Indian Ocean. In this context, this paper maps out the growing Chinese presence in Myanmar and how it is impacting India's security interests.

In 2004, China signed an agreement with Myanmar for construction of a 1,250 km pipeline, connecting the Myanmar's deepwater port at Sittwe in the Bay of Bengal to Kunming in China. China has executed dredging projects across the Irrawaddy River in a concerted effort to reach the Bay of Bengal. China is also upgrading facilities in Great Coco Islands, which was leased in 1994, on the periphery of Andaman islands, besides improving facilities in ports of Hyangyi, Kyankpyu and Mergui to berth larger displacement vessels. Kunming, the capital of Yunnan Province is the strategic hub, enabling China to link these facilities inland by connecting Mekong and Irrawaddy Rivers, as well as roads and railways. China's strategic interests in Myanmar also include upgrading the airfields in Mandalay and Pegu, to facilitate landings of IL-76 aircraft. In 1992, China commenced the 'Great Mekong Sub Region Programme', with Cambodia, Laos, Myanmar, Thailand, Vietnam and its own Yunnan Province. The designated route identified was Kunming - Chiang Rai via Laos; Kunming - Chiang Rai via Myanmar and Kunming – Hanoi - Hai Phong, with Mekong River being the main artery for these inland waterways.

Sri Lanka

Hambantota Port lies 150 miles South East of Colombo. Major Powers in the world seem not to consider the Hambantota project; 80 percent of which has been financed by China; merely as an economic venture, given the geographical location of Sri Lanka. The country lies astride the major sea lanes of communication from Europe to East Asia and the oil tanker routes from the oil producing countries of the Gulf to China, Japan and other Pacific countries. In the military sense it is important to the US as these same sea routes are used for transference of naval power from the Pacific Ocean to the Indian Ocean and the Gulf. China's involvement in Sri Lanka has inevitably raised speculation that Hambantota is the latest jewel in its "string of pearls" that will pave the way for China's rapidly expanding navy to operate routinely in the Indian Ocean from secure bases in the region.[29]China has a burgeoning defence relationship with Sri Lanka, which includes provision of training facilities and major supplies of military equipment.

Construction of the port began in January 2008 with the aim of becoming Sri Lanka's largest port, after the Port of Colombo; serving ships travelling along the east-west shipping route which passes six to ten nautical miles (19 km) south of Hambantota. However, the Hambantota dream hasn't quite worked out as designed. It has so far contributed to a monumental debt trap that's rattled the country to its financial core and prompted a recent IMF bailout. Nearly the entire infrastructure built in Hambantota was done with Chinese money, bringing Sri Lanka's debt to over $8 billion. As a result in 2016, 80% share of the port was leased to 'China Merchants Ports' holding company in a debt-for-equity swap who will invest $ 1.12 Billion to revive the port under a Private-Public Partnership.[30] Mattala International Airport today is known as the world's emptiest because of the region's inability to attract passengers.[31]

However, Sri Lankan cabinet has decided to re-negotiate the deal with China as a result of the heated public controversy over the issue and also President Maithripala Sirisena's recent steps to subject the existing deal to a review.[32]

Bangladesh

China supplies 20% of its overall arms exports to Bangladesh.[33] However, it is not restricted to supply of military hardware alone. It also includes other diverse aspects like exploration of natural resources and connectivity between Kunming and Dhaka. The Chinese interest in the Chittagong Port, where extensive work is in progress to develop the harbour as a container port, are indicative of the Chinese intent of having extensive naval and commercial access in the region. The Belt and Road initiative is the formalisation of China's strategy for securing and bolstering their commercial trade routes, and Bangladesh is a major part of its maritime agenda.[34] China is also interested in the untapped natural gas of Bangladesh reserves estimated to be about 60 trillion cubic feet. Due to the close proximity of these reserves to Myanmar, China has commenced negotiations with Bangladesh, for a gas pipeline that will connect Sittwe to Kunming through Bangladesh.

Possible Motivations for China's Establishment of Strategic Footprints

China's Grand Strategy

China's grand strategy of achieving global pre-eminence in the long term envisages unrelenting pursuit of its economic interests, reducing its energy vulnerabilities and developing its military strength, to include enhanced strategic reach, while simultaneously, undermining its potential rivals and adversaries. The underlying message it probably wants to convey to countries located along its Asian SLOC is that China's influence in the region as a self-appointed guarantor of security should be preferable to that of the US. Also, China continues to establish its foot prints in energy and market rich nations, while simultaneously undermining US interest's and also appeasing Chinese nationalism in an effort to help the regime maintain its hold.

China's pro-active attempts to gain access to port and airfield facilities as also to forge a multi-faceted strategic partnership with countries the world over appear to be motivated it's One Belt One Road Initiative; and certain key considerations discussed in the succeeding paras.

Economic

Essentially, China's increased global influence and growing military might is economy driven. Maintaining high growth rates presents a tremendous challenge to the Chinese leadership, as they manage the turmoil of massive structural, technological and social changes in the country. China's biggest strategic concerns of regime survival, territorial integrity, and domestic stability are also inexorably linked to its economy. China's greatest strength and also its vulnerability is its economy, and therefore, form the centre piece of China's foreign policy and strategy. Hence, it is axiomatic that China would spare no efforts to protect its economic interests.

Energy Security

The quest for energy security remains a key consideration in China's strategic thinking. In the event of a war, or war-like situation, such as in the Taiwan Strait, China's energy security could be seriously threatened. This is especially true due to the fact that the US has relatively more effective power projection capabilities, which could block and control crucial SLOC, which are vital to meet China's energy needs. Vulnerability of the SLOC is perceived by China as a geo-political risk. Energy security has compelled China's foreign policy to forge new alliances, for ensuring security of its SLOC as it graduates towards upgrading its navy to a true blue water navy in the real sense.

Malacca Dilemma

Nearly 80% of China's oil imports and other trade items pass through the Straits of Malacca. The Strait of Malacca is considered by the Chinese as a crucial choke point that could enable the US to seize crucial geostrategic advantage, restrict China's growth, and control the flow of energy. The Chinese are apprehensive that the US and Japan could seal off the Straits as a coercive measure against China, if the need so arises.

US Footprints

China has devoted substantial attention to the security dilemma it faces due to the US naval presence in the region and its dominance of the high seas stretching from the Persian Gulf to the South China Sea. This is to be seen in context of the visible US foot prints along the first island chain emanating from Japan South ward – through the Philippines and the Indonesian archipelago to Diego Garcia and the second chain, which runs from Guam to Australia. The perceived threat to China gets exacerbated with the US attempts to gain major footprints in South Asia. This may be a crucial factor for establishment of bases by China, in order to secure its

SLOC and thereby secure its energy interests against an overwhelming US presence in the region.

Enhancing Power Projection Capability

The modernisation of the People's Liberation Army (PLA) is a tangible manifestation of China's growing national power. According to the US 2006 Quadrennial Defence Review, "China has the greatest potential to compete militarily with the US and field disruptive military technologies that could offset the traditional US advantage". PLA's modernisation efforts appear to be aimed specifically at combating US maritime forces, which might come to Taiwan's aid and at denying the US access to its regional military bases such as Japan and South Korea. The enhanced Chinese capability threatens not only Taiwan, and therefore the US, but also poses a challenge to the US allies throughout the Western Pacific, South East Asia and South Asia.

The India Factor

Sino-India relations have been steadily improving since the last decade. Geopolitical calculations have been the main drivers for the improved bilateral ties. However, it is obvious that China perceives that India's dominance in the IOR and its growing power potential could challenge China's supremacy in the long term. China is also concerned about India's possible geopolitical ambitions beyond the IOR, and views India's 'Act East Policy' as impinging upon its maritime interest. Chinese scholars perceive that India is currently focusing on economic cooperation, but could well expand its 'Act East Policy' into the political and security realms, at a later stage. The Chinese are of the opinion that Indo-ASEAN cooperation on counter terrorism, maritime security and transnational crime fighting are part of India's 'grand strategy' to dominate the IOR, particularly the Straits of Malacca.

Is there a Pattern to these Footprints?

Is there a 'String of Pearls' being Established?

An analysis of Chinese activities indicates that China, rather than awaiting empirical proof of its soft power strategy to gain influence in the IOR, has resorted to a more pronounced option of seeking access to geo-strategic facilities, thus projecting the possibility of a more vigorous future strategy. It is doing so by cultivating close relations with these countries. It is apparent that China's pattern of activities is not restricted to acquisition of bases and sea ports along its SLOC but also undertaking infrastructure development projects in these countries.

To that extent, the 'string of pearls' formulation does help in explaining the Chinese strategic interests and defining the motivations behind the strategy. It is obvious that the Chinese forays into West Asia, Africa, Iran, CARs and Latin America are linked to securing her energy requirements, as also to protect itself from US hegemony. It also appears that China is keen to develop alternate land routes to bypass the Malacca choke point in pursuit of her energy security. Further, based on the pattern of its activities in South Asia, it can also be argued that the Chinese string of pearls strategy appears to be aimed at India in addition to being part of its grand strategy aimed at challenging the US.

A Counter to the US?

The Chinese pattern could also be explained by its consideration of the US as the paramount threat to its energy security and economic stability. China has effectively engaged Africa, a region which it perceives as an alternate supplier of energy, more so in view of the unstable conditions in West Asia. In Iran, China has signed a 25 year deal to develop natural gas reserves, despite threats of US led sanctions due to Iran's nuclear programme. China views the quadrilateral alliance of the US, Japan, Australia and India as a major threat in the South China Sea and the IOR, and its securing footholds in the littorals could be aimed at countering this perceived threat. China views that the latent US-China competition will ultimately prompt the US to adopt a proactive strategy to contain China, which could be put into effect by controlling the SLOC. Possibly, this strategic competition has compelled China to establish relationships which extend from Latin America to Africa, West Asia, the IOR, South Asia and the CARs.

Containment of India?

The question that needs to be answered is whether China has any interest in containing India. Undoubtedly, the answer is in the affirmative, considering China's policies in the past, where, at one stage, it even stoked insurgencies in India's North East. Further, it has provided Pakistan much of the military and strategic resources with which it could confront India. It is also apparent that in the realm of foreign policy, China has always attempted to undermine India's role and status. Its efforts at negating India's quest for a permanent seat in the UN (in collaboration with Pakistan),obstruction to India's membership in the Nuclear Suppliers Group and prevention of Mazoor Azhar being declared a terrorist; are an indicator of China's deep rooted concerns about an emerging India. The pattern of China's activities in India's periphery and the IOR, indicates the possibility of a Chinese 'game plan' to contain and marginalise India's influence in the region. It appears that, by effectively engaging India's immediate neighbours diplomatically, economically and militarily, China aims to limit Indian influence in the IOR. Besides, China is wary of the growing Indo-US partnership, which it perceives has great potential to threaten China's national security. It is in this context that the `string of pearls' strategy could also be considered as India centric.

US Views on China's String of Pearls Strategy

China's Grand Strategy

The US perceives that China has identified three stages of planned development with a time horizon of 50 years. From 2000 to 2010, to double the GDP; from 2010 to 2020, double the GDP again, such that the GDP on per capita bases is expected to be US $3,000, and finally from 2020 to 2050, join the rung of advanced nations as a prosperous and modernised socialist country. China would then, claim to have achieved 'peaceful development'.

Peaceful Development

'Peaceful development' was a strategy adopted by China in the mid-1990s, to enable economic growth and modernisation, while mitigating the risk that other nations might perceive from China's rise as a threat.

The Chinese had realised that a multipolar world was not going to emerge at the end of the Cold War and that the US would remain preeminent as the global hegemon in a unipolar world. As such, China would be forced to operate in an environment where the US could frustrate its ambitions. China realised its weakness in fields of industrial capacity, force modernisation and technology, as compared to the leading nations of the world. The possibility of adverse international reaction to a rising China and the possibility of the US adopting a Cold War type of containment towards China was a cause of concern for a rising China. Moreover, tensions over Taiwan, in the backdrop of likely US intervention had to be catered for.

The US Dilemma

The US dilemma arises from the question whether China will become a 'responsible stake holder' in the existing international system or will it emerge as a disruptive, revisionist power, determined to alter the international equation to its advantage. Since 1988 China, has been articulating the emergence of a multipolar world in its 'new security concept', implying the end of US unipolarity. This new security concept is indicative of China's discomfort with the growing US alliances with Japan, Australia and other regional nations. The US views the concept as 'anti-US' rhetoric. Moreover, the increasing assertiveness of China in South and East China Sea, its ambitious 'One Belt, One Road(OBOR)' initiative, articulation of its 'China Dream', its unprecedented military modernisation and now the transformation of its military; have added to US concerns.

The Chinese Intent

Currently, China's military modernisation and power projection capabilities lag behind that of the US. However, China's latent and potential capabilities, when considered in the geopolitical context of East Asia, can pose serious problems for the US. If the 'string of pearls' is an effort at regional hegemony, then China is likely to pursue a patient, deft and subtle approach in this regard. Undoubtedly the US would be alarmed, if the 'string of pearls' results in states being forced to distance themselves from the US and gravitate towards China. China's relation with the so called 'rogue states' is also reflective of China's intentions in the regard. The US is visibly concerned of the intentions behind the modernisation drive of China's armed forces, especially the PLA Navy.

US-China Rivalry

Competitive pursuit of energy security may play an increasingly critical role in the US-China relationship, possibly eclipsing other major concerns like Taiwan and bilateral trade. From Sudan to Venezuela, both the US and China are competing for global resources in a tussle to remain the world's economic powerhouse. While China has identified the US as a 'paramount threat to its energy security and economic stability', the US perceives, that once China has established substantial control over Asian SLOC or developed alternatives, it may well move on to some of the world's key oil reserves, which may not be in the best interests of the US. Many in Pentagon are of the view and especially after the unfolding of OBOR initiative that, the "Chinese and have the tendency to see securing their energy security as a zero sum game", which will bring it into confrontation with US interests in the future.

US Perception of the Malacca Strait

The US views China's naval aspiration as vital to China's economic rise. It is in this context, that the US wants to control the strategic waterways from the Straits of Hormuz to the Malacca Straits, through which one third of the total world trade passes. The US continues its forward deployment of B-1B Lancer heavy strategic bombers on Guam[35], with additional aircraft carriers and submarines in the Pacific, as part of a 'hedge' strategy aimed at countering the Chinese 'string of pearls'. The US views the Malacca Straits as the centre of gravity for its strategy against China. If, hypothetically during a crisis, either power controls the Straits, then the other would suffer. China clearly has much to lose, with its economic clout clearly dependent on the oil imports and trade, which transits through the Malacca Straits. It is perhaps, in this context, the US has set up the Proliferation Security Initiative (PSI) and the Regional Maritime Security Initiative (RMSI) to patrol these waterways.[36] Thus, it may be assumed that the motive behind the US presence in the region, other than the stated objectives of fighting sea piracy and nuclear proliferation, could be to limit China's access to oil and raw material along the strategic maritime choke point of the Malacca Strait.

Rise of the Dragon

Since the last decade, China has indicated that it would use its veto power in the UNSC to buttress its minimalist agenda of national territorial integrity and sovereign claims, specifically related to its claim on Taiwan. Lately, China has shown confidence and resolve in using this veto power to safe guard its energy security as well. As a subtle, yet direct, hint to the US, China supported Iran in the standoff on the nuclear issue, and also expressed strong opposition to the sanctions against Sudan, by threatening to veto the US proposals on this issue.[37]It is challenging an emerging India's desire to be part of the coveted Nuclear Suppliers Group and has prevented Mazoor Azhar being declared a terrorist by the UNSC. These have added new dimensions to the Chinese approach, which earlier was confined to building bilateral political and economic relations, but now aims to undermine not only the US interests in the strategic spectrum but other emerging powers like India as well.

Strategic Highways

Apart from the various energy related relationships with Kazakhstan, Russia and other Central Asian nations, as part of OBOR China is building numerous new highways, connecting Xinjiang to major Central Asian markets and also giving it access to the Arabian sea through the China-Pakistan Economic Corridor (CPEC). When completed, these highways will connect Urumqi with Tashkent, Mashad (in Iran), Istanbul, and ultimately Europe and Xianjiang to Gwadar.[38] These developments have also to be viewed in the context of the emergence of SCO as a perceived counter to the NATO in the region.

Future Manifestations of China's 'String of Pearls' Strategy'

China could leverage its informal strategic alliances with countries that have granted it 'basing facilities', to counter-balance US power, check India's rise, monitor maritime activities, have access to markets, and more importantly, protect its SLOC. The 'string of pearls' would continue to aim at either bypassing the Straits of Malacca or identifying alternate avenues for oil and gas. The Chinese have also been aggressively acquiring blue water naval capabilities to protect its vital SLOC in order to secure her energy interests, while also aiming to keep the US at bay.

Snowballing the US

China while increasingly demonstrating its propensity to take risks, is likely to develop a 'hedging strategy' against the US to avoid military face off. It will continue to establish relations across the globe to safeguard its energy and trade interests. The Chinese strategy would aim at projecting itself as a 'peaceful global player', while marginalising US influence in CARs, Asia- Pacific, Latin America and Africa, and bide time till it can match the US militarily.[39] It is in this context that China has accorded the highest priority towards modernisation of its navy, the strategic forces and space capabilities.

Crystal Gazing for India

China is likely to continue to exert its soft power diplomacy with regard to India's neighbours and the littorals of the IOR, aimed at marginalising the Indian influence in the region. These engagements would also be aimed at enlarging its footprints in these countries to enhance the scope of its presence and influence in the region. It is envisaged that China is likely to continue her soft power strategy in the IOR as a counter to India's rising status as a regional and global power.

Fragility of the Pearls

China has undoubtedly established physical imprints in the IOR by providing monetary credit facilities, technological know-how and skilled workforce to set up infrastructural facilities, with the additional motive of utilising them to further its economic and security interests. However, China as yet, not forged any formal military alliance with these states, which will allow it to utilise these bases for 'forward deployment' of its forces in the military context. Given China's stated policy of 'opposing military alliances', as also 'following an independent foreign policy of peace and development', it is unlikely that China will forge overt alliances with these nations to use these bases to further its military strategic reach. The efficacy of these pearls, however, would be substantially enhanced and would increase the Chinese strategic reach, if these nations allow the Chinese to use these bases in the militarily context in the eventuality of a conflict involving China. However, this is not an assured outcome, as these nations have to safeguard their own security interests and would not like to be embroiled in a conflict with the US.

Strategic Reach?

Currently, the Chinese power projection capabilities are limited. However, major reforms and revamping is underway to enhance the strategic reach of the PLAN and PLAAF. It is however getting increasingly, feasible for China to deploy its naval assets in the IOR. It is in the process of honing up its skills in aircraft carrier operations making it a 'blue water navy' in the true sense. China's ability to sustain the logistic infrastructure of these so called 'bases' abroad, is debatable but it is aggressively pursuing the same through modernisation of its Navy and Air Force.

Conclusion

The China factor in the strategic stability of South Asia has become pronounced as China continues with its stated 'Peaceful Rise' while it continues to make strategic inroads in the region. It's 'higher than the mountains and deeper than the seas friendship' with Pakistan, a state known for abetting terrorism as part of its state policy, itself raises questions on the Chinese intentions. These concerns get further accentuated when seem in light of China's unprecedented military modernisation and transformation of its armed forces, its increasing assertiveness in South and East China sea. Growing nationalism and its desire to ruthlessly achieve its "China Dream" has made the world closely monitor the rise of the 'Dragon'. As far as India is concerned Chinese increasing footprints in its strategic neighbourhood as part of its 'String of Pearls' policy in an overall climate of mutual distrust are viewed with suspicion. Though the string of pearls policy on the look of it is primarily to serve China's economic aspirations and secure its energy needs; these are bound to have strategic ramifications in South Asia.

Undoubtedly, China perceives the US as a paramount threat to its energy security and economic stability, and has therefore adopted the 'string of pearls' strategy to safeguard the SLOC from the Persian Gulf to the South China Sea. It is likely that once China controls Asia's SLOC, it may move on to some of the world's key oil reserves, perhaps even replacing the US as Saudi Arabia's patron and protector. This would present a complex strategic situation, which could impact the future direction of China's relationship with its neighbours as well as the US. Overcoming the potential challenges and integrating China as a responsible stakeholder in the international arena is hence essential for future prosperity and security in South Asia, the IOR as well as the world at large.

Endnotes

1 (2016) "Deterrence by Design: Sino-Pak Strategic Cooperation in Gwadar". Accessed 11 Feb 2017 URL : http://southasianvoices.org/deterrence-by-design-sino-pak-strategic-cooperation-in-gwadar/

2 Small, Andrewl, "The China-Pakistan Axis: Asia's New Geopolitics" (London: C Hurst & Co Publishers Ltd, 2015).

3 (2016) "What to Make of China's Latest Meeting With the Taliban". Accessed 11 Feb 2017 URL : http://thediplomat.com/2016/08/what-to-make-of-chinas-latest-meeting-with-the-taliban/

4 (2016) "Council for Foreign Affairs Backgrounder on China – Pakistan relations". Accessed 13 Feb 2017 URL :   http://www.cfr.org/china/china-pakistan-relations/p10070, accessed 28 August, 2016

5 (2016) "China is the world's fastest-growing arms exporter—thanks to the nations surrounding India". Accessed 14 Feb 2017 URL : http://qz.com/621884/china-is-the-worlds-fastest-growing-arms-exporter-thanks-to-the-nations-surrounding-india/

6 (2016) "Satellite to be launched for monitoring CPEC projects" Accessed 16 Feb 2017 URL : http://www.dawn.com/news/1253323

7 (2009) "Why China Helped Countries Like Pakistan, North Korea Build Nuclear Bombs". Accessed 16 Feb 2017 URL : http://www.usnews.com/news/world/articles/2009/01/02/why-china-helped-countries-like-pakistan-north-korea-build-nuclear-bombs

8 (2016) "China moved N-missiles and launchers via Karakoram highway to Pak in 2005: Indian intelligence reports" Accessed 16 Feb 2017 URL : http://blogs.timesofindia.indiatimes.com/nandygram/china-moved-n-missiles-and-launchers-via-karakoram-highway-to-pak-in-2005-indian-intelligence-reports

9 (2016) "Chinese Dream". Accessed 18 Feb 2017 URL https://en.wikipedia.org/w/index.php?title=Chinese_Dream&oldid=723729046.

10 (2016) "One Belt, One Road". Accessed 16 Feb 2017 URL : https://en.wikipedia.org/w/index.php?title=One_Belt,_One_Road&oldid=732943554.

11 (2016) "The Grand Design of China's New Trade Routes" Accessed 20 Feb 2017 URL: https://www.stratfor.com/analysis/grand-design-chinas-new-trade-routes

12 (2016) "Pakistan Army chief promises firm crackdown on Uyghur militants to protect China-Pak corridor" Accessed 21 Feb 2017 URL : http://indianexpress.

com/article/world/world-news/pakistan-china-economic-corridor-army-chief-raheel-sharif-promises-firm-crackdown-on-uyghur-militants-2953525/

13 (2016) "China's Military Strategy" Accessed 22 Feb 2017 URL : https://i1.wp.com/news.usni.org/wp-ontent/uploads/2013/05/Liaoning-16-Chinas-first-aircraft-carrier.jpg?ssl=1

14 Naravane, Manoj (2015) "War Zone Campaign Doctrine- A Revisit". Accessed 24 Feb 2017 URL : http://www.claws.in/images/journals_doc/SW%20i-10.10.2012.71-79.pdf

15 (2016) "China's Road & Belt Initiative: Indian Perspective". Accessed 23 Feb 2017 URL : http://www.vifindia.org/article/2016/may/19/chinas-road-and-belt-initiative-indian-perspective

16 Mizokami, Kyle(2015) "A Look at China's Growing International Arms Trade". Accessed 25 Feb 2017 URL : https://news.usni.org/2015/05/07/a-look-at-chinas-growing-international-arms-trade

17 (2015) "Press release of ISPR". Accessed 26 Feb 2017 URL : https://www.ispr.gov.pk/front/main.asp?o=t-press_release&date=2015/4/21

18 (2016) "Press release of ISPR" Accessed 26 Feb 2017 URL : https://www.ispr.gov.pk/front/main.asp?o=t-press_release&date=2016/2/19

19 (2016)"Pakistani army chief assures full security for CPEC" Accessed 27 Feb 2017 URL : http://news.xinhuanet.com/english/2016-04/13/c_135274538.htm

20 (2016)"Chinese army spotted along Line of Control in Pakistan-occupied Kashmir". Accessed 27 Feb 2017 URL : http://timesofindia.indiatimes.com/india/Chinese-army-spotted-along-Line-of-Control-in-Pakistan-occupied-Kashmir-say-sources/articleshow/51380359.cms

21 (2016)"Chinese engineer and driver injured in Karachi separatist bombing" Accessed 01 Mar 2017 URL : https://www.theguardian.com/world/2016/may/30/chinese-worker-driver-injured-karachi-bombing-claimed-separatists

22 (2016) "Joint patrol along China-Pakistan border- People's Daily". Accessed 01 Mar 2017 URL : http://en.people.cn/n3/2016/0721/c98649-9089345.html

23 (2016) "Military and Security Developments Involving the People's Republic of China 2016" Accessed 01 Mar 2017 URL: http://www.defense.gov/Portals/1/Documents/pubs/2016%20China%20Military%20Power%20Report.pdf

24 Tiezzi, Shannon(2016) "It's Official: China's Military Has 5 New Theater Commands" [Online : web] Accessed 05 Mar 2017 URL : http://thediplomat.com/2016/02/its-official-chinas-military-has-5-new-theater-commands/

25 (2016) "India's Trade Deficit with China" Commands" [Online : web] Accessed 05 Mar 2017 URL :http://economictimes.indiatimes.com/news/economy/foreign-trade/indias-trade-deficit-with-china-jumps-to-53-billion-in-2015-16/articleshow/53492853.cms

26 (2016) "India, China to hold joint military exercise in Pune"[Online : web] Accessed 05 Mar 2017 URL : http://indianexpress.com/article/india/india-news-india/india-china-to-hold-joint-military-exercise-in-pune-4372291/

27 (2016) "Aware of Chinese submarine deployment at Balochistan's Gwadar port: Navy chief" [Online : web] Accessed 05 Mar 2017 URL : http://www.tribuneindia.com/news/nation/aware-of-chinese-submarine-deployment-at-balochistan-s-gwadar-port-navy-chief/331339.html

28 Jash, Amirita(2014) "China in India's 'Look East' - Myanmar: Strategic Interests and Security Concerns" [Online : web] Accessed 05 Mar 2017 URL : https://papers.ssrn.com/sol3/papers.cfm?abstract_id=2797128

29 (2016) "Hambantota in the eyes of major world powers"[Online : web] Accessed 05 Mar 2017 URL :http://infolanka.asia/government-and-politics/foreign-relations/hambantota-in-the-eyes-of-major-world-powers

30 (2017) "Magampura Mahinda Rajapaksa Port"[Online : web] Accessed 05 Mar 2017 URL : https://en.wikipedia.org/wiki/Magampura_Mahinda_Rajapaksa_Port

31 (2016) "Sri Lanka's Hambantota Port And The World's Emptiest Airport Go To The Chinese" Accessed 11 Mar 2017 URL : https://www.forbes.com/sites/wadeshepard/2016/10/28/sold-sri-lankas-hambantota-port-and-the-worlds-emptiest-airport-go-to-the-chinese/#6ce385ca4456

32 ibid

33 (2016) "China third largest weapons exporter, Pakistan main recipient" Accessed 11 Mar 2017 URL : http://www.hindustantimes.com/world/china-third-largest-weapons-exporter-pakistan-main-recipient/story-eiVUgDEKGKfdR7mAfA70PJ.html

34 (2016) "Bangladesh's Deep Sea Port Problem". Accessed 11 Mar 2017 URL : http://thediplomat.com/2016/06/bangladeshs-deep-sea-port-problem/

35 Gady, Franz-Stefan (2017) "The United States continues its forward deployment of B-1B Lancer heavy strategic bombers on Guam"[Online : web] Accessed 14 Mar 2017 URL: http://thediplomat.com/2017/02/us-air-force-rotates-supersonic-strategic-bombers-in-the-asia-pacific/

36 (2012) "Malacca Strait Cooperation"[Online : web] Accessed 14 Mar 2017 URL: http://www.marsecreview.com/2012/07/malacca-strait-cooperation/

37 (2016) "China Guarantees Support to Iran in 'Standoff Between Tehran, Washington"[Online : web] Accessed 14 Mar 2017 URL: https://sputniknews.com/world/201612091048372275-china-iran-sanctions/

38 (2015) "One Belt One Road' initiative"[Online : web] Accessed 13Feb 2017 URL : http://www.frontline.in/world-affairs/one-belt-one-road-initiative/article7098506.ece

39 (2014) "Hide your strength bide your time"[Online : web] Accessed 13Feb 2017 URL : http://www.aljazeera.com/indepth/opinion/2014/11/china-hide-your-strength-bide-y-201411198028498329.html

Chapter 8

Role of Major Powers in South Asia

"We sincerely hope that south Asian countries will respect and live in amity with each other, and achieve common development, and that south Asia will enjoy peace, stability and prosperity"

- Li Peng

Introduction

The strategic stability of South Asia, the land bridge between West Asia and Southeast Asia and Central Asia with the Indian Ocean is influenced in a major way by the global and regional geostrategic developments. This region has gained prominence due to reconfiguration of strategic transportation corridors and the Pan Asian Energy Grids running along both the flanks of Indian subcontinent. The Indian Ocean, which is termed as global maritime super highway, comprises 38 states (40 percent of the world's coastline) that beset fragile socio-political scenarios and multidimensional security challenges. Armed conflicts, nuclear brinkmanship, and the non-conventional threats propagated by state sponsored non-state actors complicate the security dynamics.[1] The uncertainties in Afghanistan post U.S. withdrawal, add yet another dimension to the regional security dynamics. Therefore, role of extra regional powers in South Asia to secure their own national interests is but natural.

In view of the above, the chapter will endeavour to take an appraisal of the role of extra regional powers namely the US, Russia and Iran in South Asia.

The United States of America

"South Asia is most dangerous place on the earth" The statement was made by President Clinton when he was going to visit South Asia in the year 2000 amply highlighting the growing importance of South Asia for the U.S. Before World War II, U.S. was not very much involved in this region but after the war its primary objective was to develop relations with the states of South Asia who came in to being all of a sudden after the end of World War II. After 1945 U.S. started to realize that South Asia comprised of 40 percent of the world population which could go the communist way. Main purpose of U.S. foreign policy towards South Asia is to achieve its global strategic and political goals. Its goals in the region are not shaped by the states of the region at large but how these states can be used to marginalize the influence of China and Russia.[2] An increasingly assertive China and resurging Russia pose a strategic challenge to the U.S. preeminence in the region.

Further the recent shifts in global power relationships, has made South Asia an important region not to ignore. The situation after September 11 and the Indo-U.S. strategic cooperation have changed the relationship pattern between U.S. and South Asia. Present involvement of the U.S. in Afghanistan and Pakistan, Indo-Pak rivalry, concerns about the proliferation of nuclear weapons, fight against terrorism, and the growing influence of China in the region have significantly increased the strategic importance of South Asia in the U.S. policy making circles.[3]

Thus seen in this context, today the U.S. policy interest is not anchored on a single set of issues - but on a set of core issues. These include counter-terrorism, Afghanistan, Pakistan (where counter terrorism, Afghanistan and non-proliferation communities converge), India (where commerce and diplomatic interests dominate), and the broader "rebalancing" towards Asia (where the greatest concern comes from China).[4] The U.S. is looking at a stable geopolitical order in Asia that is conducive to peace and prosperity and, by extension, the preservation of American pre-eminence internationally.[5] For this, extending America's rebalancing to include South Asia is not just important, but essential. South Asia matters because a stable, peaceful, and outward looking South Asia that joins East Asia's production networks will offer a counterpoint to China's economic predominance in the region and provide additional impetus and resilience to Asia's rise.[6]

U.S. and Afghanistan

U.S. is undoubtedly the most important player in Afghanistan. Successful transition as also stability in Af-Pak region will depend upon its policies in the region. U.S. has tried to improve the capacity and legitimacy of Afghan state and institutions, both military and civilian, as part of an overall effort to foster stability, reduce extremism and defeat Taliban.

In this regard, the U.S. interests in the region are based on the two pronged strategy. Firstly, fight against terrorism, the main reason for entering Afghanistan, the September 11 terrorist attacks on the U.S. soil, will remain the main motivation for continuing to engage with Afghanistan as long as there is possibility of return of international terrorists. Though, the U.S. does not face defeat in Afghanistan, but at the same time, there has not been any concrete political and military success so far.[7]

Secondly, to prevent a state failure. Today the U.S. is much more concerned about the possible effects of armed violence on the stability of Afghan state. The U.S. has worked to build Afghan government's capacity, legitimacy and good governance. In all these fields, progress has been significant, but not strategically decisive.[8]

Therefore as part of its strategy, in the last 10-12 years, U.S. diplomacy has followed military objectives leading to engagement with Taliban and Pakistan, relegating or neglecting engagement with India, China, Russia, Iran and Central Asian Republics; hindering regional cooperation. U.S. has decided to keep 8400 troops in Afghanistan through 2016.

The main challenges for the U.S. strategists remain shaping the future of Afghanistan, protect gains made in nation building, and preventing a return to civil war fueled by Afghanistan's neighbours as was the case in the early 1990 when the Soviet Union left Afghanistan. Today preserving a military stalemate in Afghanistan remains the biggest stumbling block to U.S. drawdown with increase in Taliban offensive and consequent loss of territory. U.S. today seeks greater role of regional stakeholders in Afghan reconciliation, albeit without losing strategic space in Afghanistan.[9]

U.S. and Pakistan

Pakistan since 1948, after the first Kashmir war, has consistently sought U.S. military assistance and ties to balance the Indian military superiority in the subcontinent. However, the U.S. interest in Pakistan remained limited during the early years. It was only by mid-1949, that some American strategists started viewing Pakistan with some military utility in balancing the Soviet Union through "the possibility of ideological and intelligence penetration of the U.S.S.R". With the election of Eisenhower to the presidency the new administration as part of 'Northern Tier Strategy' started building up the indigenous. defence capabilities of a number of "frontline states" such as Pakistan, Iran, Iraq and Turkey in order to contain the spread of Soviet influence.[10]

U.S. announced a military assistance programme for Pakistan in early 1954 and the same year, it joined the SEATO and CENTO alliance as part of Northern Tier strategy. In return for military aid and political support, Pakistan also allowed the U.S. to lease a military base in Peshawar for launching U-2 spy flights over the Soviet Union and to set up electronic listening posts. During the Eisenhower era, American efforts in Pakistan were explicitly concerned with the balancing (or containment) of Soviet and Chinese power and influence in the region.[11]

However, by the late 1950s, American military support for Pakistan began to slow down as the Congress repeatedly raised objections over the amount that Pakistan was receiving as military assistance and its utility as a bulwark against the Soviet Union. The election of Kennedy was viewed with dismay in Pakistan as Kennedy was known to have a "soft-spot" for India. The American reaction to the 1962 war between India and China also shocked and surprised the Pakistanis. The U.S. rushed military aid to India, while pressuring Pakistan not to take advantage of India's trouble. Pakistan, now increasingly distrustful of the American commitment, began turning to China to counterbalance India. After the 1965 war, U.S. military sales policy towards both the region in general and Pakistan in particular underwent significant changes. The policy of building up the Pakistan military was given up and a more neutral approach was adopted. The importance of the whole region was reduced in American strategy. Though there was a greater appreciation of India's power, stability and utility, which accompanied a more realistic and comparatively reduced place for Pakistan, there was little desire for involving India in American global strategy.[12]

However, Pakistan's pivotal geostrategic location came into prominence once again with Soviet invasion of Afghanistan. It was an imperative for the U.S. to contain the Soviet expansionism. Pakistan was indispensable for the U.S to finance and arm the Mujahideen engaged in fighting the Soviets. The prominence once again came to the forefront post 9/11, with 'Operation Enduring Freedom' wherein Pakistan's support was considered invaluable by the Americans.

However, with the drawdown of U.S. forces in Afghanistan and post Osama-bin-Laden's killing, there is lack of mutual trust between the two countries. Pakistan's continued support for resurgent militant groups hostile to the U.S. coupled with warming U.S. military and business relations with India, is sharply diminishing Islamabad's strategic importance as an ally to Washington.[13]

Pakistan too feels that it has been used by the Americans during the Afghan war and then abandoned, to deal with the aftermaths of U.S. policies, especially the increased militant movements on the Afghan-Pakistan border. There also a deep concern and anguish amongst the Pakistani media over continuing U.S. drone strikes, as they believed that these strikes were counter-productive in combatting terrorism.[14]

However, U.S. is able to neither ignore Pakistan nor abandon it. It continues to rely on Pakistan for its war in Afghanistan and appreciates that a failed Pakistan will be detrimental to its overall efforts towards regional stability. It is also a fact that U.S. will have to substantially depend upon Pakistan for its final withdrawal from Afghanistan, whenever it happens. Moreover, U.S. also feels that in the present circumstances with increasing Chinese influence in Pakistan a substantial hold is required to be maintained on Pakistan for strategic reasons.

Considering all these aspects U.S. is adopting a more conciliatory approach towards Pakistan. On the Afghan issue U.S. seems to agree with Pakistan on the overall role of Taliban and the Haqqanis in the peace reconciliation process. On the economic front, the assistance continues. However, the civilian and military aid to Pakistan, once the third-largest recipient of U.S. foreign assistance, is expected to total less than $1 billion in 2016, down from a recent peak of more than $3.5 billion in 2011. The decrease also comes amid budget constraints and shifting global priorities for the U.S., including fighting Islamic State militants, a resurgent Russia and an increasingly assertive China.[15]

The two countries have set out five strategic priorities to include Law Enforcement and Counterterrorism; Economics and Finance; Energy; Security, Strategic Stability, Non-Proliferation; and the Defence Consultative Group.[16] U.S. has offered technical assistance programme to support the development of Pakistan's domestic natural gas reserves and also U.S. support in key areas such as economic growth, agriculture, health, and education. U.S. plans to continue providing assistance and support, including training and equipment to Pakistan's military and security services, cooperation in regional maritime security, and to counter Improvised Explosive Devices (IEDs).[17]

U.S. and Bangladesh

A definitive Asia policy of U.S. is still being moulded, but its agenda will possibly include the Integration of the South Asian economy into Asian Strategy. It would try to counter Chinese inroads in South Asia and Middle East through an exclusive focus on economic and social development. Continuing with this policy Hillary Clinton's visit to Bangladesh in 2012 was an important landmark. Clinton declared the visit would "review robust U.S.-Bangladesh cooperation across the full range of political, economic and security matters".[18]

The primary objective of U.S. in Bangladesh has been defence cooperation, prevent its dependence on China and to augment Bangladesh's role in Bay of Bengal in congruence with India. As per Andrew Shapiro, U.S. assistant secretary in the bureau of political-military affairs stated, Bangladesh was also working through a military modernization plan, which includes looking to partners for affordable defense systems. This modernization effort provides an opportunity for U.S. to expand its security cooperation, especially through its 'Excess Defense Articles' program, making surplus equipment available to its partners.[19]

The most important agenda for the U.S. is to break the Chinese inroads into Bangladesh. Prior to Clinton's visit, China had agreed to give Bangladesh $1 billion of armament, which U.S. obviously wanted to, neutralize. The U.S. also stressed that "Bangladesh is a key player in maintaining security in the Bay of Bengal" and should cooperate with the U.S. to optimise opportunities within its maritime boundary and related developments to follow afterwards."[20]Clinton also urged Bangladesh to improve relations with India and Myanmar stressing, "Bangladesh is geographically situated to serve as a land bridge for trade between the dynamic Asia-Pacific region and the huge economic potential of South Asia."

However, U.S. is now getting increasingly concerned with the increase in the Islamist insurgency in Bangladesh. This if not checked may make the region vulnerable to Islamic fundamentalism and as such the civil society in Bangladesh has seen an upsurge in these radical activities. In a speech made by Secretary of State John Kerry on U.S.-Bangladesh relations at Dhaka on 29 August 2016, he clearly expressed his concern on the growing threat from Daesh and al-Qaida in Bangladesh referring to the 01 July 2016 Holey Artisan Bakery attack as well as clearly established linkages between other smaller scale attacks carried out in the last few months. These attacks were clearly designed to divide Bangladesh, and cut it off from the outside world.[21] The increasing inroad of international terrorist organisations within Bangladesh was an emerging challenge to the strategic stability of South Asia.

U.S. and Nepal

U.S. has a strong interest in helping the people of Nepal to overcome the serious political problems they face, and the developmental problems from which much of their current political crisis derives. U.S. wants Nepal to be a peaceful, prosperous and democratic country where civil liberties and human rights are protected. It also feels that preservation of the unique culture of the Himalayan Kingdom sandwiched between two regional giants is essential.

Increasing Chinese footprint in Nepal challenge U.S. influence in the country and is not conducive to its overall policy for South Asia especially when seen in light of growing U.S. and India bonhomie. Moreover, in the present geostrategic environment; Nepal with its political instability, economic turmoil, and porous borders can become a safe sanctuary for terrorists and other anti-national elements especially those with inimical intentions against India.

Therefore, keeping into view the above, the U.S. AID programs in Nepal seek to reinforce recent gains in peace and security, stabilize the transitional government, strengthen the delivery of essential social services, expand proven health interventions, and address the global challenges of food insecurity and climate change.[22] The U.S. AID is approximately $ 64 million. Post the earthquake U.S. pledged $130 million for recovery and reconstruction. U.S. through its International Military Education and Training (IMET) programmes has sought to develop Nepal's military's ability. The two countries also engage in joint military exercises. U.S. aims at bringing Nepal into the rebalancing matrix, thus trying to negate to some extent the overbearing influence of China. There exists adequate potential for India and the U.S. to align their approach to engage Nepal and limit its leanings towards China.

U.S. and India

The unprecedented economic growth and military modernisation of China is a cause of major concern for the U.S. These concerns have been further accentuated by China's growing assertiveness in South China Sea and its very well-articulated 'Chinese Dream' and it's 'Military Strategy'. Under mentioned Chinese activities in South Asia have major implications on the regions stability and in turn impact upon the U.S. interests.

- The 'One Belt and Road initiative', with particular reference to China Pak Economic Corridor.

- Increased activity in the IOR by constructing ports, establishing electronic intelligence facilities, and ship visits for securing the SLOCs.

- Strengthening Pakistan's nuclear and missile arsenals as well as making its overall military capabilities more robust.

- Enhancing military relations with Nepal by supplying arms and other defence equipment.

- Strengthening military cooperation with Myanmar by developing Myanmar's overland transport and maritime sectors.

- Enhancing defence cooperation with Bangladesh and Sri Lanka and developing strategic ports there and

- Intensify the efforts to make diplomatic relations with Bhutan normal.

U.S. views an emerging India as its lynchpin in South Asia to counter an increasingly assertive China. The two countries find themselves as natural partners sharing common views on a number of global and regional issues like proliferation of weapons of mass destruction, global war on terrorism etc. After nearly a decade of painstaking discussions, India and the U.S. signed Logistic Support Agreement, a landmark defence agreement that will increase the military cooperation between two of the world's largest democracies. The two countries look forward to increased strategic and regional cooperation, deepened military-to-military exchanges, and an expanded collaboration on defence technology and innovation.[23]

After several decades of Cold War era suspicion and chill, relations between India and the U.S. have transformed in the past decade with deepening commercial and strategic partnership after they signed the landmark civilian nuclear cooperation deal in 2008. U.S. today is the second largest defence equipment supplier to India with around $4.4 billion worth deals in the past three years. It is also India's most common partner in military exercises. [24]

Further, both countries can also work in areas where their interest conjoins like disaster response, humanitarian assistance, counter-piracy, and peacekeeping.[25]U.S. help, in the arenas of maritime domain awareness, space security, cyber warfare, electronic warfare, and ballistic missile defense, promise a dramatic increase in India's own military effectiveness which cannot be secured currently by autonomous Indian efforts. India could reexamine its policy on operational cooperation with the United States in light of its own larger strategic interest.[26].

Despite India-U.S. strategic partnership, there are issues of divergence like climate change, trade barriers, U.S. lenient stand on cross-border terrorism from Pakistan and transfer of high end military technology to India. These issues can be ironed out through astute diplomacy, as was the case in Indo-U.S. nuclear deal.

Counter Terrorism

The U.S. will continue to take an active approach in countering terrorism. It will monitor the threats arising due to the activities of non-state actors; work with allies and partners to establish control over ungoverned territories and directly strike the most dangerous groups and individuals when necessary.[27]Washington continues to have a strong strategic interest in ensuring that terrorist groups cannot once again use Afghan territory as a safe heaven[28]. U.S. will be maintaining strength of nearly 8400 troops in Afghanistan through 2016 keeping into view the renewed challenge from Taliban and other terrorist organisations. It will continue its presence in certain permanent bases to ensure its military presence in South Asia and continue its war on terrorism.[29]

Prevent Oceanic Hegemony

The IOR has become a critical hub for trade and energy transfers. The U.S. perceives a relatively wide range of potential threats to its interests in the IOR, ranging from state-based threats (such as from China and Iran) to non-state actors. There are numerous security concerns, ranging from SLOC protection to nuclear proliferation, to failed states.[30] U.S. perceives China as a significant strategic concern across the entire Indo-Pacific. Significant defence cuts in the coming years will result in the reduction of U.S. resources. The majority of this capability gap needs to be filled by U.S. friends and allies. This primarily means India, although there is a hope that Australia and others such as Indonesia can assume greater responsibilities for regional security.[31] Thus India is an important cog in its IOR strategy and U.S. has offered India a slew of incentives to strengthen strategic partnership and defense cooperation much to the discomfort of China. The U.S. wants to become a dialogue partner with the Indian Ocean Rim Association for Regional Cooperation. There is a great deal of optimism that India will work with the U.S. in providing security to the region through its bilateral and multilateral naval exercises because it is of Indian interest also to counter the growing presence of Chinese navy in the IOR. In conclusion it could be stated that U.S. will continue to shape the geostrategic space of South Asia through its wide military and economic policies in congruence with its friends and allies.

Russia

Despite the demise of Soviet Union, Russia with its huge landmass, ample natural wealth, a formidable military capability and rich human resources, retains the latent ambition of a great power status. Historically, Russia has been a staunch ally of India and erstwhile Soviet Union viewed South Asia through the Indian prism.

Nevertheless, in the present geopolitical environment the Russian national interests have changed. Countries like China and European Union figure more prominently in its Foreign Policy primarily due to economic reasons. Factors like growing Indo-U.S. relations and India's quest to diversify its military hardware suppliers has also impacted adversely the Indo-Russian relations. Russia realises, that if radical elements in Afghanistan are not controlled then this will have spill over effects in Central Asia and Caucasus which form its 'soft underbelly'. Russia is also interested in the South Asian energy corridor and given an opportunity; it would like to diversify its revenues by constructing various lucrative natural gas pipelines. Resurgent Russia under Putin has initiated focused policy decisions which could impact this region vastly. The strategic interests of Russia in South Asia and its relations with important players are discussed in the succeeding paragraphs.

Diversification of Energy Markets

Russia holds the world's largest proven reserves of natural gas and continually alternates with Saudi Arabia as the top oil producer. The country supplies a third of Europe's oil and natural gas and is starting to export more to the energy-hungry East Asian markets.[32] Russia also wants to expand its supply routes to South Asia through Central Asia. Russia views India as a privileged strategic partner, Afghanistan as an important neighbour and Pakistan as an emerging regional power.[33]

Implementing CASA-1000 (the construction of electric power line from Kyrgyzstan and Tajikistan to Pakistan via Afghanistan) is important for Russia because Russian companies are actively involved in its construction. Pakistan's geostrategic position serves as an important link for the energy corridor traversing through South, Central and West Asia. Russia supported Pakistan's bid to gain full membership of SCO along with India. Russia's decision to participate in creation of energy and transport corridors in the Eurasian region has far reaching geopolitical implications. Turkmenistan-Afghanistan-Pakistan-India (TAPI) pipeline, Iran-Pakistan pipeline and Central Asia-South Asia (CASA-1000) electricity projects can fundamentally alter the energy requirements of energy deficient states.[34]

Further, the rail-road transport corridor from Tajikistan to Pakistan, cutting across Wakhan Corridor, will ensure Russia and CAR countries getting access to Arabian Sea and Indian Ocean through Gwadar[35]. This will help Pakistan economically, giving it an access to Russian and CAR markets. Russia – Pakistan relations, however, will be largely shaped by how Pakistan acts post U.S. withdrawal from Afghanistan. If it continues to support terrorism then Russia-Pakistan relations will deteriorate but if Pakistan adopts a constructive approach then Pakistan can be an important link in a system of important trade and transport routes and gas and oil pipelines running across Central Asia to the Arabian Sea ports and onwards to the large Indian market.[36]

Supply of Military Hardware

Russia's position on the world arms market is very strong. Russian arms and military equipment are supplied to 88 countries of the world, 57 of them are regular customers. India continues to remain the largest importer of Russian armaments. This strategic partnership is largely based on the arms trade and nuclear energy projects. Russia is also diversifying its arms trade as it has recently announced its decision to supply MI-35 attack helicopters to Pakistan. The countries of South and South East Asia are allocating large funds to buy Russian armaments. The demand for Russian combat aircraft remains very high.

Counter Terrorism

The rising specter of Jihadi terrorism in Af-Pak region directly impacts Russia's national security. Pakistan, ISI-al Qaeda-Taliban combine have close linkages with Muslim radical organisations of Central Asia – Xinjiang and Caucasus. Resurgence of Taliban in Afghanistan will pose a direct security threat to Central Asia and fuel terrorist movements in Chechnya and Dagestan. Central Asia is termed by Russia as its southern security belt. It has deployed its troops in Tajikistan, established air bases in Tajikistan and Kyrgyzstan. Russia has also created Rapid Reaction Forces under the aegis of Collective Security Treaty (CSTO) and set up a regional anti-terrorist centre in Bishkek to combat terrorism. In the past Russia, Iran and India had supported Northern Alliance to fight against Taliban. Russia will be keen to support any regional security framework that can counter Taliban influence in the region.

Strategic Partnership with India

India and Russia have historically shared a multi-dimensional and strong partnership. During the Cold War, India and the Soviet Union (USSR) enjoyed a strong strategic, military, economic and diplomatic relationship. After the collapse of the USSR, Russia inherited the close relationship with India, even as India improved its relations with the West after the end of the Cold War.

The erstwhile Soviet Union and now Russia have stood by India on the issue of Jammu and Kashmir over several difficult decades, vetoing one sided UN Security Council resolutions many a times. The Indo-Soviet treaty of 'Peace, Friendship and Cooperation',[37] signed before the 1971 Indo-Pak War, stood India in good stead. Though, the agreement was not a military alliance, India was perceived by the US and its Western allies to have joined the Soviet camp.

India too has been a valuable partner for erstwhile Soviet Union and now Russia. Though opposed to Soviet Union's invasion of Afghanistan in December 1979, which brought the Cold War to India's neighbourhood, it chose not to condemn the invasion publicly.[38] India maintained diplomatic neutrality and ignored the Russian interventions in Moldova in 1991, Tajikistan in 1992, Georgia in 2008 and Ukraine in 2014. Similarly, India was closer to the Russian position on Iran's violation of its NPT commitments than to the US approach of imposing sanctions and holding out military threats.[39]

India and Russia share a 'Special and Privileged Strategic Partnership' built on five major components: politics, defence, civil nuclear energy, counter terrorism cooperation and space.[40] However, 'Defence Cooperation' has been the most enduring part and the pillar of this strategic partnership with approximately 60 to 70 percent of India's defence imports, still sourced from Russia. When India was being subjected to technology denial regimes, Russia offered strategic technologies to India. The erstwhile Soviet Union had sold hi-tech weapons and defence equipment to India at 'Friendship Prices' and on the basis of barter trade to help India save its scarce foreign exchange reserves.

The 'Special and Privileged Strategic Partnership' is also qualified by the 'Annual Summit' between the Heads of Government which has been unbroken for the last 16 years. The 17th Annual Summit was held at Goa on 15 October 2016 between PM Modi and President Putin.

The traditional 'Defence Cooperation' has the potential of reenergising the strategic bilateral partnership between the two countries. India's necessity of meeting its defence hardware requirements through indigenisation and 'Make in India' concept with Russia's imperative of reviving its 'Military Industrial Complex' have the potential of seamless synergy.

India and Russia share similar views on most matters of international concern. At a time when there exist fundamental differences between Russia and the West and apprehensions about China's growing assertiveness intensify; an emerging India probably remains one of Russia's most reliable partners on the global stage. For India, Russia is a long time tested friend which is a key pillar of its foreign policy.

However, Post-Cold War, despite the numerous issues of convergences between India and Russia, the international relations have undeniably been a litmus test for the bilateral relations between the two countries. With the emergence of a new international system, the foreign policies of both the countries have vacillated to explore new avenues of partnerships with other international players.

While defining the trends in the bilateral relations between the two countries, the strategic community has been questioning as to whether the relationship can remain as special and strategic as it had been in the past. Though in the National Interest, India has to diversify its engagements; an emerging India with regional and global aspirations can ill afford to lose its old time tested strategic partner in the prevailing geopolitical environment.

Relations with Pakistan

A Russian-Pakistani renaissance started in 2014 when the Kremlin removed its arms embargo against Islamabad. In 2015, Moscow agreed to sell four Mi-35M helicopters to Pakistan and welcomed Islamabad to join the Shanghai Cooperation Organisation (SCO).[41] It is not a secret that Russia is extremely alarmed by the growth of ISIS and a possible collapse of Afghanistan, to the extent that it is even ready to engage with the Taliban. Russia fears that radicalization of Afghanistan will lead to instability in its 'soft underbelly' in Central Asia and the Caucasus. By actively coordinating with Pakistan, Moscow should be able to halt the radical jihadists' future spillover to Central Asia. Therefore, Russia is trying to portray its own security concerns as the raison d'être behind the rapprochement.[42] Russia aims at strengthening Pakistan's anti-terrorism capacity to undertake operations in its north areas near Afghanistan. It needs Pakistan to fight the Taliban and other extremists. Russia also advocated the entry of Pakistan and India as permanent members of Shanghai Corporation Organisation (SCO).

However, Kremlin probably is also aiming at slowing down the impending downward trend of its relations with India and leverage its influence over New Delhi, by skillfully utilizing the 'Pakistan card'. By engaging with Pakistan, Russia leaves New Delhi with a hard choice: to honor its strategic commitment to Russia and make concessions or to observe Russian-Pakistani rapprochement, which could potentially erode India's military advantage.[43] However, the larger understanding between India and Russia has not been affected due to Russia's overtures to Pakistan as it is aimed at stabilizing Afghanistan, which is in Indian interests as well.

Iran

Iran enjoys pivotal geostrategic importance in the region in terms of continental bridge that connects Central Asia, West Asia and South Asia. It provides access to Russia, China, Central Asian States and Afghanistan to the warm water ports of Arabian Sea. Iran is strategically located near the Strait of Hormuz. It is a major source of energy and the epicenter of Shia Islam. Iran is a major player in the Middle East crisis and ongoing conflict in Afghanistan. The Iran nuclear issue and the ongoing West Asia criseshas brought Iran at the center stage of global geopolitics.

Strategic Interest

- **Diversification of Energy Markets**

  South Asia is an energy starved region which offers Iran a major opportunity to supply oil and gas to the regional countries, mainly India. Iran is one of the main energy suppliers to India and the energy cooperation between India- Pakistan and Iran could increase if the Iran- Pakistan – India gas pipeline becomes a reality.

- **Access to Central Asia and Afghanistan**

  With the completion of North- South Corridor and Chahabhar-Zaranj-Delaram projects, Iran will become the major transit hub of commerce and trade between the Indian subcontinent-Afghanistan and Eurasia.

- **Security in Afghanistan**

  Iran is a major stakeholder in the security of Afghanistan. Post 2014, after the U.S. withdrawal, Iran together with India, Central Asian States, Russia and China can play a major role in the security and economic reconstruction of Afghanistan. However, given its close relations with Pakistan and some elements of Taliban, it could seek a rapprochement with a new regime as long as its interests are protected.

- **Balancing Saudi Arabia**

  Saudi Arabia enjoys close relations with Pakistan and supports adherents of Wahabi- Salafi ideology in Afghanistan. Increased Saudi influence in South Asia is perceived contrary to Iran's Shia ideology. Building good relations with South Asian countries and Shia Diasporas is yet another strategic objective of Iran.

- **Ending Diplomatic Isolation**

  With the easing out of economic sanctions post Iran – U.S.nuclear agreement, the region provides Iran multitude of opportunities to build multi-dimensional, politico-diplomatic and economic relations with regional countries.

Endnotes

1   Admiral D K Joshi(2013) "Role of Indian Navy in Maintaining Peace in Indian Ocean Region"[Online: web] Accessed 21Nov 2016 URL:http://www.idsa.in/keyspeeches/RoleofIndianNavyinMaintainingPeaceinIndianOceanRegion_CNS

2   Alamgir Mohammad(2011) "America's Interests in South Asia [Online: web] Accessed   21Nov 2016 URL: https://muhammadalamgir.wordpress.com/2011/08/19/america%E2%80%99s-interests-in-south-asia/

3   Rajagopalan, Rajesh(2000) "U.S. Policy towards South Asia :The Relevance of Structural Explanations" Online: web] Accessed 21Nov 2016 URL:http://www.idsa-india.org/an-mar00-1.html

4   Evans, Alexander(2012) "The United States And South Asia After Afghanistan [Online : web] Accessed 21Nov 2016 URL:http://asiasociety.org/files/pdf/as_U.S._southasia_exec_sum.pdf

5   Tellis, Ashley J(2005) "The U.S.-India ''Global Partnership": How Significant for American Interests?" [Online: web] Accessed 21Nov 2016 URL:http://carnegieendowment.org/2005/11/16/u.s.-india-global-partnership-how-significant-for-american-interests-pub-17693

6   Nehru, Vikram(2013) "The Rebalance to Asia: Why South Asia Matters" http [Online : web] Accessed   21Nov 2016 URL::://carnegieendowment.org/2013/03/13/rebalance-to-asia-why-south-asia-matters-pub-51197

7   Gojree, Mehraj Uddin (2015) "The U.S. Interests and Policies towards South Asia: From Cold War Era to Strategic Rebalancing" [Online : web] Accessed 03 Oct2016 URL: http://www.isca.in/LANGUAGE/Archive/v2/i4/2.ISCA-RJLLH-2015-017.pdf

8   ibid

9   (2016) "Enhancing Security and Stability in Afghanistan"   [Online : web] Accessed 03 Oct2016 URL: http://www.defense.gov/Portals/1/Documents/Enhancing_Security_and_Stability_in_Afghanistan-June_2016.pdf

10 Rajagopalan, Rajesh(2000) "U.S. Policy towards South Asia :The Relevance of Structural Explanations" [Online:web] Accessed 21Nov 2016 URL:http://www.idsa-india.org/an-mar00-1.html

11 ibid

12 ibid

13 Ali ,Idrees (2016) "U.S. aid to Pakistan shrinks amid mounting frustration over militants" [Online: web] Accessed 22Nov 2016 URL: http://www.reuters.com/article/U.S.-U.S.a-pakistan-aid-idU.S.KCN1110AQ

14 Rajagopalan, Rajesh(2000) "U.S. Policy towards South Asia :The Relevance of Structural Explanations" [Online: web] Accessed 21Nov 2016 URL:http://www.idsa-india.org/an-mar00-1.html

15 Ali ,Idrees (2016) "U.S. aid to Pakistan shrinks amid mounting frustration over militants" [Online: web] Accessed 22Nov 2016 URL: http://www.reuters.com/article/U.S.-U.S.a-pakistan-aid-idU.S.KCN1110AQ

16 (2013) "Joint Statement by President Obama and Prime Minister Nawaz Sharif"[Online : web] Accessed 22Nov 2016 URL:https://www.whitehoU.S.e.gov/the-press-office/2013/10/23/joint-statement-president-obama-and-prime-minister-nawaz-sharif

17 ibid

18 Barrister Harun Ur Rashid (2012)"Clinton's visit to Bangladesh: A long-waited one"[Online : web] Accessed 22Nov 2016 URL:http://www.thedailystar.net/news-detail-232748

19 Shapiro, Andrew J (2012) "Talks With India and Bangladesh"[Online : web] Accessed 22Nov 2016 URL:http://www.state.gov/t/pm/rls/rm/188522.htm

20 Barrister Harun Ur Rashid (2012)"Clinton's visit to Bangladesh: A long-waited one"[Online : web] Accessed 22Nov 2016 URL:http://www.thedailystar.net/news-detail-232748

21 Kerry, John (2016) "U.S. – Bangladesh Partnership" [Online : web] Accessed 22Nov 2016 URL: https://bd.U.S.embassy.gov/u-s-secretary-state-john-kerry-delivers-speech-u-s-bangladesh-relations/

22 (2016) "Nepal" [Online : web] Accessed 22Nov 2016 URL: https://www.U.S.aid.gov/nepal

23 (2016) "How U.S. Scored Landmark Military Agreement With India: Foreign Media" [Online : web] Accessed 22Nov 2016 URL: http://www.ndtv.com/india-news/india-U.S.-deepen-defense-ties-with-landmark-agreement-1452220

24 ibid

25 S. Amer Latif (2012) "U.S.-India Defense Trade: Opportunities for Deepening the Partnership", [Online : web] Accessed 22Nov 2016 URL: https://csis-prod.s3.amazonaws.com/s3fs-public/legacy_files/files/publication/120614_Latif_U.S.IndiaDefenseTrade_Abbreviated_Web.pdf

26 Tellis, Ashley(2013) "Opportunities Unbound .Sustaining the transformation in U.S.-Indian Relations" [Online : web] Accessed 22Nov 2016 URL: http://carnegieendowment.org/2013/01/07/opportunities-unbound-sU.S.taining-transformation-in-u.s.-indian-relations-pub-50506

27 S. Amer Latif (2012) "U.S.-India Defense Trade: Opportunities for Deepening the Partnership", [Online : web] Accessed 22Nov 2016 URL: https://csis-prod.s3.amazonaws.com/s3fs-public/legacy_files/files/publication/120614_Latif_U.S.IndiaDefenseTrade_Abbreviated_Web.pdf

28 ibid

29 Auken, Bill Van(2013) "Permanent U.S. Bases in Afghanistan" [Online : web] Accessed 22Nov 2016 URL: http://www.globalresearch.ca/karzai-reveals-us-plan-for-permanent-afghanistan-bases/5334680

30 Brewster, David (2012) "U.S. strategic thinking about the Indian Ocean" [Online: web] Accessed 22Nov 2016 URL:https://www.lowyinstitute.org/the-interpreter

31 ibid

32 **Lauren Goodrich and Marc Lanthemann** (2013) "The Past Present and Future of Russian Energy Strategy" [Online : web] Accessed 22Nov 2016 URL:**https://www.stratfor.com/weekly/past-present-and-future-russian-energy-strategy**

33 Topychkanov, Petr (2016) "Russian policy on India and South Asia"[Online : web] Accessed 22Nov 2016 URL:http://carnegie.ru/2013/02/27/russian-policy-on-india-and-south-asia-pub-51283

34 ibid

35 Radyuhin, V (2010) "Changing face of Russia-Pakistan ties" " [Online : web] Accessed 22Nov 2016 URL:http://www.thehindu.com/opinion/lead/changing-face-of-russiapakistan-ties/article621447.ece

36 Bakshi, Jyotsna(2014) "Russian Policy Towards South Asia" " [Online : web] Accessed 22Nov 2016 URL: http://www.idsa-india.org/an-nov9-9.html

37 (2011) "The Indo-Soviet Friendship Treaty and its Legacy" [Online : web] Accessed 22Nov 2016 URL:http://www.mainstreamweekly.net/article2989.html

38 Bakshi, Jyotsna(2014) "Russian Policy Towards South Asia" " [Online : web] Accessed 22Nov 2016 URL: http://www.idsa-india.org/an-nov9-9.html

39 (2016)"Russian Approach to Iran Nuclear Programme" [Online : web] Accessed 22Nov 2016 URL:http://www.rusemb.org.uk/in4b/

40 Sajjanhar, Ashok "India and Russia — special and privileged strategic partnership" [Online : web] Accessed 22Nov 2016 URL: http://www.orfonline.org/expert-speaks/india-and-russia-special-and-privileged-strategic-partnership/

41 Frolovskiy, Dmitriy(2016) "What's Behind Russia's Rapprochement With Pakistan?" [Online : web] Accessed 22Nov 2016 URL: http://thediplomat.com/2016/05/whats-behind-russias-rapprochement-with-pakistan/

42 Frolovskiy, Dmitriy (2016) "What's Behind Russia's Rapprochement With Pakistan?" [Online : web] Accessed 22Nov 2016 URL: http://thediplomat.com/2016/05/whats-behind-russias-rapprochement-with-pakistan/

43 ibid

Chapter 9

Strategic Stability in South Asia: Options For India

"New norms never enter a normative vacuum but instead emerge in a highly contested normative space"

- Finnemore and Sikkink

Introduction

South Asia despite its historical, cultural and economic linkages does not have a shared security perception. The region has seen partition, large scale migration, wars, and great games of the Great Powers in a short span of time. India realised in the early 1990s that a paradigm shift was called for if it had to play an important role in the international arena. The success of India's economic reforms, with marked improvement of relations with US and the West and its outreach via its "Act East" policy has given a new direction and impetus to India's global outlook, which has profound effect on the geopolitics of the Indian subcontinent and its extended neighbourhood.

As per PM Modi, India is presently at an exciting moment of change, with a high tide of hope and optimism in the country with new levels of international confidence. India has become the fastest growing major economy in the world. In an interdependent world, India's transformation is closely linked with its international partnerships and   so is its security. Today across the world, India is seen not just as a new bright spot of the global economy but also as an anchor for regional and global peace, security and stability. Therefore, India's responsibilities are no longer confined to its borders and coastlines; but extend to its interests and citizens, spread across the world. It is but natural that as India's security horizons and responsibilities extend beyond its shores and borders; it must prepare its forces for range and mobility." [1]

India's strategic vision is in natural harmony with our traditional character as a peaceful, responsible nation that has abjured aggression and played a constructive, mainstream role in international relations. Moreover, India is a multicultural democracy on the path of rapid economic growth and it is but natural that as it grows economically and technologically, gets to harness the demographic potential of its people and spread the soft power of its culture and values with no extra territorial ambitions and no desire to transplant its ideology on others; it will a play a significant role in the emerging world order.

The recommended outlook for India towards regional stability is discussed in the subsequent paras.

Emerging India: Relatively Stable yet Vulnerable

An emerging India continues to face myriad socio-political, religious and ethno – regional fault lines. Good governance, inclusive growth, dealing with the Left Wing Extremism, containing proxy war in Kashmir and pan India terrorism are the major internal security challenges faced by India.

The primary reason for these challenges is lack of or no political consensus in a democratic India on national security issues. For instance, there is no consensus on how to treat challenges from Pakistan and China. The government's policies on these issues have fluctuated. To give another example, there is little agreement on how to deal with Maoism. Similarly, the views of political parties on Kashmir and insurgencies in the North East differ widely.[2]But interestingly, in South Asia, India is the only state that has witnessed democratic rise, economic growth and overall relative internal stability.

However, the strategic community feels that to sum up, India lacks a strategic culture with absence of a well-defined long term national security strategy. There is no common understanding among various segments of the government of what national security constitutes. Definitely, India needs a National Security Strategy urgently. The world is changing very fast.

New security challenges have arisen. In the absence of a coherent strategy, the government's responses will remain ad hoc and partial which may prove costly.[3] There is urgent need to build a broad political consensus on national security issues. An official National Security Strategy document, for the next 10 years, is urgently needed. This will help clarify confusion over national security matters and consolidate government's responses. More important, it will generate informed debate which may help build consensus.[4]

Anyhow India is demonstrating a strong desire to play a proactive role in South Asia. The Invitation to SAARC leaders at the swearing-in ceremony of PM Modi indicates the same. PM Sheikh Hasina's visit to N Delhi in April, 2017 her gesture to honour the war veterans of '1971 Liberation War of Bangladesh' acknowledging India's role, reflects a new dynamic role of India emerging in South Asia.[5]

Moving beyond the neighbourhood, India engaged all major powers with PM Modi visiting all P-5 countries as well as Japan and Germany. India's 'Act East Policy' manifested itself in the deepening of economic and strategic partnerships with ASEAN Countries and the extended East Asia region. India's relations with West Asia, home to over 7 million-strong Indian diaspora and the source of over 70 per cent of the country's oil imports, moved into an upward trajectory. India showcased its deep desire for integration with the African continent by hosting the third India-Africa Forum Summit in October 2015 by inviting all 54 African countries.

India's "Connect Central Asia" policy too moved upwards with PM Modi visiting all five Central Asian states in July 2015, sending a strong message on the importance of building on India's civilizational links with this resource rich, strategically located region. The likely hood of an early operationalisation of International North South Transport Corridor will substantially increase economic activities between India and the resource-rich Russia as well as markets of Europe.[6]

India also revitalised its Latin American and Caribbean ties. Similarly, in the Pacific, PM Modi visited Fiji to attend the first meeting of the Forum for India-Pacific Islands Cooperation (FIPIC). Apart from bilateral diplomatic engagement, India is having a robust engagement in the world's leading multi-lateral forms to include UNGA, G-20, BRICS, SCO, ASEAN and EAS, and COP21 in Paris.

Strategic Choices for India

In the emerging geopolitical environment India has to make some strategic choices. It will have to accept a China driven South Asia if its economy does not grow to a level wherein it positively impacts the country's Comprehensive National Development (CND) and acts as a deterrent to China. Moreover sustained CND for India is vital to economically and diplomatically influence its neighbours. In this scenario it is but natural that China's gravitational pull in South Asia and the Sino-Pak nexus against India will see an increase. China will dominate the strategic space of South Asia and India will have to accept it, since it will lack power and resources to maintain its influence in the region. This would seriously undermine India's stature as a regional power and an emerging global player. Indian neighbours, in such a scenario, will ally with China to maximise their national interest.

US would continue to remain an important player in South Asia. It considers India as a lynchpin in its 'Asia Pivot Strategy' for containing China. Therefore, the common strategic objectives have brought the two countries closer to each other in a strategic partnership, much to the discomfort of China and also somewhat Pakistan. However, regional stability demands that both India and China take steps towards enhancing mutual trust and tide over the issues of divergence through peaceful negotiations. Therefore, India has to decide for itself whether it is in its interest to allow itself to become the linchpin of the US Asia Pivot Strategy? Will China be deterred from such a move and seek rapprochement with India, or will such a strategic move irk China and its hostility towards India will grow further? Will the US risk its relations with China if there is a standoff between India and China? India would be constrained to accommodate the US interests in the Asia-Pacific and would be seen as a pawn of US in its neighbourhood resulting in a loss of influence.

India has followed the non-alignment policy in its foreign affairs. India is too big a country to come under the tutelage of any external power. Therefore, it has to develop her CNP, attain credible deterrence on her own and also seek interest based strategic alignments with the US, East Asian and ASEAN countries, while working towards a multi-polar Asia, interlocking India's collaborative security and economic interest(s) with those of the western world. This is essentially a strategy of necessity and seeking cooperative relations and an attempt to maintain her own position and relevance in the tilting balance of power in Asia. This strategy demands sustained internal development, astute and pro-active diplomacy and credible deterrence capabilities. This will enhance India's prominent role in South Asia and force the South Asian nations to maintain a balance between India and China.

Politico-Diplomatic Measures

Internal Focus

Domestic geopolitics plays an important role in the conduct of foreign policy in any country especially the democracies. The cases in point are fiery debates over 123 Nuclear Agreement, FDI in the retail sector, resolution of disputes on the border settlement, water sharing and illegal migrations with Bangladesh, Tamil ethnicity factor in bilateral relations with Sri Lanka etc.[7] Increasingly regional parties are playing a larger role in the foreign policy making and therefore there is a need to evolve a mechanism to ensure that the legitimate concerns of the state are addressed before making a foreign policy initiative.

India's free and extremely vibrant media both electronic and social has over a period of time started playing a very important role in shaping public perceptions which at times adversely impacts the country's foreign policy. Therefore, it is an imperative that a theme for the media is conjointly worked out by the media houses and the Public Diplomacy division at the MEA. This will result in an enlightened steering process with informed discussions on India's foreign policy initiatives thus increasing people's awareness and educating them on issues of national concern; thus facilitating public consensus.

Apart from the above it is essential that the shortage of diplomatic cadre is made up to augment the overall strength of India's foreign policy apparatus. Induction of officers from the Armed forces, who by the nature of their job, training and exposure do demonstrate a flair for these assignments, should be undertaken. Conceptualisation, planning and completion of important projects in a time bound manner is absolutely essential to enhance our credibility in terms of deliverance, particularly in the eyes of smaller neighbouring countries who look up to India for assistance and support.

External Focus

Geopolitical and strategic centrality mandates that an emerging India defines the destiny of its smaller neighbours by creating an India-centric South Asia. India should ideally emerge as a net security provider, a fulcrum of regional economic integration and as a lucrative socio-political and economic role model for other   South Asian States.

India has to balance the great power aspirations in the region by getting into strategic partnerships; albeit without losing focus on its strategic autonomy. India should take a lead in creation of new forums and steering the existing institutions to face the non-traditional security issues in South Asia, like climate change, pandemics etc. Initially India should forge consensus on these issues bilaterally with each of the South Asian countries to create a favourable public opinion.

However, it is increasing Chinese economic footprints in India's immediate neighbourhood, which have long-term strategic ramifications. It is challenging India's traditional sphere of influence and threatens to wean away these countries into Chinese orbit and need an appropriate response. The neighbouring countries themselves too use the Chinese card against India both as leverage and a hedge. Further, nationalist sentiments continue to present a challenge. However, India while continuing with its endeavours, being the status quo power should not worry too much about the highs and lows in its relations with its neighbours. While it should genuinely invest at regional integration and development, it should not shy away from behaviour correction of these sovereign states by exercising influence in their domestic politics.

In order to achieve a strategic balance India has come up with its 'Neighbourhood First Policy' to seek congruence between legitimate aspirations of the countries in our neighbourhood with India's abiding strategic objectives. Towards this end, a comprehensive collective approach has been articulated for positive engagement to include political and diplomatic priority, provision of support in the form of resources, equipment, and training, greater connectivity and integration and promotion of a model of India-led regionalism with which its neighbours are comfortable.

The other areas of focus of the Modi government's foreign policy are to leverage international partnerships to promote India's domestic development, ensuring a stable and multipolar balance of power in the Indo-Pacific; "Act East", dissuading Pakistan from supporting terrorism and advancing Indian representation and leadership on matters of global governance.[8]These are logical initiatives in the right direction and need to be pursued with vigour.

The traction of the policy is evident from the regular leadership meetings in India and on the side-lines of multilateral summits. India's support to Nepal during the 2015 Earthquake; completion of the land boundary agreement and improvements in energy connectivity with Bangladesh; the BBIN initiative; South Asia satellite and enhanced economic activity are a few examples which highlight India's intent. However, these concerted efforts have so far had mixed results. Bangladesh and Bhutan have clearly been positive stories for India while ties with Sri Lanka have proved a mixed bag and Maldives more difficult. But the regional outlier has been Nepal, which has been the most vexing foreign policy problem facing the Indian government over the past year.

To this end, success of India's 'Connect Central Asia' policy, 'Act East Policy' and proactive engagement with Myanmar, Bangladesh, Maldives and other IOR littorals is paramount to maximise our options and consequent politico-economic and diplomatic influence. An emerging India's strategic autonomy has ensured that it can simultaneously engage with US and Russia in bringing synergy in their South Asia outlook.

Certain country wise specific recommendations/suggestions are discussed in the subsequent paras.

Afghanistan

Af-Pak region has infamously come to be known as an epicentre of international terrorism. Biggest challenge emanates from Pakistan in form of state sponsored cross border terrorism directed towards Afghanistan. Resurgence of Taliban, a weak polity marred by corruption and an armed forces struggling for capacity and capability development further accentuates the issue. Though debatable, scenarios that could range from virtual Taliban rule in Pashtun belt or a simmering civil war degenerating into balkanization of the country along ethnic lines cannot be ruled out.

The strategic importance of Afghanistan for India cannot be understated. Afghanistan is an important buffer against the rising menace of Islamist crescent. Like Iran, Afghanistan is essential to India's "Connect Central Asia Policy", energy security and fight against Jihadi terrorism. Resurgence of Taliban in Afghanistan and an apparent consolidation of China - Pakistan nexus is a major challenge for India's strategic objectives in the region.

India is playing a significant role in reconstruction of Afghanistan and enjoys good-will of majority of the population. However, the question to be asked is whether this is enough? The problem is despite the world knowing Pakistan's complexity in the overall imbroglio still finds Pakistan invaluable in their efforts to fight the war in Afghanistan. India has to remember that it is only Afghanistan and India which are suffering from Pakistan's policy of state sponsored terrorism. To that extent India has failed to expose Pakistan in a way that it is forced to mend its ways.

The rise of IS in Afghanistan and the belief of Russia, China, Iran and Pakistan that Taliban could be a counter to its rise and hence needs to be courted; is a dangerous development, much to India's discomfort. The development has portends to change the dynamics of the ongoing war against terrorism in the region. While it will marginalise the writ of the legitimate government in Afghanistan it will further strengthen Pakistan's role despite its track record. India has to use its influence with Russia and Iran to prevent their courting with Taliban while it has to work with US to keep the larger dynamics and mistrust between Russia and US over Syria out of Afghanistan imbroglio.

Further, India has to realise that it will gradually lose out on its traditional strategic space in Afghanistan to other regional players if it does not substantially increase its footprint in Afghanistan both for security and development projects. India, a major stakeholder in peace and development in Afghanistan; which sees early fructification of energy and trade corridors from Central Asia via Afghanistan and Iran to South Asia, can ill afford to do so.

India should take comprehensive measures to strengthen the democratically elected regime in Afghanistan and take a lead role in creating a regional collaborative security framework in conjunction with Central Asian States, Iran, Russia and even China. However, this is possible only if India is prepared to exercise some robust military diplomacy initiatives. The Indian policy makers need to consider an enhanced role for the Indian Armed Forces in Afghanistan for capacity and capability building of its armed forces without boots on grounds in the actual sense. Embedding of trainers and advisors alongside the US and NATO forces is one such example which could be considered. Another could be transfer of Russian origin weapons and equipment to ANDSF for its capacity building in consultation and cooperation with Russia. This will also help bring Russia and India closer with cooperation on Global War on Terrorism in the real sense.

An enhanced presence of security personnel in Afghanistan will also serve as a confidence building measure for the Indian investors, businessmen and entrepreneurs who shy away due to security dilemmas. Enhanced Indian endeavours coupled with largely accepted peaceful and well-meaning credentials of India can help bridge gaps between regional as well as extra regional stakeholders. Bilaterally, enhanced Indian influence in Afghanistan may to some extent give certain spin offs in its relations with China and Pakistan as well.

A sustained Indian influence will also drive a wedge in Pakistan -China nexus and at the same time shape the strategic space in Afghanistan to perpetuate a two front dilemma for Pakistan. Keeping the contested status of "Durand line" and aspirations of Pashtun homeland alive will ensure that Pakistan's military remains embroiled on its western front. This is necessary to create an imbalance in Pakistan military on its western posture border and mitigate own two front dilemma. To sum up, though there are no two opinions that India's present soft power approach in Afghanistan has been in the right direction; it probably now needs to become more bold and robust in synch with the other players in the region.

Pakistan

Pakistan is in the mid of a serious internal crisis. Sunni and Shia sectarian conflict, secessionist movements in Baluchistan and Khyber–Pakhtunkhwa and rising spectre of Jihadi violence are threatening the very existence of Pakistan as a viable nation state. This harsh reality compelled Pakistan to embark upon a major counter insurgency campaign (Zarb-e-Azb) against Tehrik-e-Taliban of Pakistan (TPP) and other militant groups linked to al-Qaeda on June 15, 2014. As per Pakistan the operations resulted in more than 3,500 militants being killed, around 490 soldiers losing their lives, destruction of 992 militant hideous, confiscation of 253 tonnes of explosives, dismantling of 7,500 bomb factories, removal of 2,800 mines and recovery of 3,500 rockets and mortars during the first two years of the operations.[9] However, the success of this military adventure remains questionable.

A volatile internal security scenario coupled with failing economy is a recipe for collapse of Pakistan. The region also faces threat of nuclear terrorism. Pakistan's nuclear weapons face the risk of falling into the hands of terrorists. Pakistan's proxy war in Kashmir is testing Indian patience and has portends to seriously impact the regional peace and stability. India has to rethink its strategy to dissuade Pakistan from its policy of state sponsored terrorism aimed at bleeding India through thousand cuts.

Though India has been pushing for diplomatic isolation of Pakistan for perpetrating terrorism in the region, much in this regards should not be anticipated keeping into view Pakistan's all weather friendship with China and the perceived indispensability of its role in the security situation in Afghanistan by the US and to a large extent even Russia and Iran; the regional stakeholders. Further, Kashmir is perceived as a disputed territory between India and Pakistan by the international community wherein the role of Pakistan in destabilizing the security situation in the state and consequently the entire region is not overtly acknowledged the way India will want it to be.

Therefore, it may be prudent to rework our present strategy. India should try and bring down the overt levels of its animosity with Pakistan by avoiding a constant rhetoric of its role in fomenting trouble in Kashmir. India should gradually shape the international environment and take Kashmir out of focus. In other words India should think of delinking the Kashmir issue from Pakistan which has given an Islamic radicalized complexion to the whole issue. Debatable but merits a thought. This requires shaping of the environment within Kashmir as well by getting its population and main stream political parties into nation building, while isolating the Hurriyat and pushing it into oblivion.

These endeavours should be augmented by an enhanced level of people to people contact between India and Pakistan. Educational and cultural exchange programmes, religious and medical tourism, liberal visa regimes for certain segments of the population, enhanced business opportunities, positive control over the media of both the countries can go a long way in improving the overall environment. Further, India should strengthen the democratic institutions in Pakistan by engaging with them whatever maybe the situation in Kashmir; this will in turn marginalize the nefarious designs of Pak Army. Leveraging of India's soft power proactively to help create pro-India constituencies in Pakistan can render Pakistan Army's strategy against India meaningless.

To create goodwill amongst the population in Pakistan, India should also overtly delink itself from the issues in Balochistan, Gilgit-Baltistan and the instability along the Durand line; though covert sympathies should be maintained. As far as 'Indus Water Treaty' is concerned, threat of its abrogation leads to mistrust amongst the local population, vitiates the entire environment and needs to be avoided. It is a tool available with India and can be employed, if the relations deteriorate further.

However, the hostilities along the line of control to bleed the Pakistan Army should to be increased. The calibrations of these hostilities need to be delinked with the situation in Kashmir valley. Till such time Pakistan Army stops abetting terrorism in Kashmir, its sustenance along the line of control should be made difficult by means of unpredictable heavy fire assaults, covert cross border raids etc. However, these should be out of the media glare to bring in deniability. No political mileage should be gained from such actions.

At the same time if there is a change of heart in the Pakistan Army, it could be responded evenly by encouraging military to military links to facilitate a better understanding of its mind-set and view point. Interaction at National Defence College level, sports exchanges and discussions on improvement of confidence building along the line of control could be considered.

India while looking at a genuine behaviour correction of Pakistan and its Army has to invest in developing a multi spectrum contact and non-contact, clandestine, and lethal punitive deterrence capability against Pakistan. Prosecution of non-contact warfare strategy will demand a high degree of sophistication. It should be couched in multiple layers of plausible deniability yet credible enough to demonstrate India's will and capability.

Nepal

Despite considerable Indian assistance in the aftermath of 2015 devastating earthquake, that reportedly included over 1,700 tonnes of relief material and medical assistance to thousands; Nepal's constitutional crisis severely set back relations. The crisis was not of India's making, it was primarily the product of differences between Nepal's hill elites and the Madhesis with common ethnicities on either side of the porous border. Therefore, fearing a long drawn Madhesi agitation and its adverse impact on the Indian side of the border,India had to urge Kathmandu to revisit the more contentious aspects of the constitution, risking the immense goodwill that it had built up over the previous year. New Delhi was pronounced guilty of responding late to fast-moving developments and despite successfully pressuring Kathmandu to amend some aspects of the contentious constitution, it has not been able to overcome continuing mistrust or resolve the remaining constitutional differences.[10] However, maintaining influence in the domestic politics of Nepal is a necessity which cannot be ignored by India.

Even though China is still far behind India in terms of overall investment in Nepal, it is likely to catch up soon. China's economic control over Nepal can make India vulnerable to Chinese pressures. India has to realise the implications of the fact that the mighty Himalayas are no more a border between Nepal and China. India has to further realise that in the present political and economic environment in Nepal, wherein almost half the population is unemployed and more than half is illiterate, with more than 30 per cent of the people living in abject poverty, Nepal surely has serious business to engage with China. Therefore, it is imperative that India seriously works towards regaining the 'Strategic Space' in Nepal, which it is losing out to China, by making Nepal a part of India's economic dynamism.

Further strengthening of traditional bonds with the people, Indian army veterans and the military establishment is essential. Aspiration of Nepal to connect with Bangladesh across land corridor near Siliguri should be favourably considered. India should also supply military hardware to Nepal and enhance all dimensions of military to military cooperation in order to engage the Nepal Army which is an important stakeholder in the country. Untapped hydel power potential of Nepal needs to be harnessed. There is a need to better manage Indo-Nepal open border to check anti-India activities from there.

Apart from the above, India should clearly articulate the importance for Nepal to keep its national assets and potential growth in its hands rather than letting these be controlled by China for seeking short-term gains which could virtually mean a sell-out. Defending territorial sovereignty under international law is different from protecting economic rights under the tenets of market liberalisation. India at the same time should try and take a lead for trilateral economic engagement with China and Nepal to reduce existing competitions and pave path for implementation of mutually beneficial trade and commerce policies for overall regional development.

Bhutan

Indo-Bhutan relations are a shining example of India's successful foreign policy. However, we need to regard rising democratic aspirations and pronounced sense of sovereignty in Bhutan. While it is conceded that it is in Bhutan's National interest to settle the boundary dispute with China, any further deepening of ties of Bhutan with China beyond a necessary minimum is a cause of concern for India. China's penchant to use aid and investment as a policy tool is well known. There is a need for actively engaging Bhutan to restrict Chinese presence in Bhutan and should continue to keep the existing channels of correspondence and briefings open to allay apprehensions of the Bhutanese leadership in this regard. An astute and benign diplomacy will ensure that Bhutan continues to heed India's security concerns vis-a-vis China and makes policy choices in congruence with India's national interests.

There is a need to broaden and deepen our engagement with Bhutan at multiple levels. India should strengthen the core competencies of Bhutan in sectors like IT, medicine, engineering and disaster management. India needs to guide Bhutan's transition to democracy and make sure that the political parties do not create and use anti-India sentiment for their domestic political gains. There is still ample hydel power potential in Bhutan that remains untapped. India should explore this aspect to further add to India-Bhutan cooperation in power sector.

While IMTRAT continues to serve as an interface with RBA for training requirements; regular joint exercises should be conducted for confidence building and greater synergy. In this regard, considering Bhutan's transition to democracy, the existing footprints of IMTRAT need to be reviewed from the standpoint of sensitivities of the local people, realistic security role and scope of a more subdued background presence.

Bangladesh

PM Sheikh Hasina's visit to N Delhi in April, 2017 and her gesture to honour the war veterans of '1971 Liberation War of Bangladesh' acknowledging India's role, reflects a new dynamic role of India emerging in South Asia.[11]Keeping in view the geopolitical significance of Bangladesh, after having amicably settled land and maritime borders with Bangladesh, India should settle the Teesta water dispute to mitigate 'mistrust' in the relationship. This would pave the way for broader cooperation on other issues such as operationalization of container corridor to the northeast, investments in infrastructure sector, illegal migrations and access to international ports (Dacca, Chittagong and Sonadia), fight against Jihadi and other anti-national elements. Great scope exists for boosting cooperation in defence and disaster management. These measures will go a long way in bridging mistrust, marginalising anti-India lobbies and developing mutually beneficial, bilateral relations. India also needs to be proactive in initiating the 'Joint Climate Change Mitigation Forum', which could help Bangladesh and its citizens with mitigation and adaptation measures. India should cooperate in energy sector in Bangladesh. India could cooperate with US in Bangladesh for balancing China. Both can invest in critical infrastructure projects and possibility of a trilateral defence agreement focusing on disaster management and capacity building of Bangladesh Navy for coastal defence could be explored by India.

Sri Lanka

Sri Lanka occupies the most critical strategic location in the IOR in terms of maritime trade and security of SLOCS. China is engaged in massive infrastructure projects and is the principal supplier of military hardware to Sri Lanka. Sri Lanka is emerging as a vital link in China's 'String of Pearls Strategy' in the IOR with a pro-China tilt clearly visible. In Sri Lanka though the LTTE has been defeated it has not led to reconciliation with alienated Tamil population, who are morally supported by Indian Tamils. Sri Lanka as a majority Sinhala state is always paranoid about a perceived threat from Tamil majority in South India across Mannar strait. These elements shape Sri Lanka's foreign policy orientation towards China to hedge against perceived hostility from India.

India has ceded strategic space to China in Sri Lanka, and outcome of its inhibited policy initiatives due to Tamil factor. This has adversely impacted the strategic balance in South Asia and IOR. Therefore it is imperative that India's Sri Lankan policy balance our domestic concerns for legitimate rights of Tamil population and Sri Lanka's expectations from India. A sustained and constructive engagement with Sri Lanka can reverse trend of its growing proximity with China. India should enhance its soft power projection and also invest in Sinhala dominated areas to be seen as a genuine well-wisher of Sri Lanka.

Maldives

Importance of Maldives in India's 'Indian Ocean strategy' cannot be understated. It is also essential for containing fundamentalist forces in the neighbourhood. Island territories of Maldives are eyed by China as important maritime outposts in its String of Pearls strategy. The uninhibited or sparsely populated islands can be used by Jihadis and other non-state actors for maritime terrorism and piracy. India's foreign policy focus in Maldives should be to promote democratic regimes, develop coastal surveillance and defence facilities, capacity building, disaster management and rendering humanitarian assistance in the event of a natural catastrophe.

Myanmar

Myanmar has a long way to go before it embraces a genuine multi – party democracy and breaks out of its decades of international isolation. The majority Burmans and other ethnicities (Kachin and Karen) remain at loggerheads. Buddhist militant nationalism has led to clashes with Rohingya Muslims. Indian insurgent groups have safe havens in Myanmar. Contraband and drug trafficking from Myanmar adds to India's security concerns in the northeast region. Myanmar seeks to diversify its foreign relations, a shift that will help the country in balancing over-dependence on China. US, Japan and Western countries are engaging Myanmar. India is presented with an excellent opportunity to deepen and broaden its relations with Myanmar, a country that holds the key to India's Act East Policy. It offers India an alternate land route to Southeast Asia.

Further, strategic interests of India and China intersect in Myanmar. The country assumes vital importance in the furtherance of China's strategic objectives such as energy security, transportation corridors to Bangladesh and Southeast Asia or forays into the Indian Ocean policy. The change of regime and onset of democracy in Myanmar offer India a plethora of opportunities to make strategic investments in that country at bilateral level and in a collaborative framework together with the US, Japan and other stakeholders. Such proactive initiative are essential to balance China and maximise own strategic space and influence in the region. India should help Myanmar's transition to democracy by sharing her expertise in strengthening democratic institutions. India should make diplomatic efforts for the 6900 km India-Bangladesh-Myanmar gas pipeline which will help our energy needs.[12] India should have a basic understanding with Myanmar and Bangladesh over the Rohingya issue, as targeting of Rohingya Muslims and the increasing strife between Buddhists and Muslims, have disturbing implications for the region and for India. Myanmar's cooperation is crucial for India to combat insurgencies in the northeast or mitigate asymmetric threats that could develop through its territory and therefore greater defence cooperation with Myanmar is an imperative.

China

An emerging India is concerned by the increasing Chinese footprints in South Asia. These have strategic implications for India especially when seen alongside the unambiguous 'Chinese Dream' and its strategy of protecting its core interests. China's overt and covert support to Pakistan poses a 'Two Front Dilemma' for India. China is using Pakistan as a proxy in Kashmir to marginalise India's rise as a regional power. As far as China is concerned, India's growing closeness with the US, Japan and the littorals of South China Sea is viewed as an effort to contain a rising China. Chinese concerns are further accentuated by India's support for the Tibetan cause.

India while endeavoring to improve its relations with China cannot allow itself to be coerced or intimidated. Multi-dimensional engagement at one level and developing and leveraging credible deterrence capability at another should therefore be the cornerstones of India's China Policy.

The bilateral trade between the countries stood at $70.73 billion in 2015-16.[13] Though, there is huge trade deficit in China's favour, the trade has the potential to rise further. Currently China seeks bigger investments in Indian markets and infrastructure sector. China's economic forays into the Indian markets should be calibrated and balanced by similar access to Indian enterprises in Mainland China. India needs to enhance her investments in the pharmaceutical and software sectors in China, more fields and opportunities should be explored to bridge the gap. Strong, vibrant and interdependent economic trade with China will perforce make that country a stakeholder in India's security.

The upcoming CPEC has become a bone of contention between China and Pakistan on one hand and India on the other as it will pass through Pakistan occupied Kashmir and thus has serious issues of sovereignty for India. Delinking CPEC from Chinese OBOR initiative is difficult; however, India risks isolation if the project materialises with other South Asia countries forming a part of it. Therefore, India could look at OBOR initiative positively and become a stakeholder wherever the interests converge. This will have a positive impact on the bilateral relations between the two states. It is possible to offer China connectivity to the Bay of Bengal along Nathula-Kalimpong-Siliguri-Kolkata Corridor. The Bangladesh–China–India–Myanmar Forum for Regional Cooperation (BCIM) aimed at greater integration of trade and investment between the four countries should be pursued with vigour. India should also look at partnering with China in the overall economic integration of South Asia. Cooperation on WTO, climate change, reformation of international institutions and engagement at BRICS, India-China-Russia Triangular Dialogue, SCO etc should be enhanced. India should also nudge China to enhance cooperation on the global commons and conversely, China needs to demonstrate the sincerity by supporting India's entry in the NSG and UNSC.

The two countries should join hands in the fight on global war against terrorism, share intelligence on Jihadi networks, work alongside US and Russia. Confidence building and mutual trust could in the times to come develop an understanding between India and China on the nefarious designs of Pakistan exposing its complicity and the damage it is doing to China's own image.

Apart from the above both China and India are old civilizations. India should invest in people to people contacts; understand the unique culture of China through institutionalised exchange of scholars, cross-fertilization of ideas and in developing mutual understanding. Such endeavours will bridge the trust deficit.

However, keeping into view China'sstrategic and military capability in Tibet and the contentious issues between India and China, it is unlikely that the relations will improve soon. The visit of Dalai Lama to Tawang in April, 2017 and aggressive rhetoric's by China indicate its sensitivity towards its core interests.[14]

When it comes to dealing with China India has to remember that China respects strength and will accommodate India's concerns only if it is itself presented with a possibility of checkmate. India should manage its relations with China in a manner that prevents any open confrontation or armed conflict. This requires engagement but also requires expanding India's deterrent capabilities.

Indian Ocean Region

The Indian Ocean is the world's third largest body of water has a number of important strategic chokepoints to include the Straits of Hormuz and Malacca through which 32.2 millions of barrels of crude oil and petroleum are transported per day, more than 50 per cent of the world's maritime oil trade.[15]Nearly 40 per cent of the world's offshore petroleum is produced in the Indian Ocean, coastal beach sands and offshore waters. Fisheries too are increasingly important for both exports and domestic consumption.

IOR has become a growing area of competition. India imports nearly 80 per cent of its energy, mostly oil, from the Middle East. China's 84 per cent of its imported energy resources passed through Strait of Malacca from the Indian Ocean in 2012. Indian Ocean is central to China's Maritime Silk Route (MSR) plan. China has deepened ties with IOR states to include influx of Chinese capital into construction projects in Bangladesh, Myanmar, Pakistan, and Sri Lanka. Since launching of counter piracy operations in 2009, Beijing has become increasingly active in the region. Transformation and modernisation of PLA especially the Navy and particularly the ongoing naval deployments in IOR indicate China's desire to protect its overseas interests. Thus diverse security challenges affect the region ranging from natural disasters to concerns over energy security, piracy, maritime terrorism and military posturing. Though the probability of military conflict in Indian Ocean remains low, escalated activities and rhetoric adversely impact upon the strategic stability of South Asia.

Mitigation of Threats

Hybrid Asymmetric Conflicts

China's rapid military modernisation and infrastructure development in Tibet, on one hand, and Pakistan's military build-up with Chinese and US help, on the other, have perpetuated India's 'Two Front Dilemma'. Pak-China strategic nexus and broad spectrum of hybrid threats; terrorism, proxy war, local conflicts, conventional full scale war under a nuclear overhang; make the regional security scenario highly complex and challenging. While China's concept of 'Unrestricted Warfare' includes means of biochemical, guerrilla terrorism, psychological, smuggling, drugs, virtual media, ideological besides others; Pakistan abides by the Quaranic Concepts of War' by Brig SK Malik which justifies the use of terrorism.[16]

China and Pakistan are together exploiting India's internal fault lines. The levels of violence in J&K have gone up exponentially with increasing Chinese economic footprints in Pakistan. Therefore a strong deterrence capability against China and Pakistan is an imperative. If push comes to shove, India needs to tackle this hybrid challenge, in a hybrid manner; developing credible defensive and offensive asymmetric warfare capabilities. At the same time it is imperative that we restructure our own law and judicial mechanisms to effectively deal with the internal miscreants. 'Political Warfare' and 'Legal Warfare' too are essential ingredients of hybrid warfare, which our adversaries are adept in exploiting. Both these means are used to isolate, erode, manipulate, exhaust, down, attrite, and create conditions to wear down the target country through all possible institutions, including judiciary.[17]

Pakistan is highly susceptible to ethno-regional fault lines. China faces similar challenge in Xinjiang and Tibet. If India's well-meaning and peaceful gestures are ignored; India should create a broad spectrum 'Non-Contact' warfare leverage to exploit these weaknesses. Strategic stability in South Asia depends on a large extent on India proactively negating the destabilising forces in the region by bridging the strategic asymmetry in the sub conventional domain.

On water issue, India enjoys leverages against Pakistan but is vulnerable vis a vis China. There is a need to devise a strategy to pressurise Pakistan on this premium resource, while at the same time persuade China to behave as responsible stakeholder in sharing of global commons. India, China and Pakistan rely heavily on the SLOCs in the IOR for trade as well as for import of energy resources. A formidable naval capability by India would therefore have the best way in achieving a favourable strategic balance in the region.

Further, India has to seriously invest its energies in developing capabilities in use of disruptive technologies, exploitation of cyber space, outer space and information space. Cyber terrorism and nuclear terrorism are a reality that demands new sets of capabilities and strategic responses. Pakistan's nuclear doctrine of "First Use" and induction of tactical nuclear warheads in its strategic arsenal have further blurred the red lines. In such milieu, it is imperative for India to maintain a favourable military balance for full spectrum of conflicts and at the same time build collaborative capacities to hedge against non-traditional security threats.

Military Diplomacy

India should invest in enhancing its military diplomacy with countries in China's backyard like Vietnam, Japan, South Korea and Philippines. Heightening of China's insecurity by orchestrating bilateral and multilateral tri service anti-terrorism exercises, disaster management exercises joint maritime patrolling and military sports should be planned.

Besides India should become the preferred destination for training of the armed forces personnel of these countries and South Asian countries at tactical, operational and strategic levels. Upcoming INDU (Indian National Defence University) should not only look at absorbing students from the friendly foreign countries but should have a diverse faculty from the armed forces of these countries especially South Asia. Government could also look at establishing of Training Teams on the lines of Indian Military Training Team in Bhutan in the littoral countries of South China Sea.

India should increase the scope and frequency of joint training exercises with its South Asian neighbours for a meaningful capability building. However, to prevent these countries to look towards China for their military arms and equipment which in turn makes them dependent on China for training as well; India has to seriously look at exporting military hardware to these countries. India could also look at partnering with its neighbouring countries in its 'Make in India' initiative.

Nuclear Challenge

Pakistan's aggressive India centric nuclear programme is escalatory in nature with a 'First use Doctrine'. This has serious global and regional implications which are further accentuated by the fact that Pakistan is a hub of terrorism and the possibility of terrorist acquiring the nuclear weapons has increased due to its policy of delegating the tactical nuclear weapons to the field commanders. Also the numbers of civilian nuclear power plants in the country have increased, which makes these power plants vulnerable to a terrorist attack. China follows a policy of 'No First Use' of nuclear weapons.

India has a nuclear doctrine which is based on the principle of 'No First Use', and 'Credible Minimum Nuclear Deterrence', which is basically retaliatory in nature. India is also not increasing its fissile material production at an alarming pace, however India has to mitigate the twin challenge of China- Pakistan nuclear nexus hence has to develop its nuclear arsenal keeping this aspect in mind. Since India's nuclear policy is based on the 'Second Strike', hence it is essential that it has a survivable nuclear arsenal which can counter the adversaries 'First Attack' hence the importance of a triad. India has stated that its nuclear policy is for deterrence and it will not initiate a strike, but will go in for a punitive response. No change in the strategy is recommended.

Non Traditional Challenges

- *Piracy*

  Unlike terrorism, no state in South Asia has supported piracy till now. The threat is faced by almost all the countries in the region and there is ample scope to cooperate on the issue. A tripartite agreement on maritime cooperation was signed by India, Sri Lanka and the Maldives in 2013. South Asia lies in the middle of two most piracy infested regions – Horn of Africa and Malacca Straits. Increase in piracy will impact the region's economy and security. There is ample scope for other countries too to pitch in for collective efforts targeting piracy in the region.

• **Disaster Management**

The Indian Subcontinent is vulnerable, in varying degrees, to a large number of natural as well as human-made disasters on account of its unique geo-climatic and socio-economic conditions. The region is highly vulnerable to floods, droughts, cyclones, earthquakes, landslides, avalanches, forest fires and even tsunamis. As part of its 'Disaster Diplomacy', India has taken a lead in Humanitarian Assistance and Disaster Relief (HADR) through an evolved Disaster Management System. The system has moved from activity-based reactive system to a proactive institutionalised structure. It consists of institutional setup right from the National level, the National Disaster Management Authority (NDMA) to the district level (DDMA). India does play an important role in the regional and globalinitiatives on disaster management. With multi-dimensional initiatives and expertise, India is taking a lead role in strengthening regional cooperation among South Asian countries for reducing disasters.

As part of its Disaster Diplomacy;[18]India has hosted a SAARC Disaster Management Centre (SDMC), set up in October 2006 at the premises of National Institute of Disaster Management in New Delhi. The Centre has the mandate to serve eight Member Countries of SAARC - Afghanistan, Bangladesh, Bhutan, India, Maldives, Nepal, Pakistan and Sri Lanka - by providing policy advice and facilitating capacity building services including strategic learning, research, training, system development and exchange of information for effective disaster risk reduction and management in South Asia.[19] SAARC is raising a Common Disaster Response Force on the lines of UN Peacekeeping Force. India has pledged two Battalions of the National Disaster Response Force (NDRF) as part of the Regional Response Force.[20]

• **Poverty, Unemployment and Health**

South Asia is home to around quarter of the world population with 1.7 billion. As per World Bank extreme poverty in South Asia is 13.5 percent based on the international poverty line of $1.90 a day.[21] South Asia has the dubious distinction of having highest number of chronically hungry people in the world.[22] The region also has high youth unemployment rate at 9.6 per cent. There is widespread mismatch between skills and education provided in the South Asian countries. Many South Asians are leaving school or university without skills that are demanded by employers.[23]

Health standards in the region too are not very good and face a number of problems. South Asia's low life expectancy and high rates of malnutrition, infant mortality, and incidence of TB and HIV/AIDS are second only to those of sub-Saharan Africa. The region faces not only these and related health problems—poor sanitation, poor maternal health, poor access to healthcare services, and widespread malaria—but also an emerging chronic disease epidemic. Despite the magnitude of these inter-related challenges, South Asian countries on average spend less than 3.2 percent of their gross domestic product on health, compared to a global average of 8.2 percent. India is contributing to the regional development as a preferred destination for skill base education, medical tourism and scientific agricultural know how and development.

- **Pandemics**

Pandemics are yet another trans-border non-traditional threat. During the 14th century Black Death in Europe cost about 200 million lives. Poor health environment in South Asia lends the region susceptible to Pandemics and its spread to neighbouring countries through porous borders. Natural disasters and Pandemics can impose an unbearable economic and human cost and therefore merit a collaborative mitigation and response strategies and mechanism.

- **Water Disputes**

Water security dominates Pakistan's security concerns vis a vis India. Despite a favourable Indus Water Treaty, which provides 81 percent of water to Pakistan, Pakistan remains sceptical about India's legitimate use of waters as per international conventions.

Water is Pakistan's Achilles heel and a key determinant in its security calculus vis a vis Kashmir policy. China, on the other hand, is building dams over Brahmaputra River that causes concerns in India and Bangladesh. India is particularly vulnerable as it directly receives more than 48 percent of its total surface water of 718 billion cubic meters from the Chinese territory every year. Diversion of Brahmaputra River is another driver of conflict between India and China. Teesta water issue remains a bone of contention between India and Bangladesh that needs early resolution through some sincere negotiations. On the whole, South Asia is a water stress zone, depletion of glaciers, diversion of waters by upper riparian states, environmental costs due to flooding or water scarcity will continue to fuel intra and inter-state tensions, if the stakeholders fail to find lasting solutions to better management of this life sustaining natural resource.

• **Energy Security**

According to World Energy Outlook published by International Energy Agency, China will account for 40 percent of growing energy consumption until 2025. The rate of energy consumption for India will grow by 132 percent and China by 71 percent. Indo-Pacific region will become increasingly reliant on Middle East for its oil. By 2030, 80 percent of China's oil will come from Middle East.[24] A fragile security environment in the Middle East and IOR will not only disrupt energy supply to these developing countries but also escalate energy price and insurance costs, thus damaging the regional economy. Assured supply of energy from the sources in Middle East and security of SLOCs in the IOR therefore become paramount in achieving sustainable security and development in the region. India and China have reason to cooperate by positively managing the emerging competitions to maintain peace and tranquillity in the region.

• **Climate Change and Sea Rise – An Existential Threat**

As per the Intergovernmental Panel on Climate Change (IPCC) report, the mean annual increase in temperature by the end of the century in South Asia is 3.3 °C.[25] Bangladesh is a low lying country (70 percent of land area is 5 meters or less above sea level) and hence is prone to cyclones, storms, floods and salt water intrusion. Maldives faces challenge of climate change, as the rising sea level may submerge this country. 80% of the area is 1 meter or less above sea level. The country's highest point is only two-meters above sea level. Likewise, India's coastal cities, which are the thriving population centres and economic hubs, run the risk of destruction with sea rise or from natural disasters like Tsunami. Rising sea levels pose an existential threat to coastal towns and can trigger an unprecedented humanitarian crisis and ipso facto should be a main collective security concern for South Asian countries.

Endnotes

1 (2015) "PM Narendra Modi addresses combined commanders' conference on board INS Vikramaditya", [Online: web] Accessed 10 April 2017 URL: http://indianexpress.com/article/india/india-news-india/pm-modi-addresses-combined-commanders-conference-onboard-ins-vikramaditya/

2 Gupta Arvind (2011) "A National Security Strategy Document for India", [Online: web] Accessed 07 May 2017 URL: http://www.idsa.in/idsacomments/ANationalSecurityStrategyDocumentforIndia_arvindgupta_201011

3 ibid

4 ibid

5 (2017) "Bangladesh PM Sheikh Hasina to honour Indian soldiers killed in 1971 war", [Online: web] Accessed 14 April 2017 URL:http://indianexpress.com/article/india/bangladesh-pm-sheikh-hasina-to-honour-indian-soldiers-killed-in-1971-war-4585862/

6 (2017) "Modi-Putin give the BIGGEST SHOCK to CHINA and Pakistan", [Online: web] Accessed 14 April 2017 URL: http://www.theresurgentindia.com/modi-putin-give-the-biggest-shock-to-china-and-pakistan/

7 Menon, Shivshankar (2016), Choices, Washington: The Brookings Institution

8 Jaishankar, Dhruva "India's Five Foreign Policy Goals: Great Strides, Steep Challenges", [Online: web] Accessed 16 April 2017 URL:https://thewire. in/38708/indias-five-foreign-policy-goals-great-strides-steep-challenges/

9 (2016) "Operation Zarb e Azb",[Online: web] Accessed 10 April 2017 URL:http:// economictimes.indiatimes.com/news/defence/490-pakistan-soldiers-3500-militants-killed-in-operation-zarb-e-azb/articleshow/52766005.cms

10 ibid

11 (2017) "Bangladesh PM Sheikh Hasina to honour Indian soldiers killed in 1971 war" ,[Online: web] Accessed 14 April 2017 URL:http://indianexpress. com/article/india/bangladesh-pm-sheikh-hasina-to-honour-indian-soldiers-killed-in-1971-war-4585862/

12 (2016) "6,900 km gas pipelines to connect Bangladesh, Myanmar, India" ,[Online: web] Accessed 21 April 2017 URL: http://economictimes.indiatimes. com/news/industry/energy/oil-gas/6900-km-gas-pipelines-to-connect-bangladesh-myanmar-india/articleshow/53695899.cms

13 (2016) "India's trade deficit with China jumps to $53 billion in 2015-16",[Online: web] Accessed 26 April 2017 URL: http://economictimes.indiatimes.com/ news/economy/foreign-trade/indias-trade-deficit-with-china-jumps-to-53-billion-in-2015-16/articleshow/53492853.cms

14 (2017) "Dalai Lama begins addressing gathering in Tawang with China hopping mad over visit", [Online: web] Accessed 10 April 2017 URL: http://indiatoday. intoday.in/story/dalai-lama-tawang-arunachal-pradesh-china/1/923709.html

15 Eleanor, Albert (2016) "Competition in the Indian Ocean", [Online: web] Accessed 04 May 2017 URL: http://www.cfr.org/regional-security/competition-indian-ocean/p37201

16 Katoch, Prakash(2017) "Kashmir stone-pelter tied atop jeep: Incident may mark a turning point in India's response to hybrid warfare", [Online: web] Accessed 16 April 2017 URL: http://www.firstpost.com/india/kashmir-stone-pelter-tied-atop-jeep-incident-may-mark-a-turning-point-in-indias-response-to-hybrid-warfare-3386028.html

17 Katoch, PC(2017) "The 'Zonkey' of Hybrid Warfare", [Online: web] Accessed 04 May 2017 URL:http://www.thecitizen.in/index.php/NewsDetail/index/4/10590/The-Zonkey-of-Hybrid-Warfare

18 (2012) "Disaster Diplomacy",[Online: web] Accessed 04 May 2017 URL: http:// www.disasterdiplomacy.org/

19 (2015) "SAARC Disaster Management Centre (SDMC), Interim Unit", [Online: web] Accessed 28April 2017 URL:www.saarc-sdmc.nic.in/

20 (2015)"India, Pak agree for SAARC disaster response force" ,[Online: web] Accessed 28 April 2017 URL: http://timesofindia.indiatimes.com/india/India-Pak-agree-for-SAARC-disaster-response-force/articleshow/50336495.cms

21 (2015) "South Asia Extreme Poverty Falls, but Challenges Remain", [Online: web] Accessed 14 April 2017 URL:http://www.worldbank.org/en/news/press-release/2015/10/15/south-asia-extreme-poverty-falls-but-challenges-remain

22 (2014)"South Asia has highest number of chronically hungry people" ,[Online: web] Accessed 14 April 2017 URL: http://www.downtoearth.org.in/news/south-asia-has-highest-number-of-chronically-hungry-people-46386

23 (2013)"Youth unemployment in South Asia as high as 9.6%",[Online: web] Accessed 14 April 2017 URL: http://timesofindia.indiatimes.com/world/south-asia/Youth-unemployment-in-South-Asia-as-high-as-9-6/articleshow/18131851.cms

24 (2015) "World Energy Outlook", [Online: web] Accessed 10 April 2017 URL: https://www.iea.org/Textbase/npsum/WEO2015SUM.pdf

25 (2014) "Climate Change 2014", [Online: web] Accessed 11 April 2017 URL: https://www.ipcc.ch/pdf/assessment-report/ar5/syr/AR5_SYR_FINAL_SPM.pdf

Conclusion

South Asia is one of the most populous and densely populated geographical regions in the world. Despite rich historical, cultural and political linkages, the region has embarrassingly poor mutual understanding and hence integration. There exists a perpetual stress due to misgivings in the not so cordial bilateral relations amongst the countries of the region. A reinvigorated South Asia has the potential to vastly improve the lives of its 1.7 billion citizens – nearly one-fourth of all humanity – particularly India, the largest country of the region. While the failure of South Asia's desired evolution as a cohesive region can be attributed to several factors ranging from terrorism, strained bilateral relations and the absence of military and strategic cooperation; India's own engagement in the region has been found wanting, even though it has evolved over the years.

India's ambitions have been confronted by external and internal challenges. Externally, the continuing tensions with Pakistan, the uncertainty over Afghanistan and the role of outside actors, notably China, pose threats to emergence of India as a regional leader. India also faces emerging challenges from politically unstable Nepal and Maldives, a not so friendly Sri Lanka and a Bangladesh in grips of Islamic radicalisation. These have major security implications.

In the present geopolitical environment, emerging challenges to strategic stability in South Asia are adversely impacting global and regional peace and stability. Therefore, countries in the region need to identify specific areas of common challenges and opportunities to foster region-wide cooperation namely infrastructure, energy, water, trade, climate change mitigation, higher education, healthcare, terrorism and even military cooperation. However, the region shall remain in the present state of 'Unpleasant Stability', in the foreseeable future. This peculiar form of stability derives substantially from the inability of both India and Pakistan, the two big players in the region, to attain what may be desired political objectives.[1]

Strategic stability in South Asia is vital for emerging India's own growth, peace and stability. However, despite India's endeavours to assume regional leadership; its proactive policies in the region shall remain marginalised due to interests of extra regional players like China, growing religious fundamentalism and dynamics of partisan bilateral relations. Though, the situation does not look very encouraging, it has potential for rejuvenation. India should continue to engage the regional countries on multiple fronts. India's overall nonaligned and soft power approach can bring solutions to divergences within the region, stimulating global and regional peace and stability by 'Bridging Gaps'.

Endnotes

1 Tellis AJ (1997) "Stability in South Asia", [Online: web] Accessed 28 April 2017 URL: https://www.rand.org/content/dam/rand/pubs/documented_briefings/.../DB185.pdf

Bibliography

1. Ghosh, Partha S,'An Enigma that is South Asia: India versus the Region', Asia Pacific review.

2. Nayak, Nihar, 'Cooperative Security Framework for South Asia', Pentagon Press, New Delhi.

3. Fair Christine, C 'Fighting To The End-The Pakistan Army's Way of War', Oxford University Press.

4. Tellis Ashley, J 'Stability in South Asia', Rand Report, Natraj Publications New Delhi.

5. Pant, Harsh 'The Rise of China: Implications for India', Cambridge University Press India Pvt. Ltd.

6. Small, Andrew, 'The China-Pakistan Axis: Asia's New Geopolitics', London: C Hurst & Co Publishers Ltd.

7. Gall, Carlotta, 'The Wrong Enemy: America in Afghanistan 2001-14"'Houghton Mifflin Harcourt Publishers Ltd.

8. Menon, Shivshankar, 'Choices', Washington: The Brookings Institution.

9. http://saf.pair.com/chess.htm.

10. https://www.scribd.com/document/331162074/SHEEHAN-The-Balance-of-Power-History-and-Theory-pdf.

11. http://www.businessdictionary.com/definition/strategic-balance.html.

12. http://csis.org/programs/international-security-program/asia-division/cross-strait-security-initiative-/strategic-ba.

13. Paul, TV (2004), "Balance of Power – Theory and Practice in 21st Century," Stanford University Press, California.

14. http://timesofindia.indiatimes.com/india/China-wants-India-in-state-of-low-level-equilibrium-PM/articleshow/6508868.cms.

15. http://www.scmp.com/article/712578/india-foils-attempt-bring-china-south-asian-group.

16. https://books.google.co.in/books?id=i5RDCwAAQBAJ&pg=PA3 28&lpg=PA328&dq=China%27s+nuanced+policy+on+No+First +Use+(NFU)[.

17. http://search.proquest.com/openview/ff7ff5cdd69ab7d316046f61 c51d5f38/1?pq-origsite=gscholar&cbl=1456373.

18. http://sspconline.org/opinion/India_Pakistans_NuclearDoc-trines_11042012.

19. http://en.wikipedia.org/wiki/Realism_(international_relations).

20. http://en.wikipedia.org/wiki/List_of_countries_by_GDP_(PPP).

21. http://www.india-seminar.com/2000/487/487%20raja%20mohan. htm.

22. http://www.thehindu.com/opinion/op-ed/reviving-the-maritime-silk-route/article5896989.ece.

23. http://www.chinausfocus.com/foreign-policy/the-string-of-pearls-and-the-maritime-silk-road/.

24. http://www.tolonews.com/en/afghanistan/25826-us-general-nicholson-submits-his-assessment-of-the-situation-in-afghani-stan.

25. http://fpif.org/the_afpak_paradox/.

26. http://www.strategicstudiesinstitute.army.mil/pubs/display. cfm?pubID=1233.

27. http://www.ecoi.net/news/188769::afghanistan/101.general-secu-rity-situation-in-afghanistan-and-events-in-kabul.htm.

28. http://www.academia.edu/824937/Af-Pak_Regional_Security_ Fault_lines.

29. http://www.ecoi.net/news/188769::afghanistan/101.general-secu-rity-situation-in-afghanistan-and-events-in-kabul.htm.

30. https://freedomhouse.org/report/freedom-world/2015/afghani-stan.

31.   https://freedomhouse.org/report/freedom-world/2016/afghani-stan.

32.   http://www.aljazeera.com/indepth/opinion/2016/02/corruption-indexes-don-afghanistan-ashraf-ghani-160204132917875.html.

33.   https://www.controlrisks.com/en/our-thinking/analysis/ethnic-fault-lines.pdf.

34.   http://www.khaama.com/the-story-of-democracy-in-afghani-stan-and-pakistan-6692.

35.   http://www.aljazeera.com/news/2016/08/afghanistan-abdullah-abdullah-chides-ashraf-ghani-160812064503457.html.

36.   http://www.usip.org/sites/default/files/PW115-Afghanistan-Na-tional-Defense-and-Security-Forces-Mission-Challenges-and-Sustainability.pdf.

37.   https://en.wikipedia.org/wiki/Economy_of_Afghanistan.

38.   https://www.cia.gov/library/publications/the-world-factbook/geos/af.html.

39.   http://www.worldbank.org/en/country/afghanistan/overview.

40.   https://www.cia.gov/library/publications/the-world-factbook/geos/af.html.

41.   http://www.worldbank.org/en/country/afghanistan/overview.

42.   http://www.defense.gov/Portals/1/Documents/pubs/1225_Re-port_Dec_2015_-_Final_20151210.pdf.

43.   http://www.securitycouncilreport.org/monthly-forecast/2016-09/afghanistan_18.php.

44.   http://foreignpolicy.com/2015/10/06top-u-s-commander-ameri-can-troops-stay-afghanistan.

45.   www.defence.gov.au/ADC/Publications/IndoPac/Kenny%20Af-ghanistan%20IPSP.pdf.

46.   http://thediplomat.com/2015/10/heres-the-most-disturbing-thing-about-thetaliban-takeover-of-kunduz..

47.   https://www.fas.org/sgp/crs/row/RL30588.pdf.

48.   URL:www.defence.gov.au/ADC/Publications/IndoPac/Kenny%20Afghanistan%20IPSP.pdf.

49. http://www.defense.gov/News/Transcripts/Transcript-View/Article/721738/department-of-defense-press-briefing-by-general-cleveland-via-teleconference-fr.

50. http://www.nytimes.com/2015/12/19/world/asia/afghanistan-ash-carter.html?_r=0.

51. http://www.defense.gov/News/Transcripts/Transcript-View/Article/721738/department-of-defense-press-briefing-by-general-cleveland-via-teleconference-fr.

52. http://www.newsweek.com/shift-tactics-isis-afghanistan-483594.

53. http://www.pajhwok.com/en/2016/10/21/ghani-issues-decree-peace-deal%E2%80%99s-enforcement.

54.   http://www.usip.org/sites/default/files/PW115-Afghanistan-National-Defense-and-Security-Forces-Mission-Challenges-and-Sustainability.pdf.

55. http://www.tolonews.com/en/afghanistan/25826-us-general-nicholson-submits-his-assessment-of-the-situation-in-afghanistan.

56. http://usiblog.in/2016/08/afghan-forces-turning-afghanistan-into-graveyard-of-terrorism-says-afghan-army-chief-of-staff.

57. http://www.firstpost.com/world/ashraf-ghani-slams-pakistan-for-harbouring-terrorists-praises-india-2913030.html.

58. http://thediplomat.com/2016/07/the-afghan-peace-talks-qcg-and-china-pakistan-role/.

59. https://www.theguardian.com/world/2016/oct/18/taliban-afghanistan-secret-talks-qatar.

60. http://thediplomat.com/2016/07/the-afghan-peace-talks-qcg-and-china-pakistan-role/.

61. http://tns.thenews.com.pk/understanding-pakistans-strategic-interests-afghanistan/#.V_IZdvl97cc.

62. http://www.defense.gov/Portals/1/Documents/Enhancing_Security_and_Stability_in_Afghanistan-June_2016.pdf.

63. http://www.firstpost.com/world/ashraf-ghani-slams-pakistan-for-harbouring-terrorists-praises-india-2913030.html.

64. http://www.cfr.org/china/east-turkestan-islamic-movement-etim/

p9179.

65.   http://www.voanews.com/a/china-military-aid-afghanistan/3402178.html.

66.   http://www.khaama.com/china-pledges-2-2-million-in-fresh-aid-to-afghanistan-01645

67.   http://america.aljazeera.com/articles/2015/7/11/chinese-company-taliban-battle-afghanistan.html.

68.   http://www.reuters.com/article/us-afghanistan-oil-idUS-BRE89K08G20121021.

69.   http://thediplomat.com/2016/01/iran-and-saudi-arabia-in-afghanistan/.

70.   http://thediplomat.com/2016/01/iran-and-saudi-arabia-in-afghanistan/

71.   http://www.enduringamerica.com/may-2009/2009/5/6/video-afghan-president-karzai-at-brookings-institution-5-may.html

72.   http://economictimes.indiatimes.com/news/politics-and-nation/afghanistan-president-ashraf-ghanis-visit-ready-to-take-forward-chabahar-port-project-says-pm-narendra-modi/articlesho.

73.   http://www.dw.com/en/russias-new-role-in-afghanistan/a-19087432.

74.   https://www.rt.com/news/359220-russia-afghanistan-us-isis/.

75.   https://www.csis.org/programs/transnational-threats-project/past-projects/northern-distribution-network-ndn.

76.   http://www.khaama.com/russia-pledges-major-investment-in-housing-construction-sector-of-afghanistan-1476.

77.   http://thediplomat.com/2015/07/central-asias-stake-in-afghanistans-war/.

78.   http://thediplomat.com/2016/05/afghanistans-growing-unrest-implications-for-indias-security/.

79.   http://www.voanews.com/a/india-promises-1-billion-dollars-in-aid-during-afghan-president-s-visit/3508969.html.

80.   https://www.bloomberg.com/quicktake/pakistans-turmoil.

81.   https://en.wikipedia.org/wiki/Khyber_Pakhtunkhwa.

82.   https://en.wikipedia.org/wiki/Federally_Administered_Tribal_Areas.

83.   https://www.osac.gov/pages/ContentReportDetails.aspx?cid=19396.

84.   http://thediplomat.com/2016/08/balochistan-the-troubled-heart-of-the-cpec/.

85.   http://www.asianage.com/editorial/balochistan-pak-s-untold-story-544.

86.   http://timesofindia.indiatimes.com/world/pakistan/Baloch-leaders-who-supported-PM-Modis-comments-booked-in-Pakistan/articleshow/53810280.cms.

87.   http://timesofindia.indiatimes.com/india/Baloch-leader-Brahamdagh-Bugti-approaches-India-for-asylum/articleshow/54432342.cms.

88.   http://www.dawn.com/news/1285404.

89.   http://indiatoday.intoday.in/story/un-rights-council-india-pakistan-uri-balochistan-human-rights-violation/1/768466.html.

90.   http://www.dailyexcelsior.com/412465-2/.

91.   http://www.tribuneindia.com/news/jammu-kashmir/community/opposition-to-china-corridor-in-gilgit-baltistan/288340.html.

92.   http://www.claws.in/1595/long-road-to-peace-in-afghanistan-pavneet-chadha.html.

93.   http://www.consilium.europa.eu/en/meetings/international-summit/2016/10/05/.

94.   http://www.pajhwok.com/en/2016/10/30/13-journalists-murdered-292-forced-suspend-jobs.

95.   http://www.claws.in/1595/long-road-to-peace-in-afghanistan-pavneet-chadha.html.

96.   http://usiblog.in/2016/10/pakistan-sidelined-afghanistan-taliban-secret-talks-at-qatar/.

97.   http://timesofindia.indiatimes.com/world/pakistan/All-top-leaders-will-be-forced-to-leave-Upset-at-being-sidelined-in-talks-Pakistan-warns-Taliban/articleshow/55162518.cms.

98. http://www.pajhwok.com/en/2016/10/31/pakistan-has-taken-no-action-against-haqqanis-zakhilwal.

99. http://www.dailymail.co.uk/news/article-3769308/Pakistan-military-admits-IS-presence-country.html.

100. http://www.claws.in/images/publication_pdf/1192209486_MP59-VMahalingam-14-03-16.pdf.

101. https://www.foreignaffairs.com/articles/afghanistan/2016-01-31/russia-and-taliban-make-amends.

102. http://www.theaustralian.com.au/news/world/the-times/taliban-leader-gains-vladimir-putins-help-at-secret-meeting/news-story/c212a1f20b685fae034c63ea7b0cdb89.

103. http://thediplomat.com/2016/08/what-to-make-of-chinas-latest-meeting-with-the-taliban/.

104. http://thediplomat.com/2016/06/the-rise-of-china-afghanistan-security-relations/.

105. http://www.tolonews.com/en/afghanistan/25826-us-general-nicholson-submits-his-assessment-of-the-situation-in-afghanistan.

106. http://www.csmonitor.com/World/Asia-South-Central/2013/1203/Pakistani-protests-threaten-NATO-supply-lines-to-Afghanistan.

107. http://tacstrat.com/content/index.php/2012/10/10/indian-predictions-for-the-next-major-conflict/.

108. http://en.wikipedia.org/wiki/China%E2%80%93Pakistan_Free_Trade_Agreement.

109. books.sipri.org/files/FS/SIPRIFS1403.pdf.

110. http://www.pewglobal.org/2014/07/14/chapter-4-how-asians-view-each-other.

111. http://www.diplomaticourier.com/news/regions/asia/2193-how-china-and-pakistan-shift-the-balance-of-power-in-south-asia

112. http://wcms.itz.uni-halle.de/download.php?down=9047&elem=1986859.

113. https://www.ukessays.com/essays/history/talibanisation-of-pakistan-a-threat-to-indias-security-history-essay.php?utm_ex-

pid=309629.

114. http://www.dawn.com/weekly/dmag/archive/060305/dmag6.htm

115. https://en.wikipedia.org/wiki/Indo-Pakistani_border#cite_note-Dawn_News_archives-1.

116. http://www.frontline.in/navigation/?type=static&page=flonnet&rdurl=fl1819/18191290.

117. http://www.siachenglacier.com/.

118. http://www.idsa.in/strategicanalysis/39_2/TheSirCreekDispute.

119. http://www.satp.org/satporgtp/countries/india/document/papers/parliament_resolution_on_Jammu_and_ Kashmir.htm.

120. http://www.idsa.in/idsacomments/complete-sealing-of-the-india-pakistan-border_gsen_181016.

121. http://www.britannica.com/EBchecked/topic/588371/terrorism.

122. http://www.thehindu.com/news/65-terror-groups-active-in-india-govt/article5064769.ece.

123. http://www.worldaffairsjournal.org/article/next-al-qaeda-lashkar-e-taiba-and-future-terrorism-south-asia.

124. http://timesofindia.indiatimes.com/india/ISI-created-Indian-Mujahideen-to-spread-terror-in-India-Anti-terrorism-squad/articleshow/13714739.cms.

125. http://www.ipcs.org/article/terrorism/the-non-traditional-nuclear-threat-in-south-asia-managing-the-3633.html.

126. http://www.newindianexpress.com/nation/2016/oct/25/pakistan-has-distinction-of-being-epicentre-of-terrorism-india-at-ipu-1531611.html.

127. http://blogs.quickheal.com/indian-businesses-lost-4-billion-due-cyberattacks-2013-2014-worse/.

128. http://www.nti.org/analysis/reports/south-asia-1540-reporting/.

129. http://www.bharatdefencekavach.com/news/beyond-headlines/story/58561.html.

130. http://idr.qburst.com/news/china-supports-pakistans-claim-on-kashmir/.

131. http://www.atimes.com/cpec-takes-step-forward-violence-surges-balochistan/?platform=hootsuite.

132. http://www.dawn.com/news/1200203.

133. http://www.tribuneindia.com/news/sunday-special/kaleidoscope/game-changers-pak-tactical-nukes-chinese-troops-in-pok/243608.html.

134. http://www.ndtv.com/india-news/off-goa-the-largest-ever-naval-exercises-with-a-focus-on-the-chinese-navy-1657264.

135. http://www.claws.in/index.php?action=master&task=580&u_id=36

136. http://www.indiandefencereview.com/news/andaman-and-nicobar-islands-a-security-challenge-for-india/.

137. http://www.un.org/africarenewal/magazine/august-2016/india-africa-rekindle-trade-ties.

138. http://www.dnaindia.com/india/comment-why-india-needs-to-expand-its-engagement-with-asean-2252804.

139. http://www.indiandefensenews.in/2017/02/pak-concerned-over-peace-in-indian.html.

140. http://www.dawn.com/news/1251723.

141. http://www.thehindu.com/specials/10-things-to-know-about-Indus-Water-Treaty/article15000672.ece.

142. http://www.kashmirawareness.org/pak-india-water-dispute-accelerates/.

143. http://usiblog.in/2016/02/south-asias-water-problem/.

144. http://www.southasiaanalysis.org/node/1654.

145. http://www.worldometers.info/world-population/maldives-population/.

146. https://en.wikipedia.org/wiki/Indians_in_the_Maldives.

147. http://timesofindia.indiatimes.com/world/south-asia/Abdulla-Yameen-sworn-in-as-new-Maldivian-president/articleshow/25953127.cms.

148. http://www.business-standard.com/article/news-ians/new-maldives-president-is-former-dictator-s-half-brother-pro-

file-113111700291_1.html.

149. http://www.theodora.com/wfbcurrent/maldives/maldives_military.html.

150. http://www.fao.org/docrep/X5623E/x5623e0r.htm.

151. http://www.maldiveisle.com/economy.htm.

152. http://securityobserver.org/the-perils-of-rising-religious-fundamentalism-in-the-maldives/.

153. http://www.tradingeconomics.com/maldives/unemployment-rate.

154. https://www.adb.org/countries/maldives/poverty.

155. https://www.unodc.org/documents/southasia/reports/National_Drug_Use_Survey_-_Report.pdf.

156. http://www.globalsecurity.org/military/world/indian-ocean/mv-forrel.htm.

157. https://www.mea.gov.in/Portal/ForeignRelation/MALDIVES_23_02_2016.pdf.

158. http://en.mihaaru.com/the-receding-dragon-the-decline-in-chinese-tourists-to-the-maldives/.

159. http://fp.brecorder.com/2016/05/2016052548846/.

160. https://www.state.gov/r/pa/ei/bgn/5476.htm.

161. http://indianexpress.com/article/india/india-news-india/india-maldives-sign-six-pacts-resolve-to-expand-defence-cooperation/.

162. http://thediplomat.com/2015/04/how-sri-lanka-won-the-war/.

163. http://www.rediff.com/news/interview/militarisation-is-still-a-problem-in-tamil-areas-in-lanka/20160525.htm.

164. http://nias.res.in/publication/engaging-post-ltte-sri-lanka-indias-policy-options.

165. http:// jeteraps.scholarlinkresearch.com/articles/Indo%20Sri%20Lanka.

166. http://www.hindustantimes.com/world/pak-thanks-lanka-for-help-in-1971-war/story-UpZWXd0fFX5eDPac0KMIYL.html.

167. http://www.hcicolombo.org/pages.php?id=28.

168. http://www.thehindu.com/news/sri-lanka-looking-at-devolution-of-power-to-tamils-within-the-constitution-wickremesinghe/article7655608.ece.

169. http://www.thenational.ae/news/world/south-asia/chinas-aid-revealed-in-sri-lankas-victory-parade.

170. http://www.vifindia.org/article/2011/may/18/Redefining-Sri-Lanka-Indian-Perspective.

171. http://tamilnation.co/intframe/tamileelam/070920oil.htm.

172. http://www.hcicolombo.org/pages.php?id=28.

173. http://www.army.lk/news/4th-india-sri-lanka-joint-training-exercise.

174. https://en.wikipedia.org/wiki/Bhutan.

175. www.bbs.bt/news/?p=15058.

176. http://indianexpress.com/article/world/world-news/china-bhutan-hold-24th-round-of-boundary-talks-aim-to-strengthen-ties-2970199/.

177. https://en.wikipedia.org/wiki/Bhutanese_Citizenship_Act_1958.

178. http://www.claws.in/985/dealing-with-doklam-prakash-katoch.html.

179. http://www.globalsecurity.org/military/world/bhutan/forrel-prc.htm.

180. http://thediplomat.com/tag/bhutan-nepal-relations/.

181. http://www.bbs.bt/news/?p=38843.

182. https://mea.gov.in/Portal/ForeignRelation/Bhutan_April_2014_eng.pdf.

183. https://www.indianembassythimphu.bt/pages.php?id=42.

184. www.ipcs.org/pdf_file/issue/IB18-OperationAllClear.pd.

185. https://www.foreignaffairs.com/articles/china/2016-02-25/nepals-balancing-act.

186. https://en.wikipedia.org/wiki/Pushpa_Kamal_DahalSecond_term_as_prime_minister.

187. https://www.telegraphindia.com/1151025/jsp/7days/story_49480.

jsp.

188.   http://www.hindustantimes.com/world-news/nepal-govt-tables-constitution-amendment-bill/story-uPiEympiSvwy9R0cTXezfI.html.

189.   https://thehimalayantimes.com/opinion/internal-security-issues-ways-address/.

190.   http://timesofindia.indiatimes.com/india/india-watches-warily-as-china-further-ramps-up-fdi-into-nepal/articleshow/57008982.cms.

191.   http://currentaffairs.gktoday.in/10th-indo-nepal-joint-military-exercise-surya-kiran-commences-11201636797.html

192.   http://currentaffairs.gktoday.in/10th-indo-nepal-joint-military-exercise-surya-kiran-commences-11201636797.html.

193.   http://www.dailypioneer.com/todays-newspaper/india-seeks-nepal-help-to-stem-isi-funded-madrasas.html.

194.   http://www.thehindu.com/news/international/nepal-inks-transit-treaty-with-china-to-have-first-rail-link/article8381195.ece.

195.   https://en.wikipedia.org/wiki/Myanmar.

196.   http://www.independent.co.uk/news/world/asia/bangladesh-islam-state-religion-government-considers-dropping-a7418366.html.

197.   https://en.wikipedia.org/wiki/Bangladesh_Jamaat-e-Islami.

198.   https://www.theguardian.com/world/2013/jul/30/bangladesh-hefazat-e-islam-shah-ahmad-shafi.

199.   https://www.trackingterrorism.org/group/islami-chhatra-shibir.

200.   http://www.satp.org/satporgtp/countries/bangladesh/terroristoutfits/Huj.htm.

201.   http://www.csmonitor.com/World/Asia-South-Central/2010/0805/Pakistani-militants-expand-abroad-starting-in-Bangladesh.

202.   https://www.trackingterrorism.org/group/jamaat-ul-mujahideen-bangladesh-jmb.

203.   https://www.un.org/sc/suborg/en/sanctions/1267/monitoring-

team/reports.

204. https://www.rsis.edu.sg/wp-content/uploads/2017/03/CTTA-March-2017.pdf.

205. http://edition.cnn.com/2016/07/03/asia/bangladesh-isis-al-qaeda/.

206. https://en.wikipedia.org/wiki/July_2016_Dhaka_attack.

207. http://www.thedailystar.net/city/police-boss-refutes-existence-1375225.

208. https://www.rsis.edu.sg/wp-content/uploads/2017/03/CTTA-March-2017.pdf.

209. http://www.buddhistpeacefellowship.org/the-969-movement-and-burmese-anti-muslim-nationalism-in-context/ .

210. https://www.hrw.org/news/2013/04/22/burma-end-ethnic-cleansing-rohingya-muslims.

211. https://www.trackingterrorism.org/group/harkat-ul-jihad-al-islami-arakan-burma.

212. https://qz.com/866665/rohingya-crisis-a-new-terror-group-has-emerged-in-myanmar-and-india-should-be-worried/.

213. http://www.idsa.in/idsastrategiccomments/Unholyalliancein-NorthEastIndia_MASingh_190209.

214. www.hvk.org/2002/0502/64.html.

215. https://www.telegraphindia.com/1140107/jsp/frontpage/story_17760386.jsp#.WNJFc2-GPcc.

216. http://southasianvoices.org/deterrence-by-design-sino-pak-strategic-cooperation-in-gwadar/.

217. http://thediplomat.com/2016/08/what-to-make-of-chinas-latest-meeting-with-the-taliban/.

218. http://www.cfr.org/china/china-pakistan-relations/p10070, accessed 28 August, 2016.

219. http://qz.com/621884/china-is-the-worlds-fastest-growing-arms-exporter-thanks-to-the-nations-surrounding-india/.

220. http://www.dawn.com/news/1253323.

221. http://www.usnews.com/news/world/articles/2009/01/02/why-china-helped-countries-like-pakistan-north-korea-build-nuclear-bombs.

222. http://blogs.timesofindia.indiatimes.com/nandygram/china-moved-n-missiles-and-launchers-via-karakoram-highway-to-pak-in-2005-indian-intelligence-reports.

223. https://en.wikipedia.org/w/index.php?title=Chinese_Dream&oldid=723729046.

224. https://en.wikipedia.org/w/index.php?title=One_Belt,_One_Road&oldid=732943554.

225. URL : https://www.stratfor.com/analysis/grand-design-chinas-new-trade-routes.

226. http://indianexpress.com/article/world/world-news/pakistan-china-economic-corridor-army-chief-raheel-sharif-promises-firm-crackdown-on-uyghur-militants-2953525/.

227. https://i1.wp.com/news.usni.org/wp-ontent/uploads/2013/05/Liaoning-16-Chinas-first-aircraft-carrier.jpg?ssl=1.

228. http://www.claws.in/images/journals_doc/SW%20i-10.10.2012.71-79.pdf.

229. http://www.vifindia.org/article/2016/may/19/chinas-road-and-belt-initiative-indian-perspective.

230. https://news.usni.org/2015/05/07/a-look-at-chinas-growing-international-arms-trade.

231. https://www.ispr.gov.pk/front/main.asp?o=t-press_release&date=2015/4/21.

232. https://www.ispr.gov.pk/front/main.asp?o=t-press_release&date=2016/2/19.

233. http://news.xinhuanet.com/english/2016-04/13/c_135274538.htm.

234. http://timesofindia.indiatimes.com/india/Chinese-army-spotted-along-Line-of-Control-in-Pakistan-occupied-Kashmir-say-sources/articleshow/51380359.cms.

235. https://www.theguardian.com/world/2016/may/30/chinese-worker-driver-injured-karachi-bombing-claimed-separatists.

236. http://en.people.cn/n3/2016/0721/c98649-9089345.html.

237. http://www.defense.gov/Portals/1/Documents/pubs/2016%20 China%20Military%20Power%20Report.pdf.

238. http://thediplomat.com/2016/02/its-official-chinas-military-has-5-new-theater-commands/.

239. http://economictimes.indiatimes.com/news/economy/foreign-trade/indias-trade-deficit-with-china-jumps-to-53-billion-in-2015-16/articleshow/53492853.cms.

240. http://indianexpress.com/article/india/india-news-india/india-china-to-hold-joint-military-exercise-in-pune-4372291/.

241. http://www.tribuneindia.com/news/nation/aware-of-chinese-submarine-deployment-at-balochistan-s-gwadar-port-navy-chief/331339.html.

242. https://papers.ssrn.com/sol3/papers.cfm?abstract_id=2797128.

243. http://infolanka.asia/government-and-politics/foreign-relations/ hambantota-in-the-eyes-of-major-world-powers.

244. https://en.wikipedia.org/wiki/Magampura_Mahinda_Rajapaksa_ Port.

245. https://www.forbes.com/sites/wadeshepard/2016/10/28/sold-sri-lankas-hambantota-port-and-the-worlds-emptiest-airport-go-to-the-chinese/#6ce385ca4456.

246. http://www.hindustantimes.com/world/china-third-largest-weapons-exporter-pakistan-main-recipient/story-eiVUgDEKG-KfdR7mAfA70PJ.html.

247. http://thediplomat.com/2016/06/bangladeshs-deep-sea-port-problem/.

248. http://thediplomat.com/2017/02/us-air-force-rotates-supersonic-strategic-bombers-in-the-asia-pacific/.

249. http://www.marsecreview.com/2012/07/malacca-strait-coopera-tion/.

250. https://sputniknews.com/world/201612091048372275-china-iran-sanctions/.

251. http://www.frontline.in/world-affairs/one-belt-one-road-initia-tive/article7098506.ece.

252. http://www.aljazeera.com/indepth/opinion/2014/11/china-hide-your-strength-bide-y-201411198028498329.html.

253. http://www.idsa.in/keyspeeches/RoleofIndianNavyinMaintain-ingPeaceinIndianOceanRegion_CNS.

254. https://muhammadalamgir.wordpress.com/2011/08/19/america%E2%80%99s-interests-in-south-asia/.

255. http://www.idsa-india.org/an-mar00-1.html.

256. http://asiasociety.org/files/pdf/as_U.S._southasia_exec_sum.pdf.

257. http://carnegieendowment.org/2005/11/16/u.s.-india-global-partnership-how-significant-for-american-interests-pub-17693.

258. http://carnegieendowment.org/2013/03/13/rebalance-to-asia-why-south-asia-matters-pub-51197.

259. http://www.isca.in/LANGUAGE/Archive/v2/i4/2.ISCA-RJLLH-2015-017.pdf.

260. http://www.reuters.com/article/U.S.-U.S.a-pakistan-aid-idU.S.KCN1110AQ.

261. https://www.whitehoU.S.e.gov/the-press-office/2013/10/23/joint-statement-president-obama-and-prime-minister-nawaz-sharif.

262. http://www.thedailystar.net/news-detail-232748.

263. http://www.state.gov/t/pm/rls/rm/188522.htm.

264. https://bd.U.S.embassy.gov/u-s-secretary-state-john-kerry-deliv-ers-speech-u-s-bangladesh-relations/.

265. https://www.U.S.aid.gov/Nepal.

266. http://www.ndtv.com/india-news/india-U.S.-deepen-defense-ties-with-landmark-agreement-1452220.

267. https://csis-prod.s3.amazonaws.com/s3fs-public/legacy_files/files/publication/120614_Latif_U.S.IndiaDefenseTrade_Abbrevi-ated_Web.pdf.

268. http://carnegieendowment.org/2013/01/07/opportunities-un-bound-sU.S.taining-transformation-in-u.s.-indian-relations-pub-50506.

269. https://csis-prod.s3.amazonaws.com/s3fs-public/legacy_files/files/publication/120614_Latif_U.S.IndiaDefenseTrade_Abbrevi-

ated_Web.pdf.

270. http://www.globalresearch.ca/karzai-reveals-us-plan-for-perma-nent-afghanistan-bases/5334680

271. https://www.lowyinstitute.org/the-interpreter.

272. https://www.stratfor.com/weekly/past-present-and-future-rus-sian-energy-strategy.

273. http://carnegie.ru/2013/02/27/russian-policy-on-india-and-south-asia-pub-51283.

274. http://www.thehindu.com/opinion/lead/changing-face-of-rus-siapakistan-ties/article621447.ece.

275. http://www.idsa-india.org/an-nov9-9.html.

276. http://www.mainstreamweekly.net/article2989.html.

277. http://www.idsa-india.org/an-nov9-9.html.

278. http://www.rusemb.org.uk/in4b/.

279. http://www.orfonline.org/expert-speaks/india-and-russia-spe-cial-and-privileged-strategic-partnership/.

280. http://thediplomat.com/2016/05/whats-behind-russias-rap-prochement-with-pakistan/.

281. http://indianexpress.com/article/india/india-news-india/pm-mo-di-addresses-combined-commanders-conference-onboard-ins-vikramaditya/.

282. http://www.idsa.in/idsacomments/ANationalSecurityStrategy-DocumentforIndia_arvindgupta_201011.

283. http://indianexpress.com/article/india/bangladesh-pm-sheikh-hasina-to-honour-indian-soldiers-killed-in-1971-war-4585862/.

284. http://www.theresurgentindia.com/modi-putin-give-the-biggest-shock-to-china-and-pakistan/ .

285. https://thewire.in/38708/indias-five-foreign-policy-goals-great-strides-steep-challenges/.

286. http://economictimes.indiatimes.com/news/defence/490-paki-stan-soldiers-3500-militants-killed-in-operation-zarb-e-azb/ar-ticleshow/52766005.cms.

287. http://indianexpress.com/article/india/bangladesh-pm-sheikh-hasina-to-honour-indian-soldiers-killed-in-1971-war-4585862/.

288. http://economictimes.indiatimes.com/news/industry/energy/oil-gas/6900-km-gas-pipelines-to-connect-bangladesh-myanmar-india/articleshow/53695899.cms.

289. http://economictimes.indiatimes.com/news/economy/foreign-trade/indias-trade-deficit-with-china-jumps-to-53-billion-in-2015-16/articleshow/53492853.cms.

290. http://indiatoday.intoday.in/story/dalai-lama-tawang-arunachal-pradesh-china/1/923709.html.

291. http://www.cfr.org/regional-security/competition-indian-ocean/p37201.

292. http://www.firstpost.com/india/kashmir-stone-pelter-tied-atop-jeep-incident-may-mark-a-turning-point-in-indias-response-to-hybrid-warfare-3386028.html.

293. http://www.thecitizen.in/index.php/NewsDetail/index/4/10590/The-Zonkey-of-Hybrid-Warfare.

294. http://www.disasterdiplomacy.org/.

295. www.saarc-sdmc.nic.in/.

296. http://timesofindia.indiatimes.com/india/India-Pak-agree-for-SAARC-disaster-response-force/articleshow/50336495.cms.

297. http://www.worldbank.org/en/news/press-release/2015/10/15/south-asia-extreme-poverty-falls-but-challenges-remain .

298. http://www.downtoearth.org.in/news/south-asia-has-highest-number-of-chronically-hungry-people-46386.

299. http://timesofindia.indiatimes.com/world/south-asia/Youth-unemployment-in-South-Asia-as-high-as-9-6/articleshow/18131851.cms.

300. https://www.iea.org/Textbase/npsum/WEO2015SUM.pdf.

301. https://www.ipcc.ch/pdf/assessment-report/ar5/syr/AR5_SYR_FINAL_SPM.pdf.

Index

A

Abdul Karim Tunda 111
Abdullah Abdullah 11
Actual Ground Position Line (AGPL) 58
Afghanistan-Pakistan Transit Trade Agreement (APTTA) 22
Afghanistan's National Unity Government (NUG) 39
Afghan National Army (ANA) 18
Afghan National Defence and Security Forces (ANDSF) 18, 24
Afghan National Police (ANP) 18
Afghan Security Forces 11
Af-Pak region ix, xiii, 3, 6, 10, 28, 29, 38, 40, 121, 157, 166, 181
Al-Herminie (an NGO) 105
Al-Qaeda 14, 31, 62, 111
Ansar al Islam 107, 108, 223
Arabian Sea 52
Ashraf Ghani 11, 20, 42, 45, 46

B

Baglihar dam 67
Balawaristan National Front (BNF) 35
Baloch Republican Party (BRP) 33
Banuk Karima Baloch 33
Belt and Road Initiative (OBOR) 126
Brahamdagh Bugti 33, 49

C

Chahbahar 26, 47
China-Pakistan Economic Corridor (CPEC) 4, 38, 53, 64, 125, 148
Chumbi Valley 89, 134
Cold War 2, 120, 124, 145, 146, 163, 167, 168, 171
Collective Security Organisation (CSTO) 41
Collective Security Treaty (CSTO) 166

D

Difa-e-Mussalman Arakan-Burma 109
Durand Line 10, 22, 30, 54, 128, 183, 185

E

East Turkestan Islamic Movement (ETIM) 23, 128
Exclusive Economic Zone (EEZ) 66
Exercise, 'Mitra Shakthi' 85
Exercise Suryakiran 96

F

Falah-e-Insaniyat 104
Federally Administered Tribal Areas (FATA) 23, 31, 48
Forum for India-Pacific Islands Cooperation (FIPIC) 177

G

Gaining Initiative by Striking First (GISF) 129
Gilgit-Baltistan 34
Global Relief Foundation (an NGO) 105
Gulbadin Hekmatyar 17
Gulf of Mannar 84
Gulf of Oman 52
Gwadar Port 64, 72

H

Hambantota 65, 84, 134, 140, 153
Haqqani Network 15
Harakat ul-Jihad Islami 18
Harbiyar Marri 33
Harkat-Ul-Jihad-al-Islami Bangladesh 104
Harkat ul-Mujahideen (HUM) 29, 61
Hezb-i-Islami 17
Hezb-i-Islami Afghanistan (HIA) 17
Hifazat-e-Islam (Hel) 103, 224
Hizb-e-Islami-Gulbuddin 17
Humanitarian Assistance and Disaster Relief (HADR) 196

I

Imamia Students Organization (ISO) 35
Improvised Explosive Devices 160
Indian Ocean Region (IOR) viii, 65
Indira Col 58
Indo-Nepal Treaty 96
Indo-US nuclear deal 5, 55, 126
Indus River System Authority (IRSA) 68
Internally Displaced Persons (IDP) 81
International Military Education and

Training (IMET) 162
International Security Assistance Force (ISAF) 18
Iran-Pakistan-India(IPI) 38
Islami Chhatra Shibir (ICS) 104
Islamic Movement of Uzbekistan (IMU) 17
Islamic State-Khorasan Province 16
Islamic State of Iraq and the Levant (ISIL) 106

J

Jaish-e-Mohammed (JeM) 29, 61
Jalaluddin Haqqani 15
Jamaat-e-Islami (Jel) 103
Jamaat-ul-Mujahideen 106
Jamaat-Ul-Mujahideen, Bangladesh (JMB) 105

K

Karakoram highway 64, 122
Karakoram pass 58, 59
Kargil war 123, 124
Khalistan movement 61
Khardungla pass 58
Khunjerab Pass 53, 64
Khyber Pakhtunkhwa 31, 48, 54
Konduz Province 17
Kunming-Kyaukphyu-Dhaka Corridor viii

L

Lashkar-e-Jhangvi 61
Lashkar-e-Taiba (LeT) 17, 29, 61, 70, 104
Lashkar-i-Janghvi 18
Line of Control (LoC) 57, 58, 128, 152
Loya Jirga 12

M

Maldives National Defence Force
(MNDF) 75

Manora Island 57

Markaz Dawat Wal Irshad 61

Maulana Ahmad Shafi 103

Maulana Masood Azhar 111

Metallurgical Corporation of China
Limited 24

Mohajirs 54

Muhajir 54

Mullah Haibatullah Akhunzada 14

Mullah Omar 15

Muslim Liberation Organisation of
Burma (MLOB) 110

N

Nangarhar province 16

National Disaster Management Authority (NDMA) 196

New Silk Road 28

No First Use 4, 195

North Atlantic Treaty Organization 18

Nurbakhshi Youth Federation (NYF)
35

O

One Belt and Road initiative 162

Operation Enduring Freedom 18, 159

Operation Meghdoot 58

Operation Zarb-e-Azb 131

Organization for the Prohibition of
Chemical Weapons (OPCW)
63

Osama bin Laden 31, 35, 104, 105

P

Pakistan occupied Kashmir (PoK) 57,
58, 132, 191

Palk Straits 84

Pashtunistan 22, 54

People's Liberation Army (PLA) 143

Persian Gulf 26, 66, 73, 121, 137, 142,
150

Prohibition of Chemical Weapons
(OPCW) 63

Pushpa Kamal Dahal 93, 100

Q

Qari Balal 17

Quadrilateral Coordination Group
(QCG) 20

R

Radcliffe line 57

Rakhine State 108, 109, 114

Rohingyas 106

Rohingya Solidarity Organisation 109,
110, 116

S

Salafist Sunni Muslims 73, 78

Saltoro Ridge 58, 130

Sea Lanes of Communication (SLOC)
65

Shaksgam Valley 58, 59, 123

Shanghai Cooperation Organisation
(SCO) 41, 126, 168, 169

Siachen Glacier 57

Siliguri corridor 93, 113, 134

Simla Agreement 58

Sino-Indian Conflict 122

Sir Creek 67

South China Sea xiii, 3, 137, 138, 142,
144, 150, 162, 190, 194

Strait of Hormuz 65

Strait of Malacca 53, 65, 142, 192

String of Pearls viii, 6, 8, 65, 84, 134, 137, 143, 145, 148, 150, 188, 189

T

Tehrik-e- Azadi Arakaan 110
Tehrik-e-Taliban Pakistan 14, 61, 128
Turkmenistan-Afghanistan-Pakistan-India pipeline [TAPI] 23, 38

U

Uighur 23
United Kashmir People's National Party 36
United Nations Commission for India and Pakistan (UNCIP) 35

W

Wahhabism 26
Wakhan Corridor 24, 165
Water and Power Development Authority (WAPDA) 68
Weapons of Mass Destruction (WMD) 63
Wirathu's 969 Movement 108

X

Xianjiang 148
Xinjiang-Gwadar Economic Corridor viii

Y

Yasin Bhatkal 112

Z

Zaki-ur-Rehman Lakhvi 111
Zaki Ur Rehman Lakhvi 126
Zia-ur Rehman 112

www.ingramcontent.com/pod-product-compliance
Lightning Source LLC
Chambersburg PA
CBHW031549260326
41914CB00002B/341